Tegtmeier & Papenhagen

Johann Friederick Tegtmeier b. 1821
Joachim Christian Johann Papenhagen b. 1836

Johann Frederick Tegtmeier
1821—1903

Tegtmeier & Papenhagen

A collection of United States Families

1821–2007

Compiled and written by
Sandra Taylor Bell

iUniverse, Inc.
New York Lincoln Shanghai

Tegtmeier & Papenhagen
A collection of United States Families 1821–2007

iUniverse books may be ordered through booksellers or by contacting:

iUniverse
2021 Pine Lake Road, Suite 100
Lincoln, NE 68512
www.iuniverse.com
1-800-Authors (1-800-288-4677)

ISBN: 978-0-595-44524-0 (pbk)
ISBN: 978-0-595-88852-8 (ebk)

Printed in the United States of America

Dedicated to my
Mother, Alice Tegtmeier Taylor
and
in memory of my husband, Peter Graham Bell

A special thank you to
Richard F. Davidson
2511 Charleston Lane, Reston Virginia 22091
For his incredible work on the Family Genealogy

Also, a very gracious thank you to everyone who took the time to submit biographical sketches and photos of family members. Without your help, this would have only been a series of names and dates, without the love and emotion that is inherent in families.
Stephanie Berry-Estep, West Salem, Ohio
Larry Fenton, Butler Ohio
Nancy Findley, Tecumseh, Michigan
Michael Hilborn, Fort Wayne, Indiana
Lois Hinrichs, Dickinson, North Dakota
Lester Meier, Perrysburg, Ohio
Debbie Miller, Wooster, Ohio
William Schultz, Medina, Ohio
Alice Taylor, Bradenton, Florida
Shirley Taylor, Bradenton, Florida
Dave & Rita Tegtmeier, West Salem Ohio
Harriett Tegtmeier, Fairfield Glade, Tennessee
Lucille Tegtmeier, West Salem, Ohio
Donald & Neva Tegtmeier, West Salem, Ohio
Terry Tegtmeier, Boliva, Ohio

Published in U.S. by
iUniverse.com

Contents

A Short German History of the Nineteenth Century

My grandmother, Erna Tegtmeier had always told me the reason the family left Germany was because of the wars and so many of the sons dying.

Leaving Germany in the mid 1800's was a matter of survival, and it was often said by our ancestors that they came to America to escape the wars in Germany. War was everywhere and frequent. If the family stayed in Germany, the boys would soon be in a war. But other issues were also taking place.

In 1829, Gottfried Duden, a German visitor to America, published his book, Report of a Journey to the Western States of North America. The book providing a very attractive account of German immigrant life in America. As well as describing spectacular harvests, Duden praised the intellectual freedom enjoyed by people living in America. The book sold in large numbers and persuaded thousands of Germans to emigrate.

Many people didn't have any prospects or future in Mecklenburg, since their lives were totally uprooted by the change from feudal rule to a civil-capitalist one. Serfdom was annulled in Mecklenburg in 1820/21. At that time, many landowners—titled gentry and knights—took the opportunity to get rid of a lot of their day laborers who were now considered personally free according to the law. They began to run their lands with a minimum of permanent laborers. The landowners did this so that they would not have to pay for any laborers who were injured or take care of them when they grew old.

Nearly 88.5 % of German emigrants came from rural areas. This was mostly due to the miserable social conditions caused by the Right of Abode and the Right of Establishment rules which existed almost unchanged between 1820–1860. It was very difficult for day-laborers who were thrown out to find permanent work elsewhere because they needed to receive the RIGHT OF ESTABLISHMENT from the new employer.

The GRANTING OF THE RIGHT TO MARRY also depended on the granting of the right of establishment, and all subjects needed permission to marry before they could have a family. A man or woman who did not have the right of establishment could never establish a home. Therefore, the main problem for a common Mecklenburger was to get his own "Hüsung" (housing), but many did not succeed. A lot of people that worked were refused the right of establishment by the ruling class for their whole lives. They were given only a limited right to residence—only for as long as they had work. This contributed to the inhumane conditions that existed. Mecklenburgers were homeless in their own country, not because they had no work, but this was one way the land owners could avoid responsibility toward the family.[1]

The failed German revolution in 1848 also stimulated emigration. Over the next ten years over a million people left Germany and settled in the United States. Most of these emigrants had lost confidence in its government's ability to solve the country's economic problems.

Others left because they feared constant political turmoil in Germany. One prosperous innkeeper wrote after arriving in Wisconsin: "I would prefer the civilized, cultured, Germany to America if it were still in its former orderly condition, but as it has turned out recently, and with the threatening prospect for the future of religion and politics, I prefer America. Here I can live a more quiet and undisturbed life."

THE NATIONAL GERMAN AMERICAN ALLIANCE was formed in 1901 in America to preserve the German way of living, its language and culture. By 1914 the group had a membership of over two million people.

When the United States entered into the First World War in 1917, there was a great deal of hostility toward the German-Americans. Camps were set up across the United States to imprison many suspected Germans who came to the United States after the 1900's. Towns, streets and buildings with German names were renamed, and many American-Germans changed their surnames in order to hide their native origin.

---

1 Mecklenburg Magazine 1990/0 by Dr. Sc. Klaus Baudis, translation: Daniela Garling

In 1917 the National German-American Alliance, the organization that had campaigned against United States involvement in the World War I, had its charter withdrawn. Some schools stopped teaching German as a foreign language and radio stations were encouraged not to play the music of German composers. A large number of German language newspapers, starved of advertising, were also forced to close.

TAKE A PEN IN HAND and cross out what doesn't seem to fit. There are several possibilities in some instances of family, i.e. Otto Tegtmeier who I fear I have not found as a Saloon Keeper as my mother remembers him … he exists in no records that I can find, or is he there buried beneath the census records that records only evidences of time and essentials. She may have known him as Otto, but he may have written his name for the census as Frederick. Parts of the lives of families have disappeared.

We also realize that Germans coming to America obciously don't have an understanding of English, and the American's csometimes came close to writing down what they thought they heard when interviewing families for census. At any rate, the following are sample surnames, all of which belong to this family of Tegtmeier's (pronounced Tek-my-er)

TEGTMEIER, TEGTMIER, TAEGTMEIER, TEGTMEYER, TEGETEMYER, TEGETMEYER, TAGTMEYER, TECKMYER, TIETTMEYER, and many more.

The names may have been written down and given to the immigrant so they could hold unto the spelling for later use, as many seemed to retain the spelling of their names as it was given to them at the time of immigration.

The name Tegtmeier and Papenhagen are old families in Germany, and have been traced back further than the 1600's in Germany. We will let other younger minds tackle the European Census as it becomes available and the links to family in America. Every day the internet opens more and more possible sources of information not previously available.

Much of this information is taken from ships' logs, death notices where available, and census records that at present are only available as recent as 1930 to protect the privacy of the living. These records are collected and recorded here to save time for any future genealogists to research, edit and add to as the years go by. There is nothing worse then to have a lot of names and dates with absolutely no proof to back it up.

THE TEGTMEIR FAMILY of this sketch settled primarily in the Ohio and Michigan areas. This book is in part a mystery that needs your help in solving. Parts of the lives of family have disappeared. Please advise if you can find them.

A SHORT BACKGROUND OF TEGTMEIERS IN AMERICA BEFORE 1862.

THE WAR OF 1812—earliest recorded Tegtmeier in North America.

LEWIS TEGTMEYER
Company: Thompson's Regiment Pennsylvania Militia
Rank: Induction: Private
Rank—Discharge: Private
Roll Box 206
Roll Exct: 602

CIVIL WAR TEGTMEYERS
(There were civil war swords in the attic of the old farm house in Burbank, Ohio and we were told back in the 1950's they belonged to Uncles that were in the Civil War … but no one remembered who. We also had photos on the table of men in uniform, but haven't been able to authenticate the relationships. The ones in bold are most likely immediate family.)

EDMUND TEGTMEYER
Residence: Chicago, Illinois
Enlistment Date: 26 December 1863
Distinguished Service
Side Served: Union
State Served: Illinois
Unit Numbers 239239
Service Record: Enlisted as a Private on 26 December 1863
Enlisted in Company B, 12th Cavalry Regiment Illinois on 31 January 1864
Deserted Company B, 12th Cavalry Regiment Illinois on 16 June 1865.

FREDERICK TEGTMEIER
Residence: Blue Island, Illinois
Enlistment Date: 14 January 1863
Distinguished Service:
Side Served: Union
State Served: Illinois
Unit Numbers 243 243
Service Record: Enlisted as a Private on 14 January 1863
Enlisted in Company D, 16th Cavalry Regiment Illinois on 27 March 1863.
Mustered out Company D, 16th Regiment Illinois on 19 August 1865 in Nashville, TN

FREDERICK TEGTMEIER
Residence: Marinette, Wisconsin
Enlistment Date: 16 September 1864
Distinguished service
Side Served: Union
State Served: Wisconsin
Unit Numbers 3113
Service Record: Enlisted as a Private on 16 September 1864
Enlisted in Company B, 8th Infantry Regiment Wisconsin on 16 September 1864.
Mustered out Company B, 9th Infantry Regiment Wisconsin on 05 March 1865.

FREDERICK TEGTMYER
Residence: Paris, Indiana
Enlistment Date: 17 October 1864
Distinguished Service
Side Served: Union
State Served: Indiana
Unit Numbers 582 582
Service record: Enlisted as a Private on 17 October 1864
Drafted in Company I, 31st Infantry Regiment Indiana on 17 October 1864.
Mustered out Company I, 31st Infantry Regiment Indiana on 21 June 1865.

LEWIS TEGTMIER
Enlistment Date: 18 January 1865
Distinguished Service
Side Served: Union
State Served: Ohio
Unit Numbers 1824
Service Record: Enlisted as a Private on 18 January at the age of 28
Enlisted in Company U, 186th Regiment Ohio on 18 January 1865.

WILLIAM TEGTMEYER
Company: H
Unit: 11 Ohio Infantry
Rank—induction: Private
Rank—Discharge: Private
Allegiance: Union
Notes: Teighmeier, William

CENSUS RECORDS in the United States 1870
1870 Census Ohio—Clermont—Ohio
Louis Tegtmeier, age 44, cigar maker from Germany; Julia, wife born in Germany age 40; Mary age 13. Otto age 8; Matta age 2; Henry Elhard age 19 Hanover Germany; Conrad Tegtmeier, Hanover, Germany age 21; John Deser age 29, Hanover Germany.

The 1870 Census reports the following Tegtmeier families living in the United States, names being transcribed by the census takers as best as they could into English.

Fred & Vora Yeztwin[2] (that's Frederick Johann Tegtmeier—the transcriber wrote it the way she thought it was scripted)

	Cleveland, Ohio	Deutschland
Louis & Julia Tegtmeier	Clermont, Ohio	Hanover
Fred & Louisa Tegtmeier	Pallatine, IL	Hesse
Angus & Elizabeth Tegtmeier	Camden, NJ	Hesse
August Tegtmeier & family	Philadelphia, PA	Hesse

2 1870 Census Ohio>Cuyahoga>Middleburgh: Tegtmeier (transcriber read as "Yeztwein" but if you read the original record, you can easily read "Tegtmeier") Fred, age 48 from Deutschland: Dora age 46; Henry 27; Fred 24; Ferdinand 21; Louisa 18 (b abt 1852); Adeline 7 born in Ohio.

Henry & Dora Tegtmeyer	Chicago, Cook, IL	Hanover, Germany
Fred & Stina Tegtmeyer	Palatine, IL	Hanover, Germany
Edmund & Sophia Tegtmeyer	Wyandotte, KA	Prussia
Chris(opher) & Louisa Tegtmeyer	Allegheny, PA	Prussia
Charles & Minna Tagtmeyer	Randolph, IL	Hanover
Frederick & Amelia Tegtmier	Winnebago, WI	Hanover
Ernest & Magdalena Teckmeyer	St. Louis, MO	Hanover
Frederick & Caroline Tegmeyer	Madison, IL	Prussia
Frederick Tegmeier and family	New Haven, CT	Prussia

TRAVEL TO OHIO

Unknown how the family arrived in Ohio. Railroads existed but most suffered damage between 1861–1864 from the Civil War. The Erie Canal had been completed and was safer up north, stretching from the Hudson River to Lake Erie. It was begun in 1798, and the first section completed by 1819. The entire canal was opened on October 26, 1825. It was 363 miles long, 40 feet wide and just 4 feet deep. There were 83 locks along the canal, each 90 feet by 15 feet. The canal was the first transportation route and proved faster than carts pulled by draft animals between the Eastern Seaboard of the Unites States and the western interior, and cut transport costs into what was then wilderness by about 95%. The Canal resulted in a massive population surge in western New York, and opened regions further west to increase settlement.[3]

Travel on the canal was about 4 miles an hour as the horses pulled the packetboat (for passengers) with three horses, or the lineboat (for freight) with 2 horses. From New York they would have to catch a steamer to Albany, NY.

In 1863, the cost of sailing the Canal rivaled rail passage.

The Tegtmeiers arrived in the United States during the Civil War, June 24, 1862. The B & O Railroad, though dangerous, had just been completely repaired after being severely damaged by the Confederates. They had destroyed nearly 500 cars, engines, many bridges and rails. It was probably the quickest way to get to Ohio. This was news as reported in The New York Times, which was 8 pages at a cost of three cents.

3 Wikipedia

Descendants of Johann Friedrich Tegtmeier

1 Johann Friedrich Tegtmeier b: 31 Aug 1821 in Iden, Osterburg, Prussia d: 27 Aug 1903 in Middleburg Twp, Cuyahoga OH

+Maria Dorothea Bree b: 29 Sep 1823 in Iden, Osterburg, Prussia d: 29 May 1903 in Middleburg Twp. Cuyahoga Co. OH

... 2 Johann Heinrich Tegtmeier b: 08 Jan 1844 in Iden, Osterburg, Prussia d: 24 Jan 1897 in Middleburg Twp, Cuyahoga, OH

...... +Sophia Louise Juliana Reinecke b: 19 Jan 1848 in Prussia d: 11 May 1933 in Washington Twp, Henry, OH

...... 3 Hulda Louise Maria Tegtmeier b: 21 May 1873 in Independence, OH d: 25 Feb 1968 in Adrian, Lenawee, MI

.... +Heinrich Ernst A. Ahleman b: 25 May 1869 in Riga Twp, Ottawa Lake, Michigan d: 21 Dec 1948 in Riga, MI

.... 4 Frederick Wm Ahleman b: 19 Jul 1894 in Riga Twp, Ottawa Lake, MI d: 01 Dec 1905 in Riga Twp, Ottawa Lake, MI

.... 4 Arthur G. Ahleman b: 12 Feb 1896 in Riga Twp., Riga, MI d: 11 Apr 1988 in Riga Twp., Riga, MI

.............+Olive A. Dedering b: 20 Oct 1903 in Port Huron, MI d: 08 Jan 1958

.............*2nd Wife of Arthur G. Ahleman:

.............+Adelaide Koppin b: 19 Jul 1901

.... 4 Almeta Bertha Christine Ahleman b: 26 Jan 1901 in Riga Twp, Riga, MI d: 15 Nov 1979

.............+John Bernard Meier b: 02 Jun 1887 in Toledo, OH d: 01 Jun 1969

.............5 John Arthur Meier b: 25 Dec 1922 in Curtice, OH

................+Doris Jane Metzker b: 17 Jun 1923 in Toledo, OH d: 09 Jan 2003 in Bellville, OH

................6 Ronald Arthur Meier b: 21 Feb 1946 in Toledo, OH

...................+Janice Marie Williams b: 29 Mar 1946 in Toledo, OH

...................7 David John Meier b: 24 Aug 1971 in Toledo, OH

...................7 Mark Arthur Meier b: 24 Aug 1971 in Toledo, OH

................6 Richard Allen Meier b: 06 Mar 1949 in Toledo, OH d: 18 Jun 2000

...................+Sally Helen Kolasinaki b: 02 Dec 1958 in Toledo, OH

....................7 James Andrew Meier b: 17 Jan 1982 in Toledo, OH
....................7 Paul Jacob Meier b: 17 May 1984 in Toledo, OH
....................7 William Joseph Meier b: 20 Oct 1985 in Toledo, OH
....................7 Elizabeth Jane Meier b: 20 Aug 1987 in Toledo, OH
................6 Beverly Ann Meier b: 16 Aug 1954 in Perrysburg, OH
....................+Allyn Kent Euler b: 08 Oct 1945 in Bowling Green, OH
....................7 Abel W. Euler b: 12 Sep 1976 in Bowling Green, OH
....................7 Jason Allyn Euler b: 02 Apr 1981 in Bowling Green, OH
.............5 Lucene Elsie Meier b: 15 Nov 1924 in Curtice, OH
................+Victor Junior Pyers b: 15 Dec 1919 in Lime City, OH d: 17 Jun 1993 in Fort Meigs Cemetery, Perrysburg, OH
................6 Dean Hale Pyers b: 07 Aug 1962 in Toledo, OH
.............5 Doris Hulda Meier b: 22 Oct 1925 in Curtice, OH
................+Dale Herman Hille b: 14 Aug 1924 in Wood Do., Bowling Green, OH
................6 Karen Rae Hille b: 21 Apr 1951 in Perrysburg, OH
....................+William Kristopher Roman b: 15 Oct 1949 in Canton, OH
....................7 Sarah Elizabeth Roman b: 09 Jul 1978 in Columbus, OH
....................7 Meghan Grier Roman b: 26 Oct 1982 in Columbus, OH
................6 Dennis Kay Hille b: 08 Apr 1953 in Bowling Green, OH
................6 Karlyn Sue Hille b: 19 Jul 1955 in Bowling Green, OH
....................+Terry Lee Stamper b: 09 Mar 1956 in Grayson, KY
....................7 Aaron Christopher Stamper b: 25 Jun 1981 in Stamford, CT
.............5 Lester Bernard Meier b: 07 Jan 1931 in Curtice, OH
................+Mary Lou Klebold b: 04 Jun 1932 in Columbus, OH
................6 Linda Christine Meier b: 25 Apr 1951 in Toledo, OH
....................+Jack Richard Simmons b: 05 Feb 1949 in Toledo, OH
....................7 Katherine Kramer Simmons b: 15 Jun 1970 in Bowling Green, OH
........................+Steven Scott Kirsch b: 28 Jan 1949 in South Bend, IN
........................8 Brian Scott Kirsch b: 04 Mar 1994 in Beaufort, NC
....................7 Sarah Jane Simmons b: 12 Aug 1973 in Toledo, OH
........................+Michael Raymond Fishbaugh b: 12 Feb 1971 in Toledo, OH
....................7 Megan Meier Simmons b: 22 Jun 1983 in Bowling Green, OH
....................7 Abigail Christine Simmons b: 06 Nov 1986 in Bowling Green, OH
................6 Eileen Kay Meier b: 19 Oct 1952 in Toledo, OH
....................+Barton Thomas Stamper b: 21 Aug 1949 in Denver, CO
....................7 Joshua Noel Thomas Stamper b: 27 Sep 1972 in Denver, CO
........................+Kory Lea Behny b: 01 Mar 1973 in Wheat Ridge, CO
........................8 Ansa Rachel Stamper b: 11 Jun 1996 in N. Hampton, MA
....................7 Benjamin Jacob Stamper b: 11 Apr 1975 in Denver, CO
................6 Cynthia Ann Meier b: 06 Apr 1956 in Bowling Green, OH
....................+Robert Eugene Thompson b: 16 Apr 1950 in Denver, CO

....................7 Andrew Scott Thompson b: 07 Aug 1977 in Denver, CO
....................7 Ian Robert Thompson b: 05 Oct 1979 in Denver, CO
.... *2nd Husband of Cynthia Ann Meier:
.... +Gary Allyn Dingman b: 10 Jun 1957 in Longmont, CO
....................7 Justin Cody Dingman b: 18 Jun 1997
................6 Laureen Marie Meier b: 31 May 1958 in Bowling Green, OH
...................+Douglas Charles Bauer b: 23 Mar 1956 in Denver, CO
....................7 Scott Ryan Bauer b: 10 Aug 1987 in Menlo Park, CA
....................7 William Taylor Bauer b: 08 Sep 1990 in Menlo Park, CA
.... 4 Elsie Emma Hulda Ahleman b: 20 Apr 1903 in Riga Twp., Riga MI d: 15 May 1994
.............+Elwin C. Marks b: 20 Aug 1898 in Blissfield, MI d: 01 Nov 1997 in Clayton, MI
.............5 Leola May Marks b: 12 Oct 1925 in Henry Co., OH
................+Wesley Alger Hunt b: 04 Oct 1928 in Franklyn Twp., MI
................6 Karen Jane Hunt b: 11 Feb 1962 in Adrian,MI
...................+Daniel George Shoner b: 21 Feb 1959 in Ypsilanti, MI
....................7 Michael W. Shoner b: 05 May 1992 d: 17 Sep 1992 in Saline MI.
....................7 Jenna Marie Shoner b: 26 Jan 1994 in Saline, MI
....................7 Rachel Nicole Shoner b: 21 Dec 1995 in Ann Arbor, MI d: 30 Sep 1996
.............5 William Carl Elwin Marks b: 01 Mar 1930 in Monroe Co., MI
................+Mildred Irene Emery b: 03 Jan 1933 in Adrian, MI
................6 Nancy Kay Marks b: 12 Dec 1957 in Adrian, MI
...................+Leonard J. Beaubien b: 29 Nov 1958 in Adrian, MI
....................7 Christopher J. Beaubien b: 31 Aug 1982 in Adrian, MI
....................7 Audrey Kay Beaubien b: 18 Aug 1985
................6 Judy Lyn Marks b: 04 Jun 1960 in Adrian, MI
...................+Craig Schneiderbuer b: 17 Jun 1955 in Toledo, OH
....................7 Eric Stephen Schneiderbuer b: 29 Jul 1988 in Toledo, OH
....................7 Emily Lyn Schneiderbuer b: 09 Jan 1991 in Toledo, OH
................6 Wendy Lee Marks b: 25 Jul 1964 in Adrian, MI
...................+Bentley John Laser b: 01 Dec 1958 in Wauseon, OH
....................7 Bently John II Laser b: 29 Mar 1991 in Toledo, OH
....................7 Holly Jeanne Laser b: 19 Nov 1992 in Grayling, MI
....................7 Shelby Lee Laser b: 16 Oct 1996 in Toledo, OH
.............5 Herbert Bernard Marks b: 31 Mar 1936 in Deerfield, MI
................+Janice Gibson b: 12 May 1936 in Toledo, OH
................6 Todd Bernard Marks b: 29 Nov 1957 in Hudson, MI
...................+Terry Ashdown b: 16 Mar 1958 in Pierre, S. Dakota
................6 Gregg Herbert Marks b: 18 Jan 1960 in Mt. Clemens, MI
...................+Dana Lynne Caruthers b: 17 Jun 1962 in Denver, CO

................6 Scott Edward Marks b: 18 May 1964 in Lansing, MI
...................+Marie Colleen Shupick b: 15 Oct 1965 in Eagle Butte, S. Dakota
...................7 Jaycee Marie Marks b: 03 Dec 1991 in Elgin, IL
...................7 Trevor Scott E. Marks b: 14 Jan 1994 in Elgin, IL
.............5 Stanley Arthur Marks b: 23 Jan 1940 in Deerfield, MI
................+Judith Katherine Backman b: 11 Oct 1946 in Fresno, CA
................6 Travis Stanley Marks b: 05 Sep 1981 in Fresno, CA
................6 Troy William Marks b: 31 Dec 1989 in Fresno, CA
.... 4 Walter Adolph Ahleman b: 16 Jan 1907 in Riga Twn, Riga, MI d: 17 Feb 1959 in Napolean, Henry Co.,
.............+Ethel M. Strayer b: 10 Sep 1906 in Grand Rapids, OH d: 17 Apr 1996
.............5 Florence Elsie Ahleman b: 30 Nov 1930 in Henry Co., Liberty Center, OH
................+Richard F. Henning b: 30 Oct 1929 in Napoleon, OH
................6 Chari Lynn Henning b: 29 Nov 1953 in Henry Co., OH d: 06 Jul 1959
................6 Debra Kay Henning b: 16 Oct 1956 in Napoleon, OH
...................+Joey Donald Bergstedt b: 12 Jul 1959 in Napoleon, OH
...................7 Jennifer Elizabeth Bergstedt b: 09 Jun 1984 in Wauseon, OH
...................7 Jessica Elyse Bergstedt b: 19 Apr 1985 in Wauseon, OH
...................7 Alyssa Kathleen Bergstedt b: 07 Nov 1991 in Wauseon, OH
................6 Lori Jean Henning b: 07 Oct 1959 in Wauseon, OH
...................+Alfred Coey b: 27 Sep 1956 in Wauseon, OH
...................7 Jason Tyler Coey b: 26 Mar 1980 in Wauseon, OH
...................7 Jacob Lee Coey b: 12 May 1990 in Wauseon, OH
.............5 Donald Ernest Ahleman b: 04 Mar 1934 in Liberty Center, Henry Co., OH
................+Marilyn Lou Stevens b: 03 Jul 1934 in Holgate, OH
................6 Shelly Joanne Ahleman b: 05 Aug 1967 in Toledo, OH
...................+Rodney Richard Parsell b: 24 Apr 1968 in Unionville, MI
...................7 Lucas Prescott Parsell b: 15 Jul 1994 in Napoleon, OH
................6 David John Ahleman b: 16 Oct 1969 in Toledo, OH
.... 4 Paul Ernest Ahleman b: 06 Apr 1917 in Riga Twn, Riga, MI
.............+Lola E. Huff b: 10 Aug 1908 in Toledo, OH d: 17 Apr 1954 in Henry Co., OH
.............5 Damaris Anne Ahleman b: 10 Jun 1944 in Lowrey Air Force Base, CO
................+Ronald Bromley b: 06 Jan 1940 in CA
................6 Robert Paul Bromley b: 07 Oct 1971 in Boise, ID
................6 Maria Ann Bromley b: 08 Jun 1973 in Boise, ID
.............5 Larry Ernest Ahleman b: 22 Mar 1943 in Lincoln, NE
................*2nd Wife of Paul Ernest Ahleman:
................+Pauline Snapp b: 30 Sep 1929 in Maryland

...... 3 Ida Louise (died in inf) Tegtmeier b: 21 Jan 1872 in Berea, Cuyahoga Co. OH d: 21 Jul 1872 in Berea, Cuyahoga Co. OH
...... 3 Henry William Carl Tegtmeier b: 04 Nov 1874 in Middleburg Twp., Cuyahoga, OH d: 08 Jun 1963 in Millersburg, Holmes, OH
.... +Augusta Christine Brandes b: 18 Jan 1879 in Ohio d: 02 Apr 1967 in Strongsville, Ohio
.... 4 Ruth Tegtmeier b: ABT 1913 in Ohio
.... +Francis P. Davidson b: 09 Jul 1908 in Cuyahoga Co., OH d: 05 Mar 1996 in Richfield, Summit, Ohio
.... 5 Nancy Davidson b: ABT 1935
.... +xxx Jones
.... 6 Elizabeth Jones b: Bef. 1967 in Ohio
.... 5 Richard Davidson b: ABT 1936
.... 5 Susan Davidson b: ABT 1938
.... +xxx Hahn
.... 4 Oscar Tegtmeier b: 09 Jul 1914 in Brookpark, Cuyahoga Co., Ohio
...... 3 Adeline Elizabeth Emma (died in inf) Tegtmeier b: 08 Apr 1876 in Berea, Cuyahoga Co. OH d: 18 Sep 1876 in Berea, Cuyahoga Co. OH
...... 3 Lucie Adeline Julianna Tegtmeier b: 06 Aug 1877 in Berea, Cuyahoga Co. OH d: 09 Oct 1921 in Middleburg Twp, Cuyahoga OH
.... +William R. Scrivens b: ABT 1870 in Ohio d: 07 Apr 1927 in Middleburg Twp. Cuyahoga OH
.... 4 Edwin A. Scrivens b: 24 Jan 1899 in Ohio d: Jul 1976 in Cleveland, OH
.... +Clara Hansen b: ABT 1900 in Ohio
.... 5 Mary Lou Scrivens b: Aft. 1930
.... +xxx Prechtel b: ABT 1930
.... 4 Florence Julia Scrivens b: 21 Jan 1903 in Berea, Cuyahoga Co. OH d: 04 May 1993 in Ohio
.... +Lloyd William Schultz b: 18 Oct 1899 in Ohio d: 30 Jul 1979 in Ohio
.... 5 William L. Schultz b: 02 Aug 1931 in Berea, Cuyahoga, OH
.... +Dolores Ann Hines b: 02 Dec 1934
.... 6 James William Schultz b: 05 May 1953
.... +Gloria J. Dyke
.... 6 David Alan Schultz b: 07 Apr 1956
.... +Rhonda Hughes
.... 6 Connie Ann Schultz b: 21 Jul 1954
.... +Andrew Adams
.... 6 Cynthia Sue Schultz b: 07 Jan 1958
.... +Dennis Balliet
.... 6 Timothy Ben Schultz b: 18 Mar 1960

.... 4 William A. Scrivens b: 30 Apr 1901 in Cuyahoga Co., OH d: 06 Jul 1997 in Cleveland, OH

.............+Claretta R. Konzen b: ABT 1907 in Ohio d: 24 Oct 1960 in Cleveland, Cuyahoga Co., Ohio

.............5 Peter A. Scrivens b: ABT 1934

.............5 Jay D. Scrivens b: ABT 1933

.... 4 Clayton Scrivens b: 30 Oct 1904 in Ohio d: 26 Aug 1977 in Berea, Ohio

.............+Mary Jozwiak b: ABT 1885 in Ohio d: in Berea, Ohio

...... 3 Otto Friederich Heinrich (died in inf) Tegtmeier b: 07 Jan 1879 in Berea, Cuyahoga Co. OH d: 02 Jun 1879 in Berea, Cuyahoga Co.,Ohio

...... 3 Christina Dorothea Emilie Tegtmeier b: 01 Dec 1880 in Berea, Cuyahoga Co. OH d: 17 Nov 1963 in Middleburg Hts. Cuyahoga Co. OH

.... +Julius Carl Smith b: ABT 1879 in Ohio d: 12 Dec 1949 in Longview, Texas

.... 4 Leland J. Smith b: ABT 1910 in Ohio d: 1972 in Brookpark, Ohio

.............+Alice Allen b: ABT 1910 in Ohio

.............5 Glen A. Smith b: ABT 1938 in Cleveland, Cuyahoga Co., OH

................+Carol

................6 Caria Smith

................6 Cindy Smith

................6 Gregory Smith

.... 4 Bertha Smith b: ABT 1913

...... 3 William Carl Tegtmeier b: 15 May 1882 in Middleburg Twnshp, OH d: 10 Apr 1955 in Medina Twp., Medina, OH

.... +Erna Henriette Sophie Papenhagen b: 10 Oct 1888 in Beubukow, Schwerinschen, Mecklenburg, Germany d: 30 Sep 1982 in Dickinson, Stark North Dakota

.... 4 Loretta Mattie Tegtmeier b: 26 Aug 1911

.............+Paul Franklin Berry b: ABT 1908

.............5 David Berry b: ABT 1940

................+Beverly b: ABT 1940

................6 Wesley Berry b: ABT 1960

................6 Tammy Berry b: ABT 1962

................6 Stephanie Berry b: ABT 1965

.... +Mr. Estep

.............5 Karen Berry b: ABT 1941

................+Don Boyer b: ABT 1940

................6 Bryan Boyer b: ABT 1962 in Denver, CO

................6 Bradley Boyer b: ABT 1963 in Denver, CO

................6 Lisa Boyer b: ABT 1964 in Denver, CO

.... 4 Raymond Julius Tegtmeier b: 07 Dec 1912 in Brookpark, OH d: Sep 1982 in Wayne County, Ohio

.............+Laura Anna Minichbauer b: 01 Aug 1916 in Cleveland, Cuyahoga County, Ohio d: 10 Oct 1995 in Wayne County, Ohio

.............5 Donna Mae Tegtmeier b: 01 Sep 1944
................+William Schemrich b: ABT 1928
................6 Ronnie Schemrich b: ABT 1958
................6 Dale Schemrich b: ABT 1959
................6 Shawn Schemrich b: ABT 1960
.............5 Sharon Lee Tegtmeier b: 04 Jan 1947
................+Gary Erro b: ABT 1947
................6 Jody Ann Erro
................6 Amanda Marie Erro
.............5 Daniel Howard Tegtmeier b: 23 Sep 1957
................+Beth Ann Bougher b: 14 Jan 1959
................6 Ethan Daniel Tegtmeier b: 26 Jan 1990
................6 Sarah Christine Tegtmeier b: 16 May 1993
.... 4 Julia Wihelmina Tegtmeier b: 07 Oct 1914 in Brookpark, Cuyahoga Co., Ohio d: 02 Mar 1934 in Columbus, OH
.... 4 Alice Henrietta Tegtmeier b: 28 May 1916 in Brookpark, Ohio
.............+Edward William Taylor b: 01 Aug 1914 in New York d: 22 Jan 1967 in Jost Van Dyke, US Virgin Islands
.............5 Shirley Ann Taylor b: 11 Oct 1941 in Scranton, PA
................+Eugene Barr b: 13 Nov 1935 in West Virginia
................6 Jeffrey Barr b: 03 Dec 1963 in Zanesville, Ohio
...................+M. Christina Sidwell
...................7 Blake Barr b: 04 Jul 1996
...................7 Blair Barr b: 14 Feb 2001
................6 Kathy Anne Barr b: 04 Dec 1965 in Zanesville, OH
...................+Richard Skillman
...................7 Spencer Skillman b: 04 Oct 1997
................6 Angela Lynn Barr b: 07 Oct 1969 in Zainesville, Ohio
...................+Alan Gresh
...................7 Allison Nicole Gresh b: 27 Jul 2001
...................7 Alec Conner Gresh b: 18 Jun 2004
.............5 Edward William Taylor b: 11 Jan 1944 in Alden, NY
................+Nancy Untezuber b: 03 May 1948
................6 Craig Edward Taylor b: 07 Sep 1962
...................+Debra "Cricket" Jones
................6 Christine Jean Taylor b: Nov 1974
...................+Brian Lee Slone
...................7 Abigail Slone b: 1997
...................7 Victoria Slone b: 2002
.............5 James Robert Taylor b: 22 Mar 1949 in Berea, Ohio
................+Margie Moore b: 01 May 1950 in Newfoundland, Canada
................6 Shane Edward Taylor b: 01 Aug 1978

................6 Chasta Taylor b: 21 Mar 1981
...................*2nd Wife of James Robert Taylor:
...................+Nancy
.............5 Sandra Mina Taylor b: 17 Mar 1950 in Berea, Ohio
................+Peter Graham Bell b: 29 Aug 1937 in Wauseon, Ohio
................6 Heather Lynne Bell b: 30 Sep 1984 in Sarasota, FL
................6 Joshua Taylor Bell b: 13 Oct 1986 in Miami, FL
...................*2nd Husband of Alice Henrietta Tegtmeier:
...................+John Goralsky b: in Coalport, PA d: in Cleveland, OH
.... 4 Henry Adolph Tegtmeier b: 19 Mar 1918 in Ohio d: 09 Dec 1992 in Fairfield Glade, TN
.............+Harriett Barendt b: 09 Jan 1923 in Cleveland, Cuyahoga Co., OH
.............5 Miriam Ann Tegtmeier b: 08 Apr 1946
................+Paul Camper b: ABT 1937
................6 Nicole Camper
................6 Nathan Camper
...................+Dianne
.............5 Joan Charlotte Tegtmeier b: 07 Aug 1947
................+Tom Truman b: 21 Jul 1946
................6 Tom Truman b: 14 Sep 1972
...................7 Grace Truman
...................7 Alex Truman
...................7 Abigail Truman
...................7 Jonathan Truman
................6 Jacob Truman b: 13 Sep 1974
...................+Maggie
...................7 Jacob Truman
...................7 Paige Truman
...................7 Kaitlyn Truman
................6 Ashley Truman b: 20 Apr 1976
...................+Dan McMaster
................6 David Truman b: 12 Sep 1978
...................+Sara
.............5 Paul Tegtmeier b: 03 Aug 1948
................+Sandra Rice b: 19 Jul 1953
................6 Jamie Tegtmeier b: 25 Apr 1975
...................+Richard Hartley
...................7 Thaddeus Hartley
................6 Jeremy Tegtmeier b: 30 Mar 1976
...................+Tiffany Sinderyeld
...................7 Angela Tegtmeier
......................+Adam Rice
......................8 Jonah Rice

......................8 Beth Rice
......................8 Amelia Grace Rice
...................7 Matthew Tegtmeier
.... +Alice
................6 Jerrod Tegtmeier b: 22 Oct 1984
.............5 Joel Tegtmeier b: 13 Aug 1959
................+Tammie b: 30 Jul 1959
................6 Angela Tegtmeier b: 19 Apr 1979
................6 Matthew Tegtmeier b: 03 Feb 1981
................6 Laken Tegtmeier
................6 Logan Tegtmeier
.... 4 William Edward Tegtmeier b: 06 Mar 1920 in Brookpark, Ohio d: 24 Jul 2000 in Savanah, OH
.............+Lois Genvieve Westlund b: 31 Dec 1922 in Youngstown, Ohio
.............5 Linda Jean Tegtmeier b: 24 Aug 1947 in Youngstown, OH, North Side Hospital
................+Larry Gene Fenton b: 02 Mar 1947 in Mansfield, OH
................6 Shawn Michael Fenton b: 19 Jan 1968 in Columbus, OH
...................+Sharon Ann Myers b: 30 Apr 1969 in Dayton, OH
...................7 Amanda Michelle Fenton b: 04 Jan 2001 in Dayton, OH
...................7 Rachel Elizabeth Fenton b: 21 Mar 2004 in Kettering, OH
................6 Amy Krista Fenton b: 15 May 1971 in Pittsburgh, PA
...................+Paul David Kennedy b: ABT 1970
...................7 Jack William Kennedy b: 05 Jan 2003 in Mt. Carmel West Hosp'l, Columbus, OH
.............5 Terry Tegtmeier b: ABT 1949
.............5 Timothy Tegtmeier b: 15 Sep 1955
................+Pam Honaker
................6 Christine Tegtmeier
................6 Jonathan Tegtmeier
.............5 Todd Alan Tegtmeier b: 19 Feb 1962
................+Wendy Floyd
.... 4 Harold William Tegtmeier b: 02 Mar 1921 in Brookpark, Ohio d: 18 May 2003 in West Salem, Wayne, Ohio
.............+Lucille Clarissa Herman b: 12 Sep 1922 in Hermanville, Creston, Ohio
.............5 James Herman Tegtmeier b: 14 Feb 1945 in Lodi Hospital, near Wooster, Ohio
................+Jeanne Marie Gresser b: ABT 1945
................6 Molly Marie Tegtmeier b: 24 May 1971
...................+Brad Stull b: ABT 1971
...................7 Katie Marie Stull b: 09 Jun 1999
...................7 Riley Ann Stull b: 06 Jun 2003

................6 Randy James Tegtmeier b: 24 Mar 1975
...................+Heather Eubanks
...................7 Cody James Tegtmeier b: 10 Jul 2000
...................7 Brock Gilbert Tegtmeier b: 17 Jun 2002
.............5 Donald Phillip Tegtmeier b: 14 Nov 1948 in Lodi Hospital, near Wooster, Ohio
................+Neva Nestor b: ABT 1948
................6 Adam Donald Tegtmeier b: 17 Jun 1986
................6 Heidi Rose Tegtmeier b: 12 Apr 1989
.............5 Barbara Lucille Tegtmeier b: 15 Dec 1952 in Lodi Hospital, near Wooster, Ohio
................+James Kramer b: 06 Jun 1950
................6 William Kramer b: 05 Jan 1974
...................+Erin b: ABT 1974
...................7 Madeline Kramer b: 16 Jan 1999
...................7 Grant Kramer b: 10 Oct 2001
................6 Matthew James Kramer b: 29 Sep 1982
.............5 David Harold Tegtmeier b: 15 Sep 1954 in Lodi Hospital, near Wooster, Ohio
................+Rita Kay Kamp b: 25 Feb 1959 in Ashland, OH
................6 Luke David Tegtmeier b: 11 May 1983
................6 Jill Arlene Tegtmeier b: 29 Oct 1985
................6 Mark David Tegtmeier b: 25 Apr 1990
.... 4 Richard Elmer Tegtmeier b: 03 Jan 1924 in Berea,Cuyahoga Co.OH d: 17 Oct 1995 in Crossville, TN
.............+Sandy Louise Kestner b: 26 Sep 1933 in Ashland, Ashland Co., OH
.............5 Douglas Richard Tegtmeier b: 06 Dec 1952 in Wooster, Montgomery Co., OH
................+Suzanne Gulyas b: 09 Jan 1954 in Dayton, OH
................6 Jeff Tegtmeier b: 22 Dec 1982 in Columbus, Ohio
................6 Ryan Tegtmeier b: 11 Oct 1984 in Columbus, Ohio
.............5 Debra Louise Tegtmeier b: 09 Jan 1955 in Wooster, Wayne Co. OH
................+Terry Miller b: 05 Nov 1952
................6 Jeremiah Miller b: 20 Jun 1978
................6 Jonathan Miller b: 24 Aug 1979
...................+Rebekah Wright
.............5 Dean Edward Tegtmeier b: 02 Mar 1957 in Ashland, Ashland Co., OH
................+Michele Haynes b: 15 Aug 1957 in Toronto, Ohio
................6 Celeste Tegtmeier b: ABT 1982
................6 Shawn Tegtmeier b: ABT 1984
...................+Michelle
................6 Sara Tegtmeier b: ABT 1986

...... 3 Gustav Adolph Tegtmeier b: 06 Sep 1883 in Middleburg Twp, Cuyahoga Co. OH d: 24 Nov 1937 in Erie, Erie Co. PA
.... +Alma Marie Bauer b: ABT 1893 in Ohio d: Bef. 1966
.... 4 Howard J. Tegtmeier b: ABT 1913 in Ohio
.............5 Howard Jr. Tegtmeier b: ABT 1934
.... 4 [1] Dale Peterson
.............*2nd Wife of Gustav Adolph Tegtmeier:
.............+Rose M. Welnie b: 1882 d: 27 Nov 1937 in Erie, PA
.... 4 [1] Dale Peterson
... 2 Friedrich Wilhelm Tegtmeier b: 28 Sep 1845 in Iden, Osterburg, Prussia d: 16 Jan 1909 in Cleveland, Cuyahoga Co. OH
...... +Magdelena M. Droege b: ABT 1850 in Ohio d: 04 Aug 1936 in Cleveland, Cuyahoga Co., O
...... 3 Fred C. Teckmyer b: Aft. 1882 in Ohio d: 19 Mar 1961 in Eustis, Florida
.... +Marion Lowe b: 25 May 1888 in Ohio d: May 1982 in Seffner, Hillsborough, Florida
.... 4 Fred C. Teckmyer, Jr. b: 20 Feb 1914 in Ohio d: 21 Oct 2000 in Naples, Collier, Florida
.... 4 Isabel M. Teckmyer b: ABT 1918 in Ohio
.... 4 William L. Teckmyer b: 17 Jun 1912 in Ohio d: Feb 1978 in Cleveland, Cuyahoga, Ohio
.............+Jane Arters b: 14 Aug 1915 d: Feb 1986 in Cleveland, Cuyahoga, Ohio
.............5 William L. Jr., Teckmyer b: 29 Dec 1943 in Cleveland, Cuyahoga Co., Ohio d: 21 Dec 1998
...... 3 Lena Tegtmeier b: ABT 1879 in Ohio
...... 3 Celia F. Tegtmeier b: ABT 1888 in Ohio d: 31 Aug 1960 in Lakewood, Ohio
.... +Louis Rich b: ABT 1885 d: 1943 in Lakewood, Ohio
.... 4 Celia E. Rich b: ABT 1917 in Ohio
.... 4 Louis Jr. Rich
.... 4 Daughter Rich
...... 3 Madeline Tegtmeier b: ABT 1883 d: 13 Sep 1950 in Cuyahoga Co, Ohio
.... +Henry Pfizenmayer b: ABT 1873 d: 28 Nov 1949 in Lakewood, Cuyahoga, Ohio
.... 4 Victor C. Pfizenmayer
.............5 Victor C. Pfizenmayer
.............5 Thomas David Pfizenmayer
.... 4 Ariene Pfizenmayer d: 27 Mar 1942 in Cleveland, Cuyahoga Co., Ohio
.... 4 Lucille Pfizenmayer b: ABT 1909 in Ohio d: 04 Sep 1916 in Lakewood, Cuyahoga, Ohio
...... 3 Elsie Tegtmeier b: ABT 1885
.... +Louis G. Fairbank b: in Akron, Ohio
.... 4 Robert Lewis Fairbank b: 07 Jan 1912 in Cleveland, Cuyahoga Co., OH d: 18 Sep 1998 in Ohio

. . . 2 Karl Ferdinand Tegtmeier b: 05 Feb 1848 in Iden, Osterburg, Prussia d: 03 Jul 1907 in Middleburg Twp, Cuyahoga OH

. . . . . . +Maria Fridericka Johane Bartels b: Apr 1859 in Germany d: 04 Oct 1942 in Cleveland, Cuyahoga Co., O

. . . . . . 3 Karl Ferdinand Tegtmeier b: 30 Aug 1883 in Berea, Cuyahoga Co. OH d: 09 Apr 1956 in Cuyahoga Co., OH

. . . . +LENA Lenthe b: ABT 1883 in Ohio d: Bef. 1926 in Cuyahoga Co, Ohio

. . . . 4 Adelbert E. Tegtmeier b: Jun 1913 in Ohio d: 17 Dec 1991 in Ohio

. . . . 4 Nina Tegtmeier b: ABT 1915

. . . . +xxx Bartel

. . . . 4 Norma Tegtmeier b: ABT 1915 in Ohio

. . . . +xxx Pernoja

. . . . *2nd Wife of Karl Ferdinand Tegtmeier:

. . . . +Rose Kovalik d: 19 Jun 1947 in Cleveland, Cuyahoga, Ohio

. . . . 4 Celia Tegtmeier b: ABT 1912

. . . . +xxx Hickok

. . . . 4 Rose Tegtmeier b: ABT 1914

. . . . +xxx Biller

. . . . . . 3 Frieda Magdelena Tegtmeier b: 09 Jan 1885 in Middleburg Twp. Cuyahoga Co. OH d: 09 Jul 1946 in Berea, Cuyahoga Co.,Ohio

. . . . . . 3 Ernest Arthur Tegtmeier b: 17 Nov 1886 in Middleburg Twp. Cuyahoga Co. OH d: 18 Feb 1893 in Middleburg Twp. Cuyahoga Co. OH

. . . . . . 3 Friedrich Wilhelm Tegtmeier b: 14 May 1890 in Berea, Cuyahoga Co. OH d: Dec 1967 in Brookpark, Cuyahoga Co. OH

. . . . . . 3 Erma Maria Tegtmeier b: 25 Mar 1904 in Berea, Cuyahoga Co. OH d: 16 Feb 1977 in Medina Co. Ohio

. . . . +Elmer Behner b: ABT 1904

. . . . 4 Glenn Behner b: 18 Aug 1937 in Berea, Cuyahoga Co. OH d: 29 Jan 1999 in Brookpark, Cuyahoga Co. OH

. . . 2 Augusta Maria Elizabeth Tegtmeier b: 05 Dec 1852 in Iden, Osterburg, Prussia d: 02 Oct 1894 in Cleveland, Cuyahoga Co. OH

. . . . . . +Philip J. Mutz b: ABT 1848 in Germany d: in Cuyahoga Co, Ohio

. . . . . . 3 Lena Mutz b: ABT 1872

. . . . . . 3 Robert Mutz b: ABT 1879

. . . 2 Minna Wilhelmine Albertina Tegtmeier b: 01 Oct 1856 in Iden, Osterburg, Prussia d: 12 Sep 1867 in Middleburg Twp. Cuyahoga Co. Oh

. . . 2 ADELINE Louise Tegtmeier b: 22 Aug 1862 in Middleburg Twp. Cuyahoga, Oh d: 21 Feb 1903

. . . . . . +William W. Puls b: Nov 1856 in Cuyahoga Co., OH d: 19 Jun 1926 in Cuyahoga Co, Ohio

. . . . . . 3 William H. Puls b: Jan 1884 in Cuyahoga Co, Ohio d: 18 Apr 1943 in Berea, Cuyahoga Co.,Ohio

. . . . +Anna Parker b: ABT 1885 d: 09 Sep 1963 in Cuyahoga Co, Ohio

. . . . 4 Leah Puls b: ABT 1900
. . . .+xxx Svat b: ABT 1900
. . . . 4 LaVerne Puls b: ABT 1902
. . . .+xxx Woddups
. . . . 4 Thelma Puls b: ABT 1904
. . . .+xxx Phillips
. . . . 4 William Puls b: ABT 1906
. . . . . . 3 Elsie Puls b: Dec 1888 in Cuyahoga Co, Ohio
. . . . +xxx Rohde
. . . . . . 3 Leonard Puls b: Jun 1895 in Cuyahoga Co, Ohio d: 04 Oct 1957 in Berea, Cuyahoga Co.,Ohio
. . . . +Ethel L. Pincombe b: ABT 1896 in Ohio d: 03 Mar 1956 in Berea, Cuyahoga Co.,Ohio
. . . . 4 Carol Jean Puls b: ABT 1915
. . . .+xxx Keck
. . . . 4 Arlene Puls b: ABT 1917
. . . .+xxx Byers b: ABT 1915
. . . . 4 Myrtle Puls b: ABT 1919
. . . .+xxx Malone
. . . . . . 3 Elva Puls b: ABT 1890
. . . . +xxx Rhode b: in Brookpark, Cuyahoga, Ohio
. . . . . . 3 Emile Puls
. . . . . . 3 Adeline Puls
. . . . . . 3 Loretta Puls

Descendants of Johann Friedrich Tegtmeier

Generation No. 1

1. Johann Friedrich[2] Tegtmeier *(Tegtmeier[1])* was born August 31, 1821 in Iden, Osterburg, Prussia, and died August 27, 1903 in Middleburg Twp, Cuyahoga OH. He married **Maria Dorothea Bree** ABT 1843 in Germany. She was born September 29, 1823 in Iden, Osterburg, Prussia, and died May 29, 1903 in Middleburg Twp. Cuyahoga Co. OH.

Johann Friedrich Tegtmeier raised his family in Germany, farmed the land and provided for them. But the unrest in Germany was getting worse. The country was always at war. His sons Johann and Fred were nearing the age be drafted into the military, and he could sense another war coming. Once a healthy young man reached the age of 20, he was drafted into the military for a 3 year term. He may have already lost a son, as he and his wife had already been married 21 years. A difficult time for change. His wife thought he was crazy for thinking of leaving her beloved Germany, her family and friends. But Johann was determined to save his sons from war and possible death and in April applied for emigration papers to allow the trip.

The Homestead Act allowed 160 acres for free—and all you had to do was build a house and work the land. Other lands were available at a price. Good farm land. President Lincoln signed the Act May 20, 1962, and everyone was talking about the free land in America. What better time than now to leave and start a new life, at least for the children. There was nothing here for them. If they left now, they could find a good piece of land and stake a homestead one minute after January 1, 1963 when the law would be in effect.

They knew America was in the midst of Civil War. England had reinforced its borders in Canada. But it wasn't as if the war was being fought in their own back yard like here in Germany. And if they stayed to the North of the country, they should be out of harms way.

But the Tegtmeiers couldn't let their neighbors know their plans. This was just going to be a "visit" to friends in America as recorded in the ship's log book. Germany wouldn't want its military sons leaving the country. So at the age of 41, Johann packed very little and headed for Hamburg to set sail for America. They waited for days for a ship and purchased tickets for a cabin on *Sir Robert Peel*, a small bark (a three mast sailing ship) that sailed from Hamburg, Germany to New York. They joined nearly 300 passengers on board. Six passengers died during the trip, mostly children. At least they would have a cabin.

The Tegtmeiers were the only ones on board who said they were traveling to Ohio, signing the destination papers for the journey. The farm land was said to be black and rich, the climate much like Germany, the Berea Quarry was renowned worldwide for its sandstone, and always needed men, and the German woolen manufacturing was thriving.

There is an oil painting by I. Petersen & P. Holm Gebr (1852) of the "Bark", ***The Sir Robert Peel.*** A "Bark" is a three mast schooner that the Tegtmeier family sailed for 68 days in 1862 from Germany to New York. In 1968 the painting was in the possession of the firm of M. Sloman Jr. of Hamburg, Germany as a collection of undated vessels commanded by Captain P. E. Jorgensen. Copyright not available at this time. Unknown who owns the painting in 2007 to request copyright.

The B & O Railroad (Baltimore Ohio) had just finished repairs on the rails, bridges and engines the month before the Tegtmeiers arrived in New York. Engines and cars had been severely damaged by the Confederates during the Civil War and was just completed as reported in the New York Times. It is more likely that the Tegtmeiers took the train from New York to Ohio rather than the slower Canal system as confirmed by Alice Tegtmeier Taylor. She is sure that if they had taken the Canals, they would have heard stories about that adventure.

The[4] voyage started calm enough in early April. But most of the passengers were sick with the rolling of ship. Passengers in steerage had it worse, as they were obliged to roll up their bedding and sweep the decks each morning, sick or not. Some days the ship would rock so much in the high seas that you had to stay in bed so you wouldn't fall across the decks. The children loved it as the would slide back and forth, trying to run up the deck. On such days the passengers couldn't cook on their stoves.

The stoves were lit by the stewards each morning so everyone could cook their own meals. The Tegtmeier's had a cabin with their own stove. They would be rationed out enough food and water for the day. They had beets, and dumplings or biscuits, and always sauerkraut at least once a day to prevent scurvy. Vegetables were impossible to keep for a long journey. The Captain would tour the ship and make sure everyone had what they needed, and occasionally would bring a bottle of wine around for the ladies.

About 4 in the morning the crew would be rustling about, the ship's rooster would crow, the passengers would get up about 5 or 6 in the morning and busy themselves with knitting, sewing, baking, walking, writing, smoking or chattering all day.

---

4 Information gathered from several sources of diaries and other readings of different vessels crossing…this being mostly conjecture.

Some days the waves were so high they would come over the deck of the ship and as much as a foot of water would be on deck. The people would tumble across the ship, and many times they would nearly lose a passenger.

Some days the wind would fall and it would be so quiet and hot, no breeze. The captain would have the crew repair the rigging and sails. After nearly two weeks they were no closer to America because the wind was against them.

But on a clear day with the wind full in the sails, the porpoises would race the ship at the bow and some days the whales could be seen about a mile off. Occasionally you could hear the cry of "a ship, a ship" and some would race to the rail to see. But the Captain and crew kept every one from going to the side so the ship wouldn't tip.

At night, standing on deck, the waves would glisten and were beautiful. Something about the phosphorous in the water would make the water glow. Beautiful sight with a full moon and the stars so very bright.

June 24, 1862 they arrived at Castle Gardens in New York after 68 days at sea and were processed through immigration.

Walking the streets of New York to find a boarding house for over night was difficult. But they headed towards the German part of town. They didn't have to go far when they heard their native tongue. People were talking to them in German as soon as they disembarked. Hawkers were everywhere, each trying to shout louder than the other as they all vied for new business.

The family followed one young man as he hurriedly led them to a rooming house that offered breakfast. They found it difficult to walk after being on board the ship for so long. People told him it was just "Sea legs" and everyone felt that way when they get off the boat for a few days. It just takes time to get over it. Johann found it difficult to walk straight. They rested for a few days at the boarding house, planning their next step to Ohio.

They could head North to Albany on a steam ship, then catch the canal up thru Schenectady than ferry to Cleveland. The railroad after Albany had several train changes. The trains were different gauges in New York and they didn't use the same type track, so passengers would have to walk several miles to get to the next train track. Some track was laid 4 feet wide, some 6 feet. Sometimes passengers had to walk six miles between laid tracks to catch the next train route.

There were advertisements for men who were offered $100 to bring in more volunteers. Johann had to steer his two sons away from the uniformed men at the ports offering money to those who signed up today. His sons were already mad at him for dragging them away from all there friends in Germany. They probably hadn't talked to him for weeks during the voyage.

The *New York Times* (which then was only eight pages), dated June 29, 1862 reported trains being captured, passengers killed by the Confederates. The news of the Civil War was devastating, as many of the rail roads had already been damaged. Taking the train would be risky, but it would be quicker. The trains traveled 30 miles per hour. The canal boats traveled about 4 miles an hour. The passenger cost was about the same.

They could take the train with the Baltimore and Ohio Rail Road from New York to Columbus, then change in Columbus for Cleveland. The previous year on June of 1861 Stonewall Jackson's troop took out the bridge at Harper's Ferry, shutting down the main line of the B&O until now. The route had just been completed March 30th of 1862 and was running. There were only two train changes if they could find tickets. Many of the trains were hauling troops and supplies. Even in New York, uniformed men with their rifles could be seen everywhere. Marshall law was already instituted in several cities.

After considering the sail from Germany, no one was anxious to get back on a boat. They decided on taking the Baltimore Ohio Rail road to Columbus, then up to Cleveland.—*Alice Tegtmeier was sure they had taken the train.*

COPY OF THE TRANSLATION OF EMIGRATION PAPER *(courtesy of Lester Meier)*

No. 26 of the Passport Journal
Royal Prussian Passport for Foreign Travel
Personal Description of holder for Traveling: via Hamburg

1. Place of birth (Iden) the day laborer Johann Friedrich Tegtmeier,
2. Place of residence Iden accompanied by his wife, Marie nee Bree, and the following children:

3. Year and day of birth	1821 August 31
4. Height	5'4"
5. Hair	
6. Eyebrows	dark blond
7. Eyes	gray
8. Nose	normal
9. Mouth	normal
10. Beard	clean shaven
11. Face	normal
12. Stature	medium
13. Unusual marks	None

1. Johann Heinrich, 18 years
2. Friedrich Wilhelm, 16
3. Carl Friedrich, 14
4. Maria Elisabeth, 10
5. Minna Wilhelmine, 4

Purpose of Journey: visit
to: North America

Signature of the holder:
Johann Friedrich Tegtmeier
A11 civil and military authorities are requested to allow the holder, authorized by police certification, to travel and return freely and unhindered, and if need be to grant him and support.
Issued, Magdeburg 17 April 1862
—Royal Prussian Government

Sir Robert Peel, Ship's Log

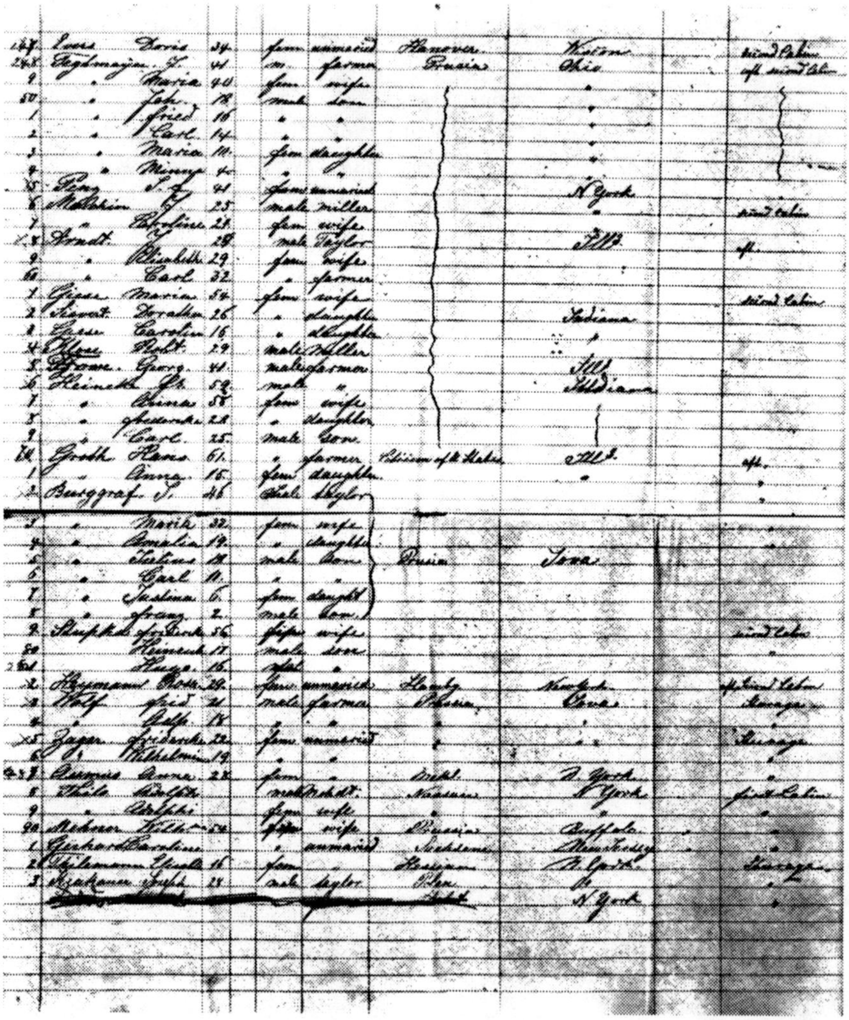

247	Evers	Doris	34	fem	unmarried	Hanover	Wiscon	second Cabin
248	Tegtmeyer	J.	41	m.	farmer	Prussia	Ohio	aft second Cabin
9	"	Maria	40	fem	wife		"	
50	"	Joh.	18	male	son		"	
1	"	Fried	16	"	"		"	
2	"	Carl	14	"	"		"	
3	"	Maria	11	fem	daughter		"	
4	"	Minna	4	"	"		"	

The only family going to Ohio …

Foreward of Passenger List

I, N. J. Jurgens * Master of the Hamb Ship S. R. Peel do solemnly, sincerely and truly swear that the following List or Manifest, subscribed by me, and now delivered by me to the Collector of the Customs of the Collection District of New York, is a full and perfect list of all the passengers taken on board of the said ship at Hamburg from which port said ship has now arrived; and that on said list is truly designated the age, the sex and the occupation of each said passenger, the part of the vessel occupied by each during the passage, the country to which each belongs, and also the country of which it is intended by each to become an inhabitant; and that said List or Manifest truly sets forth the number of said passengers who have died on said voyage, and the names and ages of those who died. Sworn to this 24 June 1862 N. J. Jurgens, so help me God. Before me Aubuclice*
List or Manifest of all the Passengers taken on board the Hamb Ship S. R. Peel whereof N. J. Jurgens is Master, from Hamburg, burthen 656 tons.

Columns represent: Name, Age, Sex, Occupation, Country to which they severally belong, Country of which they intend to become inhabitants, Part of the vessel occupied by each.

Ship's passenger list, Sir Robert Peel—1862

248	Tegtmeyer	J	41	m	farmer	Prusia	Ohio	aft second cabin
249	Tegtmeyer	Maria	40	fem	wife	Prusia	Ohio	aft second cabin
250	Tegtmeyer	Joh	18	male	son	Prusia	Ohio	aft second cabin
251	Tegtmeyer	Fried	16	male	son	Prusia	Ohio	aft second cabin
252	Tegtmeyer	Carl	14	male	son	Prusia	Ohio	aft second cabin
253	Tegtmeyer	Maria	10	fem	daughter	Prusia	Ohio	aft second cabin
254	Tegtmeyer	Minna	4	fem	daughter	Prusia	Ohio	aft second cabin

The family writes down as their destination "Ohio", according to the ship's log—who lives there they already know? They go direct to Ohio and Adeline is born in Ohio, abt 1863.

—

Advertisement for lands available.

THE HOMESTEAD ACT OF 1862 The United States government had indeed promised farms to those who wanted them. The 1862 Homestead Act essentially said that any citizen, or those seeking citizenship, of the United States could claim a designated area of land for farming. The piece of land was 160 acres in size and would be given to the person claiming it, as long as the following conditions were met:

- The individual must be over 21 years of age.
- Some kind of home must be built on the land.
- The land must be cultivated.
- The individual and/or his family must live on the claim at least 6 months every year
- All conditions must be met for a total of 5 years and the claim must be finalized within
- two years of the end of this five-year period.

NEWS from <u>the New York Times</u> (only 8 pages in 1862 at a cost of 3 cents an issue) of the Civil War the day they land in America. Actually the entire paper was filled with information from the campaigns, battles, cities instituted Marshal law, bounty for Confederates,—New York Times, 1862. It also told of the repairs completed on the B & O Railroad the previous month.

1870 Census 1870 United States Federal Census > Ohio > Cuyahoga > Middleburgh
Tegtmeier, (transcriber read this as "Yeztwin" but if you read the original record, you can easily read Tegtmeier) Fred, age 48 from Deutschland; Dora age 46; Henry age 27; Fred 24; Ferdinand 21; Louisa 18 (b abt 1852) ; Adeline 7, born in Ohio. Value of Real Estate 7000, value of personal items, 400.

1880 CENSUS: Middleburgh, Cuyahoga, Ohio
Frederick TEGETEMYER age 58 (b abt 1822), farmer, born in Prussia; Dora, wife age 56 born in Prussia, Ferdinand, age 32 born in Prussia, farmer; Adeline, age 17 born in Ohio, at home.

Johann Frederick Tegtmeier & Maria Dorothea Bree Tegtmeier
Married abt 1843 Germany

1890 Census not available, only partial records remain.

There is a cemetery by the rail road tracks that goes over a bridge at the end of Sheldon Road in Berea, Ohio, the old St. Paul's Lutheran Cemetery and you will find the gravestones of most of this Tegtmeier family there. St. Paul's Church was a dark quarried stone church with beautiful stained glass windows on Front Street in Berea, just North of Baldwin-Wallace College on Front Street. St. Paul's Church building was sold I believe in the 1960's, and a new St. Paul's Lutheran Church was built across the street from Berea High School.

Johann Friedrich Tegtmeier was a farmer and would take his produce to Cleveland to be sold. More than once he would bring home a truck of spoiled onions that heated up in the sun too much and had to be thrown away. He would throw this away before seeing his wife so she wouldn't get upset.

Children of JOHANN TEGTMEIER and MARIA BREE are:

2. i. Johann Heinrich[3] Tegtmeier, b. January 8, 1844, Iden, Osterburg, Prussia; d. January 24, 1897, Middleburg Twp, Cuyahoga, OH.
3. ii. Friedrich Wilhelm Tegtmeier, b. September 28, 1845, Iden, Osterburg, Prussia; d. January 16, 1909, Cleveland, Cuyahoga Co. OH.
4. iii. Karl Ferdinand Tegtmeier, b. February 5, 1848, Iden, Osterburg, Prussia; d. July 3, 1907, Middleburg Twp, Cuyahoga OH.
5. iv. Augusta Maria Elizabeth Tegtmeier, b. December 5, 1852, Iden, Osterburg, Prussia; d. October 2, 1894, Cleveland, Cuyahoga Co. OH.

   v. MINNA WILHELMINE ALBERTINA TEGTMEIER, b. October 1, 1856, Iden, Osterburg, Prussia; d. September 12, 1867, Middleburg Twp. Cuyahoga Co. Oh.
   Died at c. age 11. *(My mother, Alice Tegtmeier Taylor, said she died of homesickness.)*

6. vi. Adeline Louise Tegtmeier, b. August 22, 1862, Middleburg Twp. Cuyahoga, Oh; d. February 21, 1903.

Generation No. 2

2. JOHANN HEINRICH[3] TEGTMEIER *(JOHANN FRIEDRICH[2], TEGTMEIER[1])* was born January 8, 1844 in Iden, Osterburg, Prussia, and died January 24, 1897 in Middleburg Twp, Cuyahoga, OH. He married **SOPHIA LOUISE JULIANA REINECKE** April 18, 1871 in Independence, Cuyahoga Co. OH, daughter of JOHAN CHRISTOV REINECKE. She was born January 19, 1848 in Prussia, and died May 11, 1933 in Washington Twp, Henry, OH.

Johann Heinrich Tegtmeier was known as Henry and was born in 1844. He was just 18 years old when he left Hamburg, Germany. At a time when he probably had a girl friend, maybe thinking about getting married, he may have had plans on what he wanted to do. But this was Germany. Choices were slim. He may have fought leaving his home, thinking he was old enough to stay, and was probably anxious to fight as young men often are. He may have been excited about exploring a new land, not knowing what was ahead. It may not have been his choice, but he did join the family on the voyage from Hamburg to New York on the Sir Robert Peel, a three mast sailing ship in 1862. They called him "Henry" in the new world.

The family settled in Middleburg, a township just outside of Cleveland in Ohio. In 1870, Henry lived at home and worked at the Berea Quarry. The quarry was renowned for the production of grindstones. After years at the quarry, he developed asthma from the sandstone grit and had to quit and became a weaver. Many men died from breathing the sandstone grit as they cut the huge blocks into grindstones.

By April of 1871, he met and married Julia, the daughter of Johan Reinecke. She was born in Prussia and probably had a lot in common as far as leaving friends and family behind. She was four years younger than Henry. In January they had a baby girl they named Ida. She died a few months later in July. Their children were Ida, Hulda, Henry, Lucy, Otto, Christina, William Carl, and Adolph. Ida, Adeline and Otto died in infancy.

Johann Heinrick Tegtmeier
And Sophia Louise Juliana Reinecke
Married 1871, Independence, Ohio

In 1897, Henry died of asthma at the age of 53.

Julia, a widow at age 49, had five young children to look after. Her son, Henry became the head of the household, and at the age of 25 provided for his sister Christina, and brothers William and Adolph. Hulda married Heinrich Ernst A. Ahleman on March 2, 1893.

Julia is not around in 1900 for the census. Perhaps she is visiting family. In 1912 Julia married Ferdinand Staats who was four years older than she and the lived in Washington Township, Henry, Ohio. But in 1930 she has moved in with her daughter Christina and lived in Chagrin Falls, Ohio. She died May 15, 1933, Berea, Cuyahoga, OH.

1870 Census 1870 United States Federal Census > Ohio > Cuyahoga > Middleburgh
Tegtmeier, (transcriber put it down as "Yeztwin") Fred, age 48; Dora age age 46; **Henry age 27**; Fred 24; Ferdinand 21; Louisa 18 (b abt 1852) ; Adeline 7, born in Ohio.

1880 Census: Berea, Cuyahoga, Ohio—maybe (should be under "John")
Henry Tegtmier, age 36, quarry man, born in Germany; Julia age 32, wife born in Germany; Hulda age 7; Henry age 5; Lucy age 3 children born in Ohio.

Occupation: Henry worked in the Quarry at Berea but the work was hard. He later lists his occupation as a "weaver" in the obituary.

1890 CENSUS, partial census, unavailable for Cuyahoga County, Ohio

1900 Census, Middleburg Twn, Cuyahoga, page 42B
1900 Census: living next to his Uncle Ferd: Cuyahoga—other townships (Middleburgh) ed # 222—page 8 (page 47B) Henry Tegtmeir, head, farmer, single age 24, born October 1875; both parents born in Germany; Christina, sister, single, December 1880, age 19, born in Ohio; William, brother born May 1882, single, farm laborer; Adolph, brother age 16, Sept 1883, farm laborer. (I don't see Julia anywhere in this census for this county.)

(Uncle Ferdinand next door) 1900
Tegtmeier, Ferdinand, age 52, Fredricka age 41; Carl age 16; Frieda, daughter age 15, and Fred age 10.

1910 Census • Ohio • Cuyahoga • Other Townships • ED# 23 (Middleburg)
Julia Tegtmeier, age 59 widow, had 7 children, 6 survive; born in Germany; Henry age 37 son, (1873) works at a factory; William age 27, general farm; Adolph age 26 general farm; children born in Ohio.

1930 United States Federal Census > Ohio > Cuyahoga > Chagrin Falls > District 553
Smith, Julius, head, age 50, Christina, wife, age 48; Leland son age 20; **JULIA Tegtmeier**, mother in law, age 82, widowed; Bertha Smith, age 46, sister.

CEMETERY RECORDS
Id#: 0357898
Name: Tegtmeier, John H.
Date: 1897
Source: Cemetery record; Cleveland Necrology File, Reel #079.
Notes: 1844–1897. St. Paul's Lutheran Cemetery Berea, Ohio. (53 years old)
Burial: January 27, 1897, St. Paul's Lutheran Church, Berea, Cuyahoga Co. OH
Confirmed: St. Paul's Lutheran Church, Berea, Cuyahoga Co. OH
Immigration: June 24, 1862, sailed from Hamburg to NY, "Sir Robert Peel"
Occupation: Weaver

TheBerea, Ohio Quarry
The stone that was quarried in Berea was used in buildings in the United States and abroad. Quarry workers in the mid-1800s were of English, Scottish and German ancestry. The town's symbol is a grindstone, a tribute to the many sandstone grindstones that came out of its quarries. Before concrete came into wide use, sandstone was a very important construction material, and huge amounts of it came from Berea, earning it the title of "The Grindstone Capital of the World." Several lakes in the area are quarry pits that have been allowed to fill with water.

> The remains of an old quarry on Smith Road between Middleburg Hts. And Berea existed back in the 1950s near the railroad track. It was abandoned and had filled up with water. Parents didn't like the kids swimming there, saying it was too dangerous. At the bottom of the water I believe still exists the remains of a train engine that had fallen in when it was still a quarry, but due to the cost of removing or repairing, it was abandoned.

Sophia Louise Juliana Reinecke b. abt 1852
"Julia"

Bottom left: Julia and her two sisters, Wilhelmine and Augusta. Julia is sitting lower right.

Right: Grandma Reinecke in her 90s,

Phtoos courtesy of Lester Meier

Grandma (Julia Reinecke Tegtmeier) loved flowers, and had narcissus and daffodils growing all across the front of the house in Brookpark. We didn't have lawnmowers, so we would let a couple of cows graze in the front yard to mow the lawn. It greened it up with the fertilizer. Cleaning rugs, we took carpets and put them over a clothes line, then took a rug beater, a type of long wooden handle with two wires looped, and beat the hang out of 'em.

—Alice Taylor

Children of JOHANN TEGTMEIER and JULIA REINECKE are:

7. i. Hulda Louise Maria[4] Tegtmeier, b. May 21, 1873, Independence, OH; d. February 25, 1968, Adrian, Lenawee, MI.

ii. IDA LOUISE (DIED IN INF) TEGTMEIER, b. January 21, 1872, Berea, Cuyahoga Co. OH; d. July 21, 1872, Berea, Cuyahoga Co. OH.

Notes for IDA LOUISE (DIED IN INF) TEGTMEIER:
Died in infancy.

8. iii. HENRY WILLIAM CARL TEGTMEIER, b. November 4, 1874, Middleburg Twp., Cuyahoga, OH; d. June 8, 1963, Millersburg, Holmes, OH.

iv. ADELINE ELIZABETH EMMA (DIED IN INF) TEGTMEIER, b. April 8, 1876, Berea, Cuyahoga Co. OH; d. September 18, 1876, Berea, Cuyahoga Co. OH.

Notes for ADELINE ELIZABETH EMMA (DIED IN INF) TEGTMEIER:

9. v. LUCIE ADELINE JULIANNA TEGTMEIER, b. August 6, 1877, Berea, Cuyahoga Co. OH; d. October 9, 1921, Middleburg Twp, Cuyahoga OH.

vi. OTTO FRIEDERICH HEINRICH (DIED IN INF) TEGTMEIER, b. January 7, 1879, Berea, Cuyahoga Co. OH; d. June 2, 1879, Berea, Cuyahoga Co.,Ohio.

Notes for OTTO FRIEDERICH HEINRICH (DIED IN INF) TEGTMEIER

10. vii. CHRISTINA DOROTHEA EMILIE TEGTMEIER, b. December 1, 1880, Berea, Cuyahoga Co. OH; d. November 17, 1963, Middleburg Hts. Cuyahoga Co. OH.

11. viii. William Carl Tegtmeier, b. May 15, 1882, Middleburg Twnshp, OH; d. April 10, 1955, Medina Twp., Medina, OH.

12. ix. Gustav Adolph Tegtmeier, b. September 6, 1883, Middleburg Twp, Cuyahoga Co. OH; d. November 24, 1937, Erie, Erie Co. PA.

3. Friedrich Wilhelm[3] Tegtmeier *(Johann Friedrich[2], Tegtmeier[1])* was born September 28, 1845 in Iden, Osterburg, Prussia, and died January 16, 1909 in Cleveland, Cuyahoga Co. OH. He married Magdelena M. Droege June 25, 1878, daughter of Frederick Droege. She was born ABT 1850 in Ohio, and died August 4, 1936 in Cleveland, Cuyahoga Co., O.

Fred Tegtmeyer was born in Iden, Osterburg Prussia in 1845 and was 16 years old when he came to America with his family on the sailing ship, the Sir Robert Peel in 1862. They journeyed to Ohio and settled just outside of Cleveland where the Berea Quarry was offering jobs.

Most of the Tegtmeiers of this family went to the same church on Front Street in Berea, St. Paul's Lutheran. The Church was later sold, and the congregation built a new church across from Berea High School in the early 1960's. Fred was confirmed there along with his brothers and sisters.

Fred met and married Magdelena M. Droege in June of 1878, the daughter of Frederick Droege. They called her "Lena" and she was born in Ohio, 12 years younger than Fred. Fred moved closer into the town of Cleveland and set up a grocery store. Their children were Madeline, Fred, Elsie and Celia. They also took in borders to help ends meet and Lund Hane who was a coal dealer, born in Denmark stayed with them, as well as Fred Schultz who also worked in the store.

Fred was a grocer. Berea was a college town: German College which later became Baldwin College, then Baldwin-Wallace College. But when the town of Berea first chartered out of the lands of Middleburg, the founders decided to put a reservation on the land and not allow alcohol to be made or sold on any of the properties. This made quite a mix with the quarry men who after a long day at the Berea Quarry couldn't find a drink to quench their thirst This may be part of the reason that by the 1900 Census Fred moves to Cleveland on Lorain Street and has a saloon. By 1900, he had become a saloon keeper in partnership with Jacob Keller or Lorraine Street in Cleveland. He was 65 years old when he died in 1909.

His son, Fred married Marion Lowe of Ohio about 1911.

His daughter, Celia, married Louis Rich of Cleveland who was the Orchestra leader of the Louis Rich Winton Hotel Orchestra, producing radio programs nationwide from Cleveland, Ohio, Winton Hotel from about 1925–1935.

Notes for Friedrich Wilhelm Tegtmeier:
New York Passenger Lists, 1851–1891 > 1862 > June > Sir Robert Peel
Tegtmeijer, Fred age 41 married farmer from Prussia, destination, Ohio (second cabin)

Maria age 40
Joh male age 18
Fried 16
Carl 14
Maria 10
Minna 4

1870 United States Federal Census > Ohio > Cuyahoga > Middleburgh
Tegtmeier, (transcriber put it down as "Yeztwin") Fred, age 48; Dora age age 46; Henry age 27; Fred 24; Ferdinand 21; Louisa 18 (b abt 1852) ; Adeline 7, born in Ohio.

1880 Census Cleveland, Cuyahoga, Ohio
Fred Tegtmeier age 34, born in Prussia, retail grocer, father and mother both born in Prussia; Lena age 23, (MagdaLENA Droege) born in Ohio, parents both born in Prussia; daughter Lena, age 1 born in Ohio. Lund A Hane, age 38, border/coal dealer, born in Denmark; Frederick Schultz, age 18, border and clerk in store, born in Prussia.

1900: Cleveland, Ohio Directory
F. W. Tegtmeier and Jacob Keller, Saloon, 625 Lorain

United States Federal Census > Ohio > Cuyahoga > Cleveland > District 155
Fred Tegtmeier, age 84, saloon keeper; Lena age 48, born April 1857, married 21 years, 4 children, 4 survive; Madeline born May 1879 father born in Germany, mother born in Ohio; Frederick May 1881 age 19 at school; Elais age 13, Jan 1887; Celia April 1889

Taylor L. S. nuts and bolts, r. 364 Superior
Taylor Martin (Lockwood, Van Doorn & Miller), r. 1039 Willson av.
Taylor Mary, Miss, domestic Mary Rice
Taylor Mary, wid. William, r. al. rr. 289 Perry
Taylor Mary E. Miss, forewoman, r.42 Bolivar
Taylor May, Miss, bds. al. rear 289 Perry
Taylor Michael, engineer, bds. 23 Superior
Taylor Milton, conductor C. & P. R. R. r. 674 St. Clair
Taylor Milton, r. Highland, 3d b. e.Fairmount
Taylor M. sew. machine agt. bds. 7 Hill
Taylor Newton W. agt. Clev. Paper Co.128 St. Clair, r. 264 Prospect
Taylor Patrick, lab. r. ws. McCart, 5th b. n. Detroit, W. C.
Taylor P. N. (Taylor Bros. & Co.), r. 51 Huntington
Taylor Robert, r. 7 Floyd
Taylor Robert, salesman Coulton & Taylor
Taylor Robert A. shoemkr. r. 105 Alabama
Taylor Ruth, wid. George T. r. 260 Prospect
Taylor Samuel, contractor, r. 9 Floyd
Taylor Sarah M. Mrs. dressmkr. 316 Erie
Taylor St. Methodist Episcopal Church, 255 Taylor; Rev. T. C. Warner, pastor
Taylor S. G. clk. T. W. Brainard, bds. 316 Pearl
Taylor Thomas, molder Clev. Stove Co. r. 91 McLean
Taylor Thomas J. (Allen M. Taylor & Co.), r. 436 Superior
Taylor T. R. r. Ansel av. ne. cor. Superior
Taylor Uriah, r. Columbus, cor. Holmden av.
Taylor V. C. real est. 249 Superior, res. 1343 Euclid av.
Taylor Warren, brickmkr. bds. 219 Petrie
Taylor William (Coulton & Taylor), res. 1915 Miles pk. st.
Taylor William (Taylor Bros. & Co.) and (William Taylor & Co.), r. 18 Burnham
Taylor William (Taylor, Kilpatrick & Co.), r. 1008 Forrest
Taylor William, cook H. W. Murray, res. 134 Orange
Taylor William, molder, r. 2436 Cornell
Taylor William C. clk. H. A. Parks, res. 54 Bond
Taglor William D. salesman George Worthington & Co. r. 35 Granger
Taylor William E. bkkpr. Globe Iron Works, r. 384 Scovill av.
Taylor William E. salesman Charles H. Weed, r. 231 Detroit
Taylor William G. lawyer, room 2, 5 ws. Pub. Sqr. bds. 24 Chestnut
Taylor William M. r. 2551 Cottage
Taylor William N. with Taylor Bros. & Co. r. 18 Burnham
Taylor William R. bill clk. Wm. Bingham & Co. r. 7 Floyd
Taylor William & Co. (William and J. E. Taylor), wire cloth, Bratenahl blk.
Taylor W. lab. Clev. Roll. Mill
Taylor W. H. lawyer, room 6, 19½ ws. Pub. Sqr. r. 86 Huron
Taylor W. H. lawyer, res. Chestnut Ridge, se. cor. Brig
Taylor W. R. carpenter, r. 4 Orange
Taylor W. R. clk. r. 47 Irving
Taylor Zacharia M. bkkpr. bds. 202 Detroit
Taylor Zachary P. (Marvin, Taylor & Laird), r. 783 Logan

TAYLOR & BOGGIS, (H. F. Taylor and R. H. Boggis), Iron Founders, 65 to 73 Central Way
Teachout A. (A. Teachout & Co.), r. 13 Fulton
Teachout A. M. Miss, cutter Felsenheld Bros. r. 1 Fulton ct.
Teachout A. R. (A. Teachout & Co.), res. 314 Franklin av.
Teachout A. & Co. (A. and A. R. Teachout), doors, sash, etc. 21 Michigan
Teachout Howard E. clk. auditor's dept. L. S. & M. S. Ry. r. 65 Eagle
Tead Henry, lab. r. 32 Pear
Teadt Charles, brickmkr. R. O. White, r. 617 Clark av.
TEAGLE JOHN, (Scofield Shurmer & Teagle), r. 1625 Euclid av.
Teahan John, brakeman A. & G. W. Ry. bds. 17 University
Teal Amanda I. wid. George, boarding-house, 219 St. Clair
Teal Charles H. paper cutter Clev. Paper Co. r. Lake, cor. Seneca
Teal John E. (Teal & Sargent), r. 152 Greenwood
Teal Joseph B. turner J. B. Hervey, r. 8 W. Madison av.
TEAL & SARGENT, (John E. Teal and H. Q. Sargent), Photographic Stock, Picture Frames, etc. 179 Superior
Teaner Henry, servant William Hale
Teare E. E. salesman Potter, Birdsall & Co. r. 45 Charles
Teare Seelye, machinist, r. 56 Portland
Teare William, lab. A. & G. W. frt. depot
Teare William, watchman, r. 121 Walton av.
Teare W. H. (Potter, Birdsall & Co.), res. 45 Charles
Teckemeier Henry, blksmith. r. 56 Guitto
Teckemeier John, mason, r. 3 Branch av.
Teckemeyer Mary, wid. Gerhard, r. 48 Burton
Tedhram Fredricka, wid. Louis, r. 34 Rossiter
Tedhram Louis, mason, r. 34 Rossiter
Teed Burt, cash. *Penny Press*, r. 364 Gordon av.
Teed J. W. conductor, r. 364 Gordon av.
Teesling John, mason, r. 75 Iona
Teevin Patrick, lab. r. 70 Taylor
Tegen Christian, saloon, 338 St. Clair
Tegethoff Frank C. treas. r. 302 Sterling av.
Tegge Fritz, lab. r. 50 Guitto
Tegmar Andrew, molder, r. 48 Brooklyn
Tegrafe Henry, saloon, 1467 Cedar av.
Tegtmeier Frederick, grocer, 443 Lorain
Tegtmeyer Frederick, finisher, r. 27 Henry
Tehler George C. shoemkr. r. 365 Sterling av.
Te Hofste William, gardener, r. 32 Siegel
Teichman Charles, painter, r. 245 St. Clair
Teick August, lab. r. 104 Ver ennes
Teirmeister August, driver Kingsborough & Fisher
Tekempe John, lab. Zmich & Nahuis
Tekniepe Dora, Mrs. r. 106 Oregon
Tekniepe Frank, carpenter, r. rr. 100 Oregon
Tekniepert Barney, lab. B. W. Jenness
Tela John, wks. Clev. Rubber Co. res. 40 Brooker av.
Tela John, Jr. wks. Clev. Rubber Co. res. 28 Amos
Tela Joseph, wks. Clev. Rubber Co. res. 40 Brooker av.

More About FRIEDRICH WILHELM TEGTMEIER:
Confirmed: St. Paul's Lutheran Church, Berea, Cuyahoga Co. OH
Immigration: June 24, 1862, Sailed from Hamburg to NY, "Sir Robert Peel"
Occupation: 1880, Grocery store

Notes for MAGDELENA M. DROEGE:
1880 Census Cleveland, Cuyahoga, Ohio
Fred Tegtmeier age 34, born in Prussia, retail grocer, father and mother both born in Prussia; Lena age 23, born in Ohio, parents both born in Prussia; daughter Lena, age 1 born in Ohio.

1920 Census 1920 U.S. Census • Ohio • Cuyahoga • Lakewood
Louis Richy, head 35 years old; Celia F, wife age 30, born in Ohio; Celia E age 2 7/12 months born in Ohio; Magdalena Tegtmeier, mother in law, age 52, widow.

OBITUARY Id#: 0357900 1936
Name: Tegtmeier, Lena M.
Date: Aug 4 1936
Source: Source unknown; Cleveland Necrology File, Reel #079.
Notes: Tegtmeier: Lena M., widow of the late Fred W. beloved mother of Mrs. Henry Pfizenmayer, Fred C. Teckmyer, Mrs. Lewis G. Fairbank of Akron, O., and Mrs. Louis Rich, Aug. 1, Residence, 1099 Kenneth dr. Now at the Saxton-Daniels-Mastick Funeral Home, 13215 Detroit Ave., where services will be held Tuesday, Aug. 4, at 3 p. m.

Children of FRIEDRICH TEGTMEIER and MAGDELENA DROEGE are:

13. i. Fred C.[4] Teckmyer, b. Aft. 1882, Ohio; d. March 19, 1961, Eustis, Florida.

ii. LENA TEGTMEIER, b. ABT 1879, Ohio.

Notes for LENA TEGTMEIER:
1880 Census
Fred Tegtmeier age 34, born in Prussia, retail grocer, father and mother both born in Prussia; Lena age 23, born in Ohio, parents both born in Prussia; daughter LENA, age 1 born in Ohio. ***

1920 Census 1920 U.S. Census • Ohio • Cuyahoga • Lakewood
Louis Rich, head 35 years old; Celia F, wife age 30, born in Ohio; Celia E age 2 7/12 months born in Ohio; Magda**lena** Tegtmeier, mother in law, age 52, widow.

OBITUARY Id#: 0357900
Name: Tegtmeier, Lena M.
Date: Aug 4 1936
Source: Source unknown; Cleveland Necrology File, Reel #079.
Notes: Tegtmeier: Lena M., widow of the late Fred W. beloved mother of Mrs. Henry Pfizenmayer, Fred C. Teckmyer, Mrs. Lewis G. Fairbank of Akron, O., and Mrs. Louis Rich, Aug. 1, Residence, 1099 Kenneth dr. Now at the Saxton-Daniels-Mastick Funeral Home, 13215 Detroit ave., where services will be held Tuesday, Aug. 4, at 3 p. m.

14. iii. CELIA F. TEGTMEIER, b. ABT 1888, Ohio; d. August 31, 1960, Lakewood, Ohio.
15. iv. Madeline Tegtmeier, b. ABT 1883; d. September 13, 1950, Cuyahoga Co, Ohio.
16. v. Elsie Tegtmeier, b. ABT 1885.

4. KARL FERDINAND[3] TEGTMEIER *(JOHANN FRIEDRICH[2], TEGTMEIER[1])* was born February 5, 1848 in Iden, Osterburg, Prussia, and died July 3, 1907 in Middleburg Twp, Cuyahoga OH. He married MARIA FRIDERICKA JOHANE BARTELS January 10, 1883. She was born April 1859 in Germany, and died October 4, 1942 in Cleveland, Cuyahoga Co., O.

Karl Ferninand Tegtmeier was born in 1848 in Iden Prussia and was 14 years old when he came to America.

Notes for KARL FERDINAND TEGTMEIER:
New York Passenger Lists, 1851–1891 > 1862 > June > Sir Robert Peel
Tegtmeijer, Fred age 41 married farmer from Prussia, destination, Ohio (second cabin)
Maria age 40
Joh male age 18

Fried 16
Carl 14 (1848) In the census he is called Ferdin
Maria 10
Minna 4

(Is he called Ferdinand, or Carl?? cemetery records show Ferdinand)

1870 Census 1870 United States Federal Census > Ohio > Cuyahoga > Middleburgh
Tegtmeier, (transcriber read this as "Yeztwin" but if you read the original record, you can easily read Tegtmeier) Fred, age 48 from Deutschland; Dora age age 46; Henry age 27; Fred 24; Ferdinand 21; Louisa 18 (b abt 1852) ; Adeline 7, born in Ohio.

1880 CENSUS: Middleburgh, Cuyahoga, Ohio
Frederick TEGETEMYER age 58 (b abt 1822), farmer, born in Prussia; Dora, wife age 56 born in Prussia, Ferdinand, age 32 born in Prussia, farmer; Adeline, age 17 born in Ohio, at home.

1900 U.S. Census • Ohio • Cuyahoga • Other Townships • ED# 222—page 8 (next door)
Tegtmeier, Ferd, head, farmer, age 52 (1848), married 18 years, Feb 1848, immigrated 1862, 38 years ago, farmer; Fredrica age 41, April 1859, married 18 years, had 4 children, 3 survive, born in Germany, both parents born in Germany; immigrated 1870, 30 years ago; Carl, son age 16, born August 1883 in Ohio, at school; Frieda, age 15, Jan 1885, born in Ohio; Fred age 10, son, born May 1890 in Ohio

Id#: 0357895
Name: Tegtmeier, Ferdinand
Date: 1907
Source: Cemetery record; Cleveland Necrology File, Reel #079.
Notes: 1848–1907. Woodvale Cemetery Berea, Ohio.

Notes for Maria Fridericka Johane Bartels:
1910 U.S. Census • Ohio • Cuyahoga • Other Townships • ED# 23
Tegtmeier, Mrs. Fredrica, head, age 51, widowed, born in Germany, 5 children, 4 survive; Frieda, daughter age 35 born in Ohio; Fred age 19, general farm, Irma age 6.

1910 Census, next door to Mrs. Fredrica Tegtmeiere, SON CARL:
1910 U.S. Census • Ohio • Cuyahoga • Other Townships • ED# 23
Tegtmeier, Carl age 26, works at a factory, Lena age 24; both born in Ohio.

1930 Census: 1930 United States Federal Census > Ohio > Cuyahoga > Chagrin Falls > District 553
Fredricka J. age 71, widow; Frieda, daughter, age 44; Fred, son age 39, farmer (supports household); Erna, daughter age 26; Adelbert, son age 16; Nina, pend daughter age 15; Norma pend daughter age 15; (two adopted daughters?)

OBITUARY Id#: 0357896
Name: Tegtmeier, Fredicka
Date: Oct. 4, 1942
Source: Source unknown; Cleveland Necrology File, Reel #079.
Notes: Tegtmeier: Fredicka, at her late residence, Smith Rd., Brook Park, wife of the late Ferdinand, mother of Carl, Freida, Arthur (deceased), Fred and Erma Behner, grandmother and great-grandmother. Friends may call at the Haag Co. Chapel, 50 East Bridge st., Berea, where services will be held Tuesday, Oct. 6, at 3 p. m.

More About Maria Fridericka Johane Bartels:
Burial: Berea, Cuyahoga Co.,Ohio
Emigration: 1870, 1900 Census information

Children of Karl Tegtmeier and Maria Bartels are:

17. i. Karl Ferdinand[4] Tegtmeier, b. August 30, 1883, Berea, Cuyahoga Co. OH; d. April 9, 1956, Cuyahoga Co., OH.

ii. Frieda Magdelena Tegtmeier, b. January 9, 1885, Middleburg Twp. Cuyahoga Co. OH; d. July 9, 1946, Berea, Cuyahoga Co.,Ohio.

Notes for Frieda Magdelena Tegtmeier:
1900 U.S. Census • Ohio • Cuyahoga • Other Townships • ED# 222—page 8 (next door)
Tegtmeier, Ferd, head, farmer, age 52, married 18 years, Feb 1848, immigrated 1862, 38 years ago, farmer; Fredrica age 41, April 1859, married 18 years, had 4 children, 3 survive, born in Germany, both parents born in Germany; immigrated 1870, 30 years ago; Carl, son age 16, born August 1883 in Ohio, at

school; Frieda, age 15, Jan 1885, born in Ohio; Fred age 10, son, born May 1890 in Ohio

1910 U.S. Census • Ohio • Cuyahoga • Other Townships • ED# 23
Tegtmeier, Mrs. Fredrica, head, age 51, widowed, born in Germany, 5 children, 4 survive; Frieda, daughter age 35 born in Ohio; Fred age 19, general farm, Irma age 6.

1930 Census: 1930 United States Federal Census > Ohio > Cuyahoga > Chagrin Falls > District 553
Fredricka J. age 71, widow; Frieda, daughter, age 44; Fred, son age 39, farmer (supports household); Erna, daughter age 26; Adelbert, son age 16; Nina, pend daughter age 15; Norma pend daughter age 15;

OBITUARY Id#: 0357897
Name: Tegtmeier, Frieda
Date: Jul 9 1946
Source: Cleveland Press; Cleveland Necrology File, Reel #079.
Notes: Tegtmeier, Frieda, beloved sister of Carl, Fred and Emma Behner, Now at Davis' Home for Funerals, Berea, where services will be held Fri., July 12, at 2:30 p. m. (abt 61 years old)

iii. Ernest Arthur Tegtmeier, b. November 17, 1886, Middleburg Twp. Cuyahoga Co. OH; d. February 18, 1893, Middleburg Twp. Cuyahoga Co. OH.

Notes for Ernest Arthur Tegtmeier:
1900 U.S. Census • Ohio • Cuyahoga • Other Townships • ED# 222—page 8 (next door)
Tegtmeier, Ferd, head, farmer, age 52, married 18 years, Feb 1848, immigrated 1862, 38 years ago, farmer; Fredrica age 41, April 1859, married 18 years, had 4 children, 3 survive, born in Germany, both parents born in Germany; immigrated 1870, 30 years ago; Carl, son age 16, born August 1883 in Ohio, at school; Frieda, age 15, Jan 1885, born in Ohio; Fred age 10,

son, born May 1890 in Ohio (Three Tegtmeier families living next to each other: Temeyer, P____; Henry Tegtmeir, and Ferd Tegtmeier)—Ernest died abt 7 years old.

iv. FRIEDRICH WILHELM TEGTMEIER, b. May 14, 1890, Berea, Cuyahoga Co. OH; d. December 1967, Brookpark, Cuyahoga Co. OH.

Notes for FRIEDRICH WILHELM TEGTMEIER:
Fred Tegtmeier
Social Security in Ohio
Last Residence: 44142 Brookpark, Cuyahoga, Ohio, United States of America
Born: 14 May 1890
Died: Dec 1967
State (Year) SSN issued: Ohio (1951–1952)

1900 U.S. Census • Ohio • Cuyahoga • Other Townships • ED# 222—page 8 (next door)
Tegtmeier, Ferd, head, farmer, age 52, married 18 years, Feb 1848, immigrated 1862, 38 years ago, farmer; Fredrica age 41, April 1859, married 18 years, had 4 children, 3 survive, born in Germany, both parents born in Germany; immigrated 1870, 30 years ago; Carl, son age 16, born August 1883 in Ohio, at school; Frieda, age 15, Jan 1885, born in Ohio; Fred** age 10, son, born May 1890 in Ohio

1910 U.S. Census • Ohio • Cuyahoga • Other Townships • ED# 23
Tegtmeier, Mrs. Fredrica, head, age 51, widowed, born in Germany, 5 children, 4 survive; Frieda, daughter age 35 born in Ohio; FRED age 19, general farm, Irma age 6.

1930 Census: 1930 United States Federal Census > Ohio > Cuyahoga > Chagrin Falls > District 553
Fredricka J. age 71, widow; Frieda, daughter, age 44; FRED**, son age 39, farmer (supports household); Erna, daughter age 26; Adelbert, son age 16; Nina, pend daughter age 15; Norma pend daughter age 15;1930 Census:

More About Friedrich Wilhelm Tegtmeier:
Event 3: Residence code: Ohio
Event 4: Last residence ZIP: 44142
Occupation: Issued in: Ohio

18. v. Erma Maria Tegtmeier, b. March 25, 1904, Berea, Cuyahoga Co. OH; d. February 16, 1977, Medina Co. Ohio.

5. Augusta Maria Elizabeth[3] Tegtmeier *(Johann Friedrich[2], Tegtmeier[1])* was born December 5, 1852 in Iden, Osterburg, Prussia, and died October 2, 1894 in Cleveland, Cuyahoga Co. OH. She married Philip J. Mutz November 21, 1871. He was born ABT 1848 in Germany, and died in Cuyahoga Co, Ohio.

Notes for Augusta Maria Elizabeth Tegtmeier:
New York Passenger Lists, 1851–1891 > 1862 > June > Sir Robert Peel
Tegtmeijer, Fred age 41 married farmer from Prussia, destination, Ohio (second cabin)

Maria age 40 (Maria Dorthea)
Joh male age 18
Fried 16 (Fredrick Wilhelm)
Carl 14 (Karl Ferdinand)
Maria 10 (Augusta Maria)
Minna 4 (Minna Wilhelmina)

1870 Census 1870 United States Federal Census > Ohio > Cuyahoga > Middleburgh
Tegtmeier, (transcriber put it down as "Yeztwin") Fred, age 48; Dora age age 46; Henry age 27; Fred 24; Ferdinand 21; Louisa 18 (b abt 1852) ; Adeline 7, born in Ohio.

More About Augusta Maria Elizabeth Tegtmeier:
Education: June 24, 1862, Sailed from Hamburg to NY, "Sir Robert Peel"

Notes for Philip J. Mutz:
Philipp Mutz
Arrival Date: 07 Jul 1855
Age: 7

Gender: Male
Port of Departure: Bremen, Germany
Destination: United States of America
Place of Origin: Germany
Ship Name: Nebraska
Port of Arrival: New York
Line: 33
Microfilm Roll: 154
List Number: 612
New York Passenger Lists, 1851–1891 > 1855 > July > Nebraska
John Pete Mutz, age 36, Margr 38; Philipp 7; Johanne daughter, 21;

1880 United States Federal Census > Ohio > Cuyahoga > Cleveland > District 38
Philip Mutz, age 33, brewer, born in Baden, wife LOUISA age 28 born in Prussia, Lena daughter age 8, Robert age 1 … Louisa?—This is the only Philip I could find in the US in 1880. (1890 Census burned in fire, 1900 census not yet indexed … next census available 1910 … too late. Any information on this person would be helpful. Actually, this could be a nickname for Elizabeth …

Children of AUGUSTA TEGTMEIER and PHILIP MUTZ are:

i. LENA[4] MUTZ, b. ABT 1872.
ii. ROBERT MUTZ, b. ABT 1879.

6. ADELINE LOUISE[3] TEGTMEIER *(JOHANN FRIEDRICH[2], TEGTMEIER[1])* was born August 22, 1862 in Middleburg Twp. Cuyahoga, Oh, and died February 21, 1903. She married WILLIAM W. PULS August 29, 1883, son of JOHN PULS and TERESA. He was born November 1856 in Cuyahoga Co., OH, and died June 19, 1926 in Cuyahoga Co, Ohio.

Notes for ADELINE LOUISE TEGTMEIER:
1880 Census
ADELINE TEGETEMYER
Age: 17
Estimated birth year: <1863>
Birthplace: Ohio
Occupation: At Home
Relation: Dau
Home in 1880: Middleburgh, Cuyahoga, Ohio

Marital status: Single
Race: White
Gender: Female
1880 CENSUS: Middleburgh, Cuyahoga, Ohio
FREDERICK TEGETEMYER age 58 (b abt 1822), farmer, born in Prussia; Dora, wife age 56 born in Prussia, Ferdinand, age 32 born in Prussia, farmer; Adeline, age 17 born in Ohio, at home. ***
More About ADELINE LOUISE TEGTMEIER:
Education: Confirmed at St. Paul's Lutheran Church, Berea, Cuyahoga Co. OH

Notes for WILLIAM W. PULS:
1880 CENSUS
WILLIAM PULS
Age: 24
Estimated birth year: <1856>
Birthplace: Ohio
Occupation: Farm Hand
Relation: Son
Home in 1880: Middleburgh, Cuyahoga, Ohio
Marital status: Single
Race: White
Gender: Male
John Puls, Head, age 56 born in Mechlenberg; Teresa age 55, born in Mechlenberg; William 24, ** farmworker; Charles 22; Mina 18 and Elizabeth age 10—children born in Ohio.

1900 U.S. Census • Ohio • Cuyahoga • Other Townships • ED# 222—page 13
Puls, William age 43, born Nov 1856 in Ohio, farmer, both parents from Germany. married 17 years, Adeline, wife, age age 37, Aug 1862 born in Ohio, 6 children, 3 survive; William age 15, Jan 1884; Elsie age 11, Dec 1888; Leonard age 4, June 1895.

Id#: 0285697
Name: Puls, William W.
Date: June 19, 1926
Source: Cemetery record; Cleveland Necrology File, Reel #066.

Notes: Puls-William W., beloved husband of the late Adeline, father of William H. Puls, Mrs. Elsie Rohde, Mrs. Elva Rohde of Brook Park, O., and Leonard Puls of Berea, O., and brother of Charles Puls of Cleveland, O., at his home on Hummel road, age 69 years. Funeral from his late residence, Saturday, June 19, at 2:30 p. m. 1926. St. Pauls' Cemetery Berea, Ohio.
More About William W. Puls:
Burial: St. Paul's Lutheran Church Cemetery, Berea, Cuyahoga Co. OH

Children of Adeline Tegtmeier and William Puls are:

19. i. William H.[4] Puls, b. January 1884, Cuyahoga Co, Ohio; d. April 18, 1943, Berea, Cuyahoga Co.,Ohio.

ii. Elsie Puls, b. December 1888, Cuyahoga Co, Ohio; m. xxx Rohde.

Notes for Elsie Puls:
1900 U.S. Census • Ohio • Cuyahoga • Other Townships • ED# 222—page 13
Puls, William age 43, born Nov 1856 in Ohio, farmer, both parents from Germany. married 17 years, Adeline, wife, age age 37, Aug 1862 born in Ohio, 6 children, 3 survive; William age 15, Jan 1884; Elsie age 11, Dec 1888; Leonard age 4, June 1895.

Id#: 0285697
Name: Puls, William W.
Date: June 19, 1926
Source: Cemetery record; Cleveland Necrology File, Reel #066.
Notes: Puls-William W., beloved husband of the late Adeline, father of William H. Puls, Mrs. Elsie Rohde, Mrs. Elva Rohde of Brook Park, O., and Leonard Puls of Berea, O., and brother of Charles Puls of Cleveland, O., at his home on Hummel road, age 69 years. Funeral from his late residence, Saturday, June 19, at 2:30 p. m. 1926. St. Pauls' Cemetery Berea, Ohio.

20. iii. Leonard Puls, b. June 1895, Cuyahoga Co, Ohio; d. October 4, 1957, Berea, Cuyahoga Co.,Ohio.

iv. Elva Puls, b. ABT 1890; m. xxx Rhode; b. Brookpark, Cuyahoga, Ohio.

Notes for Elva Puls:
Id#: 0285697
Name: Puls, William W.
Date: June 19, 1926
Source: Cemetery record; Cleveland Necrology File, Reel #066.
Notes: Puls-William W., beloved husband of the late Adeline, father of William H. Puls, Mrs. Elsie Rohde, Mrs. Elva Rohde of Brook Park, O., and Leonard Puls of Berea, O., and brother of Charles Puls of Cleveland, O., at his home on Hummel road, age 69 years. Funeral from his late residence, Saturday, June 19, at 2:30 p. m. 1926. St. Pauls' Cemetery Berea, Ohio.

v. Emile Puls.
vi. Adeline Puls.
vii. Loretta Puls.

Generation No. 3

7. Hulda Louise Maria[4] Tegtmeier *(Johann Heinrich[3], Johann Friedrich[2], Tegtmeier[1])* was born May 21, 1873 in Independence, OH, and died February 25, 1968 in Adrian, Lenawee, MI. She married Heinrich Ernst A. Ahleman March 2, 1893, son of Frederick Ahleman and Fredericka Meuser. He was born May 25, 1869 in Riga Twp, Ottawa Lake, Michigan, and died December 21, 1948 in Riga, MI.

Notes for Hulda Louise Maria Tegtmeier:
1880 CENSUS: Berea, Cuyahoga, Ohio
Henry Tegtmeier, age 36, quarry man, born
in Germany; Julia age 32, wife born in Germany;
Hulda age 7; Henry age 5; Lucy age 3 children
born in Ohio.

More About Hulda Louise Maria Tegtmeier:
Burial: Riga Cemetary, Riga, MI

Hulda Louise Maria Tegtmeier
"Hulda"
Born in Independence, Ohio 1873
Died in Lenawee, Michigan 1968.
Upper photo circ. 1890.

Hulda Tegtmeier and
Heinrich Ernest A. Ahleman "Ernest"
Married March 2 1893
Upper right.

Ernest & Hulda Tegtmeier
Circ 1947
Riga Michigan
Bottom right.

Photos courtsy of les Meier.

Notes for Heinrich Ernst A. Ahleman:
1880 United States Federal Census > Michigan > Lenawee > Riga > District 166
Fredric Alhemann, age 45, farmer, born in Prussia; Fredricka age 38, born in Prussia; William 19; **Ernest 12;** Gustof 9; Emma 8/12.

1910 Michigan • Lenawee • Other Townships • ED# 77 (light copy, hard to read)
Ernest Ahleman, head, age 41, born in Michigan; Hulda age 33, born in Ohio; Arthur 14, Almeta 4; Elsie 6; Walter 2. (can't read occupation)

1920 Census • Michigan • Lenawee • Riga
Ernest Ahleman, age 51, born in Michigan, farmer; Hulda age 46, born in Ohio; Arthur age 23; Almeta age 18; Eloise (SP?) age 16; Walter age 12; Paul 2 and 7/12months; children all born in Michigan.

1930 United States Federal Census > Ohio > Henry > Washington > District 25
Walter R Ahleman, head, age 21, born in MI, farmer; Ethel, wife, age 21 born in Ohio, teacher, publci school; Ernest age 61, farmer, 24 when he first was married; Hulda, age 56, 19 when first married; Paul E. Brother, age 13 born in MI.

More About HEINRICH ERNST A. AHLEMAN:
Burial: Riga Cemetery, Riga MI, Section O. P. 497 graves 2 & 3
Occupation: 1920, Farmer/Riga, Lenawee, Michigan

Children of HULDA TEGTMEIER and HEINRICH AHLEMAN are:

i. FREDERICK WM.[5] AHLEMAN, b. July 19, 1894, Riga Twp, Ottawa Lake, MI; d. December 1, 1905, Riga Twp, Ottawa Lake, MI.

Notes for FREDERICK WM. AHLEMAN:
1920 Census • Michigan • Lenawee • Riga
Ernest Ahleman, age 51, born in Michigan, farmer; Hulda age 46, born in Ohio; Arthur age 23; Almeta age 18; Eloise (SP?) age 16; Walter age 12; Paul 2 and 7/12months; children all born in Michigan. (NO Frederick,—already moved away from home?)

More About FREDERICK WM. AHLEMAN:
Burial: Riga Cemetery, Riga, MI Section OP Lot 497, grave 1

ii. ARTHUR G. AHLEMAN, b. February 12, 1896, Riga Twp., Riga, MI; d. April 11, 1988, Riga Twp., Riga, MI; m. (1) OLIVE A. DEDERING, October 13, 1929; b. October 20, 1903, Port

Huron, MI; d. January 8, 1958; m. (2) ADELAIDE KOPPIN, June 13, 1959; b. July 19, 1901.

Notes for ARTHUR G. AHLEMAN:
1920 Census • Michigan • Lenawee • Riga
Ernest Ahleman, age 51, born in Michigan, farmer; Hulda age 46, born in Ohio; Arthur age 23; Almeta age 18; Eloise (SP?) age 16; Walter age 12; Paul 2 and 7/12months; children all born in Michigan.

More About ARTHUR G. AHLEMAN:
Burial: Riga Cemetery, Riga MI Section O P Lot 497 graves 4 & 5

Almeta (left) and Elsie Ahleman, circ 1918. Courtesy of Les Meier.

21. iii. ALMETA BERTHA CHRISTINE AHLEMAN, b. January 26, 1901, Riga Twp, Riga, MI; d. November 15, 1979.
22. iv. El sie Emma Hul da Ahl eman, b. April 20, 1903, Riga Twp., Riga MI; d. May 15, 1994.
23. v. Wal t er Adol ph Ahl eman, b. January 16, 1907, Riga Twn, Riga, MI; d. February 17, 1959, Napolean, Henry Co.,
24. vi. Paul Er nest Ahl eman, b. April 6, 1917, Riga Twn, Riga, MI.

8. HENRY WILLIAM CARL[4] TEGTMEIER *(JOHANN HEINRICH[3], JOHANN FRIEDRICH[2], TEGTMEIER[1])* was born November 4, 1874 in Middleburg Twp., Cuyahoga, OH, and died June 8, 1963 in Millersburg, Holmes, OH. He married AUGUSTA CHRISTINE BRANDES November 1,

1910, daughter of WILLIAM BRANDES and CHRISTINE BRANDES. She was born January 18, 1879 in Ohio, and died April 2, 1967 in Strongsville, Ohio.

Notes for HENRY WILLIAM CARL TEGTMEIER:
1880 Census: Berea, Cuyahoga, Ohio
Henry Tegtmeier, age 36, quarry man, born in Germany; Julia age 32, wife born in Germany; Hulda age 7; Henry age 5 **; Lucy age 3 children born in Ohio.

1900 Census: living next to his Uncle Ferd: Cuyahoga—other townships (Middleburgh) ed # 222—page 8 (page 47B)
Henry Tegtmeir, head, farmer, single age 24, born October 1875; both parents born in Germany; Christina, sister, single, December 1880, age 19, born in Ohio; William, brother born May 1882, single, farm laborer; Adolph, brother age 16, Sept 1883, farm laborer.

1910 Census • Ohio • Cuyahoga • Other Townships • ED# 23
Julia, age 59 widow, had 7 children, 6 survive; born in Germany; Henry age 37 works at a factory; **William age 27,** general farm; Adolph age 26 general farm; children born in Ohio.

1920 Census; Brookpark, Cuyahoga, OHIO
William Brandes, head, age 75, born in Ohio, Cristina, wife, age 78 born in Breman, Germany; Henry Tegtmeier **, age 45, son in law; Augusta age 40 born in Ohio; Ruth age 7 born in Ohio, granddaughter; Oscar age 6 grandson, born in Ohio; ***

Three Brothers & their wives:
Back row: Adolph & Alma Tegtmeier, William & Anna Tegtmeier
Front Row: Henry & Augusta Tegtmeier

1930 Census: Brookpark, Cuyahoga, Ohio
Cristina Brandes, age 88; Henry, age 56, son in law, truck driver, agricultural; August, daughter age 51; Ruth age 17; Oscar age 16;

OBITUARY Id#: 0752232
Name: Tegtmeier, Henry W.
Date: Jun 10 1963
Source: Plain Dealer; Cleveland Necrology File, Reel #161.
Notes: Tegtmeier. Henry W. Tegtmeier, beloved husband of Augusta, father of Ruth T. Davidson, Oscar B., and grandfather, brother of Hulda Ahleman, Christine Smith, and the late Lucy Scrivens, William and Adolph, passed away Saturday. Friends may call at the Baker Funeral Home, Berea, where services will be held Monday, June 10, at 1:30 P. M. In lieu of flowers contributions may be made to Immanuel United Church of Christ, Cleveland, O.

HENRY W TEGTMEIER
Gender: Male
Date of Death: June 08, 1963
Volume: 17325
Certificate: 46588
Marital Status: Married
Place of Death: Holmes County
Race: White
Residence: Brook Park, Cuyahoga County
Age: 88

Notes for AUGUSTA CHRISTINE BRANDES: Known as "Aunt Gustie"
1920 Census; Brookpark, Cuyahoga, OHIO
William Brandes, head, age 75, born in Ohio, Cristina, wife, age 78 born in Breman, Germany; Henry Tegtmeier, age 45, son in law; **Augusta age 40** born in Ohio; Ruth age 7 born in Ohio, granddaughter; Oscar age 6 grandson, born in Ohio;

1930 United States Federal Census > Ohio > Cuyahoga > Brook Park
Christina Brandes, 88 years old, widowed; Henry Tegtmeier, son in law, age 56, **Augusta, daughter, age 51**; Ruth granddaughter age 17; Oscar, grandson 16.

AUGUSTA C TEGTMEIER
Gender: Female
Date of Death: April 02, 1967
Volume: 18824
Certificate: 27366
Marital Status: Widowed

Place of Death: Strongsville, Cuyahoga County
Race: White
Residence: Brook Park, Cuyahoga County
Age: 88
Social Security:
Augusta Tegtmeier
Last Residence: 44142 Brookpark, Cuyahoga, Ohio, United States of America
Born: 18 Jan 1879
Died: Apr 1967
State (Year) SSN issued: Ohio (1963–1964)

OBITUARY Id#: 0752230
Name: Tegtmeier, Augusta C.
Date: Apr 4 1967
Source: Plain Dealer; Cleveland Necrology File, Reel #161.
Notes: Tegtmeier. Augusta C. Tegtmeier, age 88, beloved wife of the late Henry, dear mother of Ruth Davidson and Oscar, grandmother of Nancy Jones, Richard Davidson and Susan Hahn, great-grandmother of Elizabeth Jones, passed away Sunday. Funeral services will be held Wednesday, April 5, at 1:30 p.m. at Baker Funeral Home, Berea. Family suggests contributions be made to Immanuel United Church of Christ Building Fund, 4511 W. 130th St. Visiting Hours 3–5 And 7–9 P.M. Tuesday.

Children of HENRY TEGTMEIER and AUGUSTA BRANDES are:

+25. i. Rut h[5] Tegt meier , b. ABT 1913, Ohio.

ii. OSCAR TEGTMEIER, b. July 9, 1914, Brookpark, Cuyahoga Co., Ohio.

Notes for OSCAR TEGTMEIER:
1920 Census; Brookpark, Cuyahoga, OHIO
William Brandes, head, age 75, born in Ohio, Cristina, wife, age 78 born in Breman, Germany; Henry Tegtmeier, age 45, son in law; Augusta age 40 born in Ohio; Ruth age 7 born in Ohio (b abt 1913), granddaughter; Oscar age 6 grandson, born in Ohio; (b abt 1914)

1930 United States Federal Census > Ohio > Cuyahoga > Brook Park
Christina Brandes, 88 years old, widowed; Henry Tegtmeier, son in law, age 56, August, wife age 51; Ruth granddaughter age 17; Oscar, grandson 16.

1994 Phone Directory
OSCAR TEGTMEIER
Address: 16006 SHELDON RD,
City: CLEVELAND
State: OH
Zipcode: 44142

9. Lucie Adeline Julianna[4] Tegtmeier *(Johann Heinrich[3], Johann Friedrich[2], Tegtmeier[1])* was born August 6, 1877 in Berea, Cuyahoga Co. OH, and died October 9, 1921 in Middleburg Twp, Cuyahoga OH. She married William R. Scrivens April 28, 1898. He was born ABT 1870 in Ohio, and died April 7, 1927 in Middleburg Twp. Cuyahoga OH.

Notes for Lucie Adeline Julianna Tegtmeier:
1880 Census: Berea, Cuyahoga, Ohio
Henry Tegtmeier, age 36, quarry man, born in Germany; Julia age 32, wife born in Germany; Hulda age 7; Henry age 5; **Lucy age 3** children born in Ohio.

> *Lucy was hanging the wash out on the line when she just collapsed on Sheldon Road in Middleburg Hts., Ohio. Her sons ran to the neighbors to tell them. She was only 44 when she died.*
>
> *—Alice Tegtmeier Taylor*

OBITUARY Id#: 0321572
Name: Scrivens, Lucy
Date: October 11, 1921
Source: Source unknown; Cleveland Necrology File, Reel #073.
Notes: Scrivens-Lucy, beloved wife of William Scrivens and mother of Edward, Florence, William and Clayton, at her home on Shelton road, near Berea, O., age 44 years. Funeral Thursday, Oct. 13, at St. Paul's Lutheran church, on Front street, Berea, O., at 2 p. m. Burial Woodvale cemetery.

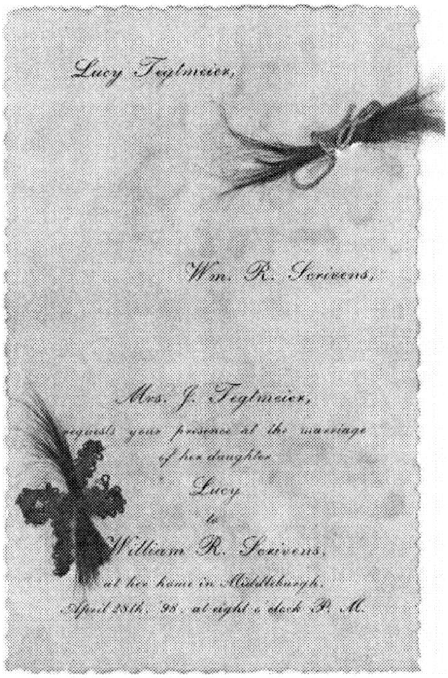
Lucy Tegtmeier,

Wm. R. Scrivens,

Mrs. J. Tegtmeier,
requests your presence at the marriage
of her daughter
Lucy
to
William R. Scrivens,
at her home in Middleburgh.
April 28th, '98, at eight o'clock P. M.

Lucy Scrivens house on Sheldon Road, Middleburgh Hts. Ohio. Lucy with Florence.

Invitation to the Wedding, Lucy Tegtmeier and William Scrivens, including locks of hair.

Scrivens Family:
Photos courtesy of William Schultz.

Lucy Tegtmeier Scrivens - Bill, Edwin, Uncle Bill, Florence, Pat cir. 1914)

Notes for William R. Scrivens:
1920 U.S. Census • Ohio • Cuyahoga • Middleburg • ED# 556
William R Scrivens**, age 49, born in Ohio, farmer; Lucy J age 42 born in Ohio; Edwin H, son age 20; William A age 18; Florence age 16; Clayton age 15; all born in Ohio.

OBITUARY Id#: 0321575
Name: Scrivens, William R.
Date: April 7, 1927
Source: Source unknown; Cleveland Necrology File, Reel #073.
Notes: Scrivens-William R., beloved husband of the late Lucy and father of Edwin, William, Clayton, and Mrs. Florence Schultz, at Community hospital Wednesday April 6, age 57. Funeral at St. Paul's Lutheran church, Front street, Berea, O., Friday, April 8, at 2:30 p. m. Burial at Woodvale cemetery.

More About William R. Scrivens:
Occupation: 1920, Farmer/Cuyahoga Co., Ohio

Children of Lucie Tegtmeier and William Scrivens are:

26. i. Edwin A.[5] Scrivens, b. January 24, 1899, Ohio; d. July 1976, Cleveland, OH.
27. ii. Florence Julia Scrivens, b. January 21, 1903, Berea, Cuyahoga Co. OH; d. May 4, 1993, Ohio.
28. iii. William A. Scrivens, b. April 30, 1901, Cuyahoga Co., OH; d. July 6, 1997, Cleveland, OH.
iv. Clayton Scrivens, b. October 30, 1904, Ohio; d. August 26, 1977, Berea, Ohio; m. Mary Jozwiak; b. ABT 1885, Ohio; d. Berea, Ohio.

Pat (Clayton) and Mary Scrivens, circ. 1964. He was known as "Pat", and he loved to hunt and fish. He was glad to have his picture taken, saying he was the only one ever taking shots, but he was never in them. He prized his dog, a red Labrador retriever who seemed to go with him every where. He had a strange round, raised mark near his temple which he told us was a bullet from the war, the doctors refusing to take it out, saying it was to dangerous to remove. He was a real rail road engineer, running the locomotives from the terminal in downtown Cleveland.

The Scrivens Family:
Photo is of Grandma (Lucy) and Grandpa (Bill) Scrivens, Uncle Ed (Edwin), bill, Pat (holding the dog.) Florence is not there. (Unknown is the young girl, other man and woman.) circ 1915. Photos courtesy of Bill Schultz, Medina, Ohio.

Clayton "Pat" and Mary Scrivens
circ 1964.
Photo courtesy Sandra Bell.

He and Mary never had children. Mary was a head nurse at Berea Hospital, which probably was within 2 miles of their house. The den was paneled in old pinewood popular in the 1940's. I probably will always remember Pat sitting in his big stuffed chair, smoking a pipe with one hand, and patting his dog with other.

—Sandra Taylor Bell

1920 U.S. Census • Ohio • Cuyahoga • Middleburg • ED# 556
William R Scrivens, age 49, born in Ohio; Lucy J age 42 born in Ohio; Edwin H, son age 20; William A age 18; Florence age 16; Clayton age 15; all born in Ohio.

Birth date: Oct 30, 1904
Death date: Aug 26, 1977
Occupation: Railroad Engineer in Cleveland, OH

More About MARY JOZWIAK:
Education: Nurse at Berea Hospital

10. CHRISTINA DOROTHEA EMILIE[4] TEGTMEIER *(JOHANN HEINRICH[3], JOHANN FRIEDRICH[2], TEGTMEIER[1])* was born December 1, 1880 in Berea, Cuyahoga Co. OH, and died November 17, 1963 in Middleburg Hts. Cuyahoga Co. OH. She married JULIUS CARL SMITH May 11, 1905. He was born ABT 1879 in Ohio, and died December 12, 1949 in Longview, Texas.

Notes for CHRISTINA DOROTHEA EMILIE TEGTMEIER:
The family called her Aunt Tina.

1900 Census: living next to his Uncle Ferd: Cuyahoga—other townships (Middleburgh) ed # 222—page 8
Henry Tegtmeir, head, farmer, single age 24, born October 1875; both parents born in Germany; **Christena,** sister, single, December 1880, age 19, born in Ohio; William, brother born May 1882, single, farm laborer; Adolph, brother age 16, Sept 1883, farm laborer.

Christina Tegtmeier, *we called her "Aunt Tina." She talked an awful lot, constantly, but was interesting, gossipy, and very likeable.*

—Alice Taylor, 2004

Alma Bauer (left) and sister in law, Christina Dorthea Tegtmeier "Tina" circ. 1925. Alma married Adolph Tegtmeier, Tina married Julius Smith

Christina married Julius Smith and they lived on Smith Road, that was kind of neat. I remember her home on the corner of Smith and Sheldon Road, a grand, two story wood house built on a foundation of good Berea sandstone quarried from nearby. I don't remember the inside of her house at all, probably because kids were bored with the grown ups talking. She loved and could grow African violets, as they covered a round, white wrought iron table in her living room by the window. (They tore down the house and made a gas station on the North West Corner of Smith and Bagley Roads.) They had a circular drive made of gravel that stretched across the back of the house connecting the two streets. There was a chicken coop full of chickens with a rounded roof made out of tin, and an old working well, with colorful marbles pressed into the top that also decorated her front yard. I always thought that the name was odd, as I remember her as a Big lady, but then again, when you're a little kid, everyone else looks enormous. I never realized that "Tina" was really part of her real name.

—Sandra Bell, 2004

Julius and Tina Smith
Circ. 1947

Notes for Julius Carl Smith:
Julius C Smith
Age: 40 years
Estimated birth year: 1879
Birthplace: Ohio
Home in 1920: Ohio • Cuyahoga • Brook Park • ED# 518

1920 Census: Julius C. Smith, age 40, Head, born in Ohio, farmer, father born in Ohio, mother born in Germany; Christina age 39, both parents born in Germany; Leland J. age 10; Bertha age 7; all born in Ohio;

1930 United States Federal Census > Ohio > Cuyahoga > Chagrin Falls > District 553
Smith, Julius, head, age 50, Christina, wife, age 48; Leland son age 20; Julia Tegtmeier, mother in law, age 82, widowed; Bertha Smith, age 46, sister.

OBITUARY Id#: 0335890
Name: Smith, Julius C.
Date: Dec 12 1949
Source: Source unknown; Cleveland Necrology File, Reel #075.
Notes: Smith, Julius C., beloved husband of Christina; father of Leland and grandfather of Glenn; brother of Bertha and the late Charles, Henry, Louisa Peterjohn, William, George, Fred, Lena Etzel, Edward and Minnie Lammermeier; passed away suddenly at Long View, Tex., Thursday. Friends may call at the Baker Funeral Home, Berea. Services at St. Paul's Lutharan Church, Tuesday, Dec. 13, at 2 p. m.

More About Julius Carl Smith:
Location: 1830, Chagrin Falls, Ohio/Census

OBITUARY
Id#: 0729062
Name: Smith, Christine A.
Date: Nov 19 1963
Source: Cleveland Press; Cleveland Necrology File, Reel #156.
Notes: Smith. Christine A. Smith (nee Tegimeier) late residence, 13780 Pleasant Valley Rd., Middleburg Heights, beloved wife of the late Julius, mother of Leland J., grandmother of Glenn A., great-grandmother of Caria, Cindy, and Gregory Smith, sister of Hulda Ahleman, the late Lucy Scrivens, Henry, William and Adolph Tegtmeier, passed away Nov. 17, age 82 years. The family will receive friends 2–4 And 7–9 P. M. Tuesday at the Baker Funeral Home, 206 Front St., Berea. Services at Redeemer Lutheran Church, 6151 Smith Rd., Brook Park, Wednesday, Nov. 20, at 2 P. M. In lieu of flowers, the family suggests contributions in her memory to Redeemer Lutheran Church.

Children of CHRISTINA TEGTMEIER and JULIUS SMITH are:

29. i. Leland J.[5] Smith, b. ABT 1910, Ohio; d. 1972, Brookpark, Ohio.

ii. BERTHA SMITH, b. ABT 1913.

Notes for BERTHA SMITH:
1920: Ohio • Cuyahoga • Brook Park • ED# 518
1920 Census: Julius C. Smith, age 40, Head, born in Ohio, farmer, father born in Ohio, mother born in Germany; Christina age 39, both parents born in Germany; Leland J. age 10; Bertha age 7; all born in Ohio;

Bertha lived with her brother when she was 46, as proved in the census. Bertha never married.

11. WILLIAM CARL[4] TEGTMEIER *(JOHANN HEINRICH[3], JOHANN FRIEDRICH[2], TEGTMEIER[1])* was born May 15, 1882 in Middleburg Twnshp, OH, and died April 10, 1955 in Medina Twp., Medina, OH. He married ERNA HENRIETTE SOPHIE PAPENHAGEN November 24, 1910 in home of her mother by Rev. Albert Zeitner Ottawa Lake, Zion Lutheran, Monroe County, OH, daughter of JOACHIM PAPENHAGEN and WILHELMINA WESTENDORF. She was born October 10, 1888 in Beubukow, Schwerinschen, Mecklenburg, Germany, and died September 30, 1982 in Dickinson, Stark North Dakota.

Notes for WILLIAM CARL TEGTMEIER:
Baptized May 25, 1882, Berea, Cuyahoga, Ohio

1900 Census: living next to his Uncle Ferd: Cuyahoga—other townships (Middleburgh) ed # 222—page 8
Henry Tegtmeir, head, farmer, single age 24, born October 1875; both parents born in Germany; Christena, sister, single, December 1880, age 19, born in Ohio; **WILLIAM,** brother born May 1882, single, farm laborer; Adolph, brother age 16, Sept 1883, farm laborer.

1910 Census • Ohio • Cuyahoga • Other Townships • ED# 23
Julia, age 59 widow, had 7 children, 6 survive;born in Germany; Henry age 37 works at a factory; **WILLIAM** age 27, general farm; Adolph age 26general farm; children born in Ohio.

William Carl Tegtmeier and Erna "Anna" Papenhagen on their wedding day, November 24, 1910.

Below: The family on the farm in Brookpark, Ohio circ 1921: Anna, Pop (William) Ray, Loretta, Julia, Alice, Henry, Bill (sitting on the block) and Harold (baby).

Tegtmeier Family circ. 1948. Back Row: Harold, Paul, Dick, Pop (William Sr.) Bill, Raymond. Sitting sisters Loey, Loretta, Alice. Mom (Anna) standing behind sisters.

William Carl Tegtmeier was born in Cuyahoga County, Ohio, where his father worked in a stone quarry. Both fathers died near the times Anna and William were confirmed, her father of asthma, his from 'consumption' caused by dust (from the mine). They lived with his widowed mother on a small farm on Smith Road. Mother made dairy products that Dad sold to customers on his route into Cleveland. All nine children were baptized at St. Paul Lutheran Church on Front Street, in Berea, OH.

—Lois Tegtmeier Hinrichs.

Erna Papenhagen (later called Anna) lived in Toledo, and did housework for Huldie Tegtmeier, William Carl Tegtmeier's sister. Pop (William Carl Tegtmeier) went to Toledo with a brother to work on the sugar beet fields as there was no work in Cleveland, and stayed with his sister, Huldie. That's where Mom and Pop met.

—Alice Tegtmeier Taylor

Pop worked in the fields all the time. When they put the Cleveland Airport in, they asked Pop to supervise putting in the waterlines. He had vericose vein and he had difficulty getting around. He had shot an owl, and had it stuffed and placed in the house in the farmhouse in Burbank.

—Alice Tegtmeier Taylor

We had enough kids to play baseball, and Mom always wanted the kids to play in our yard, so in the summer, when they sun stayed up so late, we played baseball until 10 at night. Later, Pop decided to move because the taxes were getting too high. He find land in Burbank Ohio, and before the kids graduated high school, we had to move to the farm. That was hard in our senior year.

BURBANK FARM near Kilbuck Valley. Taxes were getting to be too much, and William decided to move everyone to Burbank, Ohio where he purchased about 300 acres. Even the oldest kids were still in high school, making the move very difficult for them as they had to leave their friends.

The farm house burned down, and this painting was done from memory in 2003 by Sandra Taylor Bell and given to Alice Tegtmeier Taylor. (It's from memory, so don't shoot the artist!)

More About William Carl Tegtmeier:
Burial: April 13, 1955, Canaan, Wayne Co., OH

Notes for Erna Henriette Sophie Papenhagen:
Immigration: New York Passenger Lists, 1851–1891 > 1889 > July > Augusta Victoria
Joachim Pappenhagen, age 53, merchant
Hilhe, wife, age 40
Franz age 16
Herman age 14
Paul age 7
Marie age 6
Joh age 6 (this could be Jennie, don't have a John)
Henri age 5
Rentha age 4 (probably Bertha)
Erna age 9 months, baby
children from Mechlenburg.
Destination—New Bucklow (sp?) (New Brenen, Ohio

1900 U.S. Census • Michigan • Monroe • Whiteford • ED# 83
Pappenhagen, Jos, head, born May 1836, age 64, married 30 years, immigrated 1889; farmer, born in Germany, parents born in Germany; Minnie, wife, age 51 May 1850, married 30 years, born in Germany, parents born in Germany, had 9 children, 9 survive; Henry, son, age 17, Jan 1893; born in Germany, farmer; Bertha, daughter, June 1886, born in Germany; Annie, daughter born October 1889, age 10, born in Germany; Walter, Son born June 1892 in Ohio; (Note, Jos is 64, not 54, born 1836)

1910 Census: Whiteford Twp, Monroe, Michigan
Popenhagen, Wilhelmina, age 61, head of house, widow, had 10 children, 9 survive, born in Germany, emigrated 1889; Walter, age 17 born in Ohio; Anna***, daughter, age 21.

1930 Census 1930 United States Federal Census > Ohio > Cuyahoga > Chagrin Falls > District 553
Tegtmeier, William, head age 46, farmer, married at age 26, born in Ohio; Anna, wife, age 42, married at age 22, born in Germany; Loretta M age 18, stenographer at a garage; Raymond J age 17; Julia W age age 15; Alice L age

13; Henry A age 12; William Jr. age 10; Harold E. is 9; Richard E. is 6; Lois R. is age 2.

"Little Granny" (the Taylor's called her that) had surgery for Crone's Disease. She died in a nursing home of Crone's disease.

Social Security information
Individual: Tegtmeier, Anna
Issued in: Ohio
Birth date: Oct 10, 1888
Death date: Sep 1982
Residence code: Ohio
ZIP Code of last known residence: 44691

OBITUARY
Id#: 0752234
Name: Tegtmeier, William
Date: Apr 14 1955
Source: Source unknown; Cleveland Necrology File, Reel #161.
Notes: Tegtmeier, William, age 72, of Burbank, O., formerly of Berea; husband of Anna; father of Loretta Berry, Alice Taylor, Lois Hinrichs. Rev. Henry, William, Harold, Richard and Raymond. Friends may call at the Murray Funeral Home in Creston, O. Services Wednesday, at 2 p. m. at the Canaan Lutheran Church.

Memories of Little Granny—Erna Papenhagen Tegtmeier

Her son Ray raised his family on the farm in the valley by Killbuck River in Burbank, OH. It was there that he and Laura raised a family … Donna, Sharon and Danny. They had about 300 acres and raised corn and cattle, sheep on the hillsides. I remember visiting on long weekends. They had no closets upstairs in the old farmhouse, just nails driven into a long board across the wall. But it was enough to hang all the clothes up that needed hanging. There was the neatest little attic along side the front of the house, had to go thru a little door to get in, but the greatest of treasurers inside. Even found an old Edison Victrola that was given to the family by a banker in earlier days, and an old tin doll house with windows that really opened.

Farmhouse in Burbank, Ohio. Alice Taylor missed the old farm, so I painted this one from memory. The farm house was nestled in a valley, with Kilbuck River trailing at the bottom of the hills, fed by the constant spring waters from the hills. You could go up the hill and dig just about any where, and water would fill the spot where you dug just a few moments. There is a wooden bridge just a few feet in front of this view. It was an old wooden plank bridge, and it covered a really neat stream that cut about eight feet down. It was filled with sandstone fossils, and my brother and I and Ray's kids could spend hours in the stream, building dams. The stream went way back into the hills. The cellar was carved out of the dirt, and was always cool, even in the summer. Laura's mother and Little Granny had the down stairs bedrooms. Their was a player piano in the front room next to Little Granny's bedroom.

The kitchen had a huge Grandfather's clock. The wringer-washer was tucked into the corner next to it, and had to be wheeled over to the kitchen sink on wash day.

There were no closets, but the clothes were hung on nails driven through a 3" board nailed into the wall about a foot down from the ceiling. The house and barn burned down after it was sold. There is a back porch, but it doesn't show up very well in black and white.

- Water color, Sandra Bell.

In the 1960's we could tromp through the fields after the corn was harvested. Field corn was good when young. You would always find arrow heads in the valley. Up on the hills, you could sculpt out a clump of dirt from the side of the hill, and it would fill up with cool spring water quicker than the leaves would fall. We would find the greatest fossils in the sandstones of the creek bed that ran through the hills and by the side of the house. And up on top of the hill, my brother would collect sheep skulls and bones from the unfortunates who didn't make it the previous years. There was an old wrought iron fence on the top of one hill, with about 5 family grave stones in it, but nobody remembered what family. And on another hill, there was a great, spooky abandoned farm house that didn't seem to belong in the middle of no where, without a driveway or sidewalk.

In the springtime, we would go up the side of the hill to clean the spring—a 50 gallon steel drum dropped on end into the hillside used to collect water. We would clean out the frogs, sometimes dead snakes and such. I often wondered at the stuff we pulled out of that spring, and the water in the kitchen still smelling fresh.

The kitchen was fantastic, with a large dining table in the same room, and an old, large, black grandfather clock keeping time next to the wringer for clothes. There was a great walk-in pantry off the kitchen, with plenty of light pouring in from the window where the flour and all foods could be stored. Outside the house, if you pulled the large door open to the cellar underneath, you would find a dirt floor, a large heater, and a cool place even in summer to store potatoes and onions.

But the best thing I loved—'course the adults hated it, 'cause it dried out the hay—we made fabulous mazes in the hay loft that you could crawl through—it was a time when hay was still stacked in rectangles. It would scratch like hang in, but half the fun was building them, and the other half was getting on your stomach and pulling your body through it.

"Little" Granny was always small boned, and seemed to get thinner and thinner with age. But spry, she could still throw my 20 year old sister over the couch when she was over 60. She had very long, white, thin hair that she used to comb out at night, but it was so thin, she curled it all on top of her head and placed a matching hair net on to keep it together. I once mailed a letter to "Little Granny, Burbank Ohio" and she got it! (Hey, I was young!)

I don't remember her ever being sick, or taking the time to be sick, until the end. Her needlework was incredible, sort of a lost art these days. She sewed often, and cross-stitched aprons, pillow cases, crocheted afghans—didn't care for "crewel" work which became popular in the 1960's, but she always stayed busy.

—Sandra Taylor Bell, 2004

1948 Tegtmeier Reunion *(immediate family in italic)*
Back Row: David Berry, Paul Berry, *Bill Tegtmeier* holding Linda, Ed Taylor holding Jim. *Dick Tegtmeier* and wife Sandy Kestner Tegtmeier, *Raymond Tegtmeier*, *Harold Tegtmeier*, *Henry Tegtmeier* holding Miriam (Absent are *Lois Tegtmeier* and her husband Pete Hinrichs who were living in North Dakota.)
Second Row: *Loretta Tegtmeier* Berry, Lois Westlund Tegtmeier, *Alice Tegtmeier* Taylor, *Anna Papenhagen Tegtmeier*, *Pop (Will Carl Tegtmeier)*, Laura Minichbauer holding Sharon, Lucille Herman Tegtmeier holding Donald, Harriet holding Joan and Paul
Front Row: Karen Berry, Ed Taylor, Shirley Taylor, Donna Tegtmeier, James Tegtmeier

More About Erna Henriette Sophie Papenhagen:
Burial: October 3, 1982, Canaan, Wayne, CH
Emigration: 1889, "Augusta Victoria" July 1889, Hamburg to US

Children of William Tegtmeier and Erna Papenhagen are:

30. i. Loretta Mattie[5] Tegtmeier, b. August 26, 1911.
31. ii. Raymond Julius Tegtmeier, b. December 7, 1912, Brookpark, OH; d. September 1982, Wayne County, Ohio.
iii. Julia Wihelmina Tegtmeier, b. October 7, 1914, Brookpark, Cuyahoga Co., Ohio; d. March 2, 1934, Columbus, OH.

Julia was born October 7, 1914. She had strong features with dark brown hair. I recall teasing her under the kitchen table while she swept the floor. A kind lady at our Church lent Julia money to go to college. She also did housework and cared for children of two families along with her studies and classes. Finishing her second year at Capital University, our Church College in Columbus, she suddenly became ill and was hospitalized. Loretta and Paul took Mother and Dad to see her. Mother stayed to comfort her. It was March and we had deep snow. Julia died a week later on Harold's birthday, March 2. Her funeral was on March 6, Bill's birthday. Roads had turned so muddy from heavy rain that the service was held at the Funeral Home. The strong scent of flowers permeated the air. To this day when I see or smell hyacinths, I immediately think of Julia's funeral. She had taken an art class and doctors thought she had developed blood poisoning from lead in the paint. Mother had been at the grave of her mother in January and sister Jenny in February, now her daughter in March.

The spring days hung heavy with sadness. Dad and Ray cut firewood outdoors. Alice and the rest of my brothers were in school. I can still see the tears silently roll down Mother's cheek as she peeled potatoes for supper. She often remarked had it not been for our deep faith in the promise of our risen Lord ...

—Lois Tegtmeier Hinrichs

OBITUARY Id#: 0357899
Name: Tegtmeier, Julia W.
Date: Mar 4 1934
Source: Source unknown; Cleveland Necrology File, Reel #079.
Notes: Tegtmeier: Julia W., beloved daughter of William and Anna, at Columbus, O., Friday, March 2, at 8 p. m., aged 19 years. Remains at the funeral home of John C. Murray, Creston, O., where friends may call. Funeral at Canaan Lutheran Church, Creston, O., Monday, March 5, at 2 p. m.

More About Julia Wihelmina Tegtmeier:
Burial: March 6, 1934, Canaan Lutheran Church, Creston, O
Cause of Death: Bloodpoising from oil paints she used studying to be an artist.

32. iv. Alice Henrietta Tegtmeier, b. May 28, 1916, Brookpark, Ohio.
33. v. Henry Adolph Tegtmeier, b. March 19, 1918, Ohio; d. December 9, 1992, Fairfield Glade, TN.
34. vi. William Edward Tegtmeier, b. March 6, 1920, Brookpark, Ohio; d. July 24, 2000, Savanah, OH.
35. vii. Harold William Tegtmeier, b. March 2, 1921, Brookpark, Ohio; d. May 18, 2003, West Salem, Wayne, Ohio.
36. viii. Richard Elmer Tegtmeier, b. January 3, 1924, Berea, Cuyahoga Co.OH; d. October 17, 1995, Crossville, TN.
37. ix. Lois Ruth Tegtmeier, b. March 18, 1928, maybe Brookpark, OH.

12. Gustav Adolph[4] Tegtmeier *(Johann Heinrich[3], Johann Friedrich[2], Tegtmeier[1])* was born September 6, 1883 in Middleburg Twp, Cuyahoga Co. OH, and died November 24, 1937 in Erie, Erie Co. PA. He married (1) Alma Marie Bauer ABT 1910. She was born ABT 1893 in Ohio, and died November 24, 1937 in Erie, PA. He married (2) Rose M. Welnie ABT 1920. She was born 1882, and died November 27, 1937 in Erie, PA. They died in a car crash in Pennsylvania.

Notes for Gustav Adolph Tegtmeier:
1900 Census: living next to his Uncle Ferd: Cuyahoga—other townships (Middleburgh) ed # 222—page 8
Henry Tegtmeir, head, farmer, single age 24, born October 1875; both parents born in Germany; Christena, sister, single, December 1880, age 19, born in Ohio; William, brother born May 1882, single, farm laborer; ADOLPH, brother age 16, Sept 1883, farm laborer.

1910 Alma Tegtmeier
Age in 1910: 16
Estimated Birth Year: 1893
Birthplace: Iowa
Home in 1910: DOUGLAS TWP, BREMER, Iowa

Race: White
Gender: Female
Series: T624
Roll: 393
Part: 2
Page: 15B

1910 Census • Ohio • Cuyahoga • Other Townships • ED# 23
Julia, age 59m widow, had 7 children, 6 survive; born in Germany; Henry age 37 works at a factory; William age 27, general farm; Adolph age 26 ** general farm; children born in Ohio.
1920 U.S. Census • Ohio • Cuyahoga • Brook Park • ED# 518
Adolph Tegtmier age 37, machinist at motor company; Alma age 27; Howard, age 7 all born in Ohio; Adolph and Alma's parents born in Germany;

1930 Brook Park, Cuyahoga, Ohio
Adolph G Tegtmeier, age 48, first married when he was 28, machinst in the auto factory (probably Ford Motor Company headquartered in Brookpark at that time; wife Alma, age 37, first married when she was 18; Howard J age 17

OBITUARY Id#: 0357894
Name: Tegtmeier, Adolph—Died with Rose in a car crash in Pennsylvania.
Date: Nov 27 1937
Source: Source unknown; Cleveland Necrology File, Reel #079.
Notes: Tegtmeier: Adolph, of 15421 Brook Park rd., Brook Park, O., beloved husband of the late Rose M. (nee Weinle), father of Howard Tegimeier and Dale Peterson, suddenly at Erie, Pa., age 54 years. Friends may call at the Emil C. Haag Funeral Home, 50 E. Bridge st., Berea, O., until Saturday noon. Services at Evangelical Church on W. 130 st., Saturday, Nov. 27, at 2:45 p. m.

Adolph was married first to Alma Marie Bauer. They divorced.

Second marriage to Rose M. Welnie.
(husband and wife both died same day.—Died in auto accident while traveling to/from Buffalo New York.

Notes for Rose M. Welnie:
OBITUARY ID# 0357902
Date: Nov 27, 1937
Source unknown: Cleveland Necrology Fie, Reel # 079
Notes: Tegtmeier: Rose M. (nee Welnie) of 19431 Brookpark Rd., Brook Park, O. beloved wife of the late Adolph, mother of Dale Peterson and Howard (sic)? suddenly at Erie, PA, age 55 years. Friends may call at Emil C. Haag Funeral Home, 50 E. Bridge Street, Berea, O until Saturday noon. Services at Evangelical Church on W 130 Street, Saturday, Nov. 27 at 2:45 pm.

More About Gustav Adolph Tegtmeier:
Census: 1920, Brookpark, Cuyahoga, Ohio
Occupation: 1920, Machinist, Motor Company

Notes for Alma Marie Bauer:
1930 Census:
Alma U Tegtmeier
Age: 37 years
Estimated birth year: 1892
Relation to Head-of-house: Wife
Home in 1930: Brook Park, Cuyahoga, Ohio
Tegtmeier, Adolph, age 48, 28 years old when first married, born in Ohio, machinist in an auto factory.
Alma U. age 37, age 18 when first married, wife, born in Ohio, Howard age 17 born in Ohio. Married first to Adolph Tegtmeier; Second marriage to Fred R. Koch.

OBITUARY Id#: 0581702
Name: Koch, Fred R.
Date:?
Source: Source unknown; Cleveland
Necrology File, Reel #125.
Notes: Koch. Fred R. Koch, former residence, Aylesworth Dr., Parma Heights, O., beloved husband of the late Alma (nee Bauer), stepfather of Howard J. Tegtmeier Sr. of Dayton, O., and grandfather, brother of the late Marie Vogel, passed away Sunday at Xenia, O. Friends may call at The Baker Funeral Home, 206 Front St., Berea, where services will be held Wednesday, April 13th.

Children of GUSTAV Adolph TEGTMEIER and ALMA BAUER are:

38. i. Howar d J.[5] Tegt meier , b. ABT 1913, Ohio.

Notes for HOWARD J. TEGTMEIER:
1930 Brook Park, Cuyahoga, Ohio
Adolph G Tegtmeier, age 48, first married when he was 28, machinst in the auto factory (probably Ford Motor Company headquartered in Brookpark at that time; wife Alma, age 37, first married when she was 18; Howard J age 17. (I Don't see Dale …)

ii. DALE PETERSON, step son, son of Rose Welnie from Rose's first marriage.

13. FRED C.[4] TECKMYER *(FRIEDRICH WILHELM[3] TEGTMEIER, JOHANN FRIEDRICH[2], TEGTMEIER[1])* was born Aft. 1882 in Ohio, and died March 19, 1961 in Eustis, Florida. He married MARION LOWE ABT 1911. She was born May 25, 1888 in Ohio, and died May 1982 in Seffner, Hillsborough, Florida.

Notes for FRED C. TECKMYER:
1920 U.S. Census • Ohio • Cuyahoga • Lakewood
Fred Techmyer, age 38, secretary for steel treating company, born in Ohio, father born in Germany, mother born in Michigan; Marion L. wife, age 31 born in Ohio, father born in Ohio, mother born in Canada;
Fred C. Jr. age 5 born in Ohio; Isabel age 1 2/12; Anna Vargo, servant, age 16; William P. age 7. Children all born in Ohio.

1930 Census Lakewood Cuyahoga Ohio
Teckmyer, Fred C. head, rail road, owns own home, 48 years old; married when he was 29, born in Ohio father from Germany, mother from Michigan; secretary for Steel company, $ 10,000 per year; Marion L. wife, age 41, born in Ohio, father from Ohio, mother from Canada; age 22 when first married; William L 17, son, Fred C., Jr. 16; Isabel M. age 11, children all born in Ohio.

OBITUARY Id#: 0752130
Name: Teckmyer, Fred C.
Date: Mar 23 1961
Source: Plain Dealer; Cleveland Necrology File, Reel #161.

Notes: Beloved husband of Marion (nee Lowe); father of Isabel? Fred, Jr. and William; grandfather of seven; brother of Elsie Fairbank and the late Cecelia Rich and Madeline Pfizenmayer; passed away Sunday, March 19, at Eustis, Fla. Friends received at the Daniels Funeral Home, 15800 Detroit Ave., Lakewood, where services will be held Thursday, March 23, at 1:30 p. m. Interment Lakewood Park Cemetery. In lieu of flowers, send donations to the Cancer Society.

Notes for MARION LOWE:
Marion Teckmyer
Last Residence: 33583 Seffner, Hillsborough, Florida, United States of America
Born: 25 May 1888
Died: May 1982
State (Year) SSN issued: Florida (1962)

Children of FRED TECKMYER and MARION LOWE are:

i. FRED C.[5] TECKMYER, JR., b. February 20, 1914, Ohio; d. October 21, 2000, Naples, Collier, Florida.

Notes for FRED C. TECKMYER, JR.:
1920 U.S. Census • Ohio • Cuyahoga • Lakewood
Fred Techmyer, age 38, secretary for steel treating company, born in Ohio, father born in Germany, mother born in Michigan; Marion L. wife, age 31 born in Ohio, father born in Ohio, mother born in Canada; Fred C. Jr. age 5 born in Ohio; Isabel age 1 2/12; Anna Vargo, servant, age 16; William P. age 7. Children all born in Ohio.

Fred C. Teckmyer
Last Residence: 34110 Naples, Collier, Florida, United States of America
Born: 20 Feb 1914
Died: 21 Oct 2000
State (Year) SSN issued: Ohio (Before 1951)

ii. Isabel M. Teckmyer, b. ABT 1918, Ohio.

Notes for Isabel M. Teckmyer:
1920 U.S. Census • Ohio • Cuyahoga • Lakewood
Fred Techmyer, age 38, secretary for steel treating company, born in Ohio, father born in Germany, mother born in Michigan; Marion L. wife, age 31 born in Ohio, father born in Ohio, mother born in Canada; Fred C. Jr. age 5 born in Ohio; Isabel age 1 2/12; Anna Vargo, servant, age 16; William P. age 7. Children all born in Ohio.

39. iii. William L. Teckmyer, b. June 17, 1912, Ohio; d. February 1978, Cleveland, Cuyahoga, Ohio.

14. Celia F.[4] Tegtmeier *(Friedrich Wilhelm[3], Johann Friedrich[2], Tegtmeier[1])* was born ABT 1888 in Ohio, and died August 31, 1960 in Lakewood, Ohio. She married Louis Rich ABT 1910 in Ohio. He was born ABT 1885, and died 1943 in Lakewood, Ohio.

OBITUARY Id#: 0752130
Name: Teckmyer, Fred C.
Date: Mar 23 1961
Source: Plain Dealer; Cleveland Necrology File, Reel #161.
Notes: Beloved husband of Marion (nee Lowe); father of Isabel? Fred, Jr. and William; grandfather of seven; brother of Elsie Fairbank and the late Cecelia Rich and Madeline Pfizenmayer; passed away Sunday, March 19, at Eustis, Fla. Friends received at the Daniels Funeral Home, 15800 Detroit Ave., Lakewood, where services will be held Thursday, March 23, at 1:30 p. m. Interment Lakewood Park Cemetery. In lieu of flowers, send donations to the Cancer Society.

Id#: 0690643
Name: Rich, Mrs. Louis
Date: Aug 31 1960

OBITUARY: Source: Plain Dealer; Cleveland Necrology File, Reel #149.
Notes: Services for Mrs. Louis Rich, widow of widely known orchestra leader of more than 30 years here, will be at 1:30 p.m. tomorrow in the Saxton funeral home, 13215 Detroit Avenue, Lakewood. She died Monday night in Lakewood

Hospital, where she had been a patient for five weeks. She was 71. The family home is at 1375 Bunts Road, Lakewood. After the musician's death in 1943, Mrs. Rich catalogued his library of several thousand orchestrations, for distributions to Crile Veterans Hospital, to West Germany and to the Cleveland Public Library. She was active in service organizations. For about 40 years she was a member of the Auxiliary Board of Eliza Jennings Home. She long was active in the Children's Aid Society and in Lakewood PTA groups. The former Celia Tegtmeier, she was a member of an early West Side family. She is survived by a son, Louis Rich, Jr.; two daughters, Mrs. Joseph E. Woodworth and Mrs. F. J. Webster; four grandchildren and two brothers. Her family would appreciate contributions to the Eliza Jennings Home here

Notes for Louis Rich:
1920 Census 1920 U.S. Census • Ohio • Cuyahoga • Lakewood
Louis Rich, head 35 years old; Celia F, wife age 30, born in Ohio; Celia E age 2 7/12 months born in Ohio; Magdalena Tegtmeier, mother in law, age 52, widow.

Orchestra leader, the Louis Rich Winton Hotel Orchestra, produced radio programs nationwide from Cleveland, Ohio, Winton Hotel from about 1925–1935.

1930 United States Federal Census > Ohio > Cuyahoga > Lakewood > District 626
Address on Kenneth Drive
Louis Rich, age 44, Director of orchestra, had a radio set (part of the questionnaire) $30,000 value; was 29 when first married; born in Ohio, parents born in Germany; Celia age 39, age 24 when first married, born in Ohio, both parents born in Ohio; Louis age 10; Celia age 12; Shirley M age 4.

More About Louis Rich:
Occupation: Bet. 1920–1930, Louis Rich Orchestra, national radio show

Children of CELIA TEGTMEIER and LOUIS RICH are:

- i. Celia E.[5] Rich, b. ABT 1917, Ohio.
- ii. Louis Jr. Rich.
- iii. Shirley Rich. B abt 1926.

15. MADELINE[4] TEGTMEIER *(FRIEDRICH WILHELM[3], JOHANN FRIEDRICH[2], TEGTMEIER[1])* was born ABT 1883, and died September 13, 1950 in Cuyahoga Co, Ohio. She married HENRY PFIZENMAYER, son of CARL PFIZENMAYER and LOUISA. He was born ABT 1873, and died November 28, 1949 in Lakewood, Cuyahoga, Ohio.

OBITUARY Id#: 0276695
Name: Pfizenmayer, Madeline M.
Date: Sep 13 1950
Source: Cleveland Press; Cleveland Necrology File, Reel #064.
Notes: Pfizenmayer, Madeline M., (nee Testmeler), wife of the late Henry, beloved mother of Victor C., the late Ariene and Lucille, grandmother of Victor C. and Thomas David, sister of Fred C. Teckmyer, Mrs. L. G. Fairbank of Akron, O., and Mrs. Louis Rich, formerly of 12974 Harlan Ave., Lakewood. Friends may call at the Daniels Funeral Home, 15800 Detroit Ave., where services will be held Friday, Sept. 15, at 1:30 p. m.

OBITUARY Id#: 0276691
Name: Pfizenmayer, Renry (should be Henry)
Date: Nov 28 1949
Source: Source unknown; Cleveland Necrology File, Reel #064.
Notes: Pfizenmayer, Renry, beloved husband of Madeline M. [nee Tegtmeler (sic)]; father of Victor C. and the late Arline; grandfather of Victor C. and Thomas David; brother of John, Willard, Carl, Florence VonKrogh, Laura Miller and Lula Helmrich. Residence, 12974 Harlan Ave. Friends may call at the Daniels Funeral Home, 15800 Detroit Ave., where services will be held Monday, Nov. 28, at 3 p. m.

Children of MADELINE TEGTMEIER and HENRY PFIZENMAYER are:

40. i. Victor C.[5] Pfizenmayer.

ii. ARIENE PFIZENMAYER, d. March 27, 1942, Cleveland, Cuyahoga Co., Ohio.

Notes for ARIENE PFIZENMAYER:
OBITUARY Id#: 0276689
Name: Pfizenmayer, Arline Louise
Date: Mar 27 1942
Source: Source unknown; Cleveland Necrology File, Reel #064.

Notes: Pfizenmayer: Arline Louise, beloved daughter of Henry and Madeline (nee Tegtmeier), sister of Victor; residence, 12974 Harlan ave. Friends may call at Wm. R. & Roy A. Daniels' Funeral Home, 15800 Detroit ave., where service will be held Friday, March 27, at 3 p. m.

iii. LUCILLE PFIZENMAYER, b. ABT 1909, Ohio; d. September 4, 1916, Lakewood, Cuyahoga, Ohio.

Notes for LUCILLE PFIZENMAYER:
OBITUARY Id#: 0276693
Name: Pfizenmayer, Lucile
Date: September 7, 1916
Source: Source unknown; Cleveland Necrology File, Reel #064.
Notes: Pfizenmayer-Lucile, beloved daughter of Henry and Madeline (nee Tegtmeier), Monday Sept. 4, age 7 years 7 months. Funeral Thursday, Sept. 7, at 2 p. m., from 1427 Lincoln ave.; Auto funeral.

16. ELSIE[4] TEGTMEIER *(FRIEDRICH WILHELM[3], JOHANN FRIEDRICH[2], TEGTMEIER[1])* was born ABT 1885. She married LOUIS G. FAIRBANK. He was born in Akron, Ohio.

Id#: 0752130
Name: Teckmyer, Fred C.
Date: Mar 23 1961
Source: Plain Dealer; Cleveland Necrology File, Reel #161.
Notes: Beloved husband of Marion (nee Lowe); father of Isabel? Fred, Jr. and William; grandfather of seven; brother of Elsie Fairbank ** and the late Cecelia Rich and Madeline Pfizenmayer; passed away Sunday, March 19, at Eustis, Fla. Friends received at the Daniels Funeral Home, 15800 Detroit Ave., Lakewood, where services will be held Thursday, March 23, at 1:30 p. m. Interment Lakewood Park Cemetery. In lieu of flowers, send donations to the Cancer Society.

Elsie Teckmeyer **
SSN: 167-01-5948
Last Residence: 16412 Edinboro, Erie, Pennsylvania, United States of America

Born: 28 Jan 1887
Last Benefit: 16412 Edinboro, Erie, Pennsylvania, United States of America
Died: Dec 1977
State (Year) SSN issued: Pennsylvania (Before 1951)

Child of ELSIE TEGTMEIER and LOUIS FAIRBANK is:

i. ROBERT LEWIS[5] FAIRBANK, b. January 7, 1912, Cleveland, Cuyahoga Co., OH; d. September 18, 1998, Ohio.

Notes for ROBERT LEWIS FAIRBANK:
Robert Lewis Fairbank
Gender: Male
Date of Death: 18 September 1998
Birth Date: 07 January 1912
Volume: 31685
Certificate: 074492
Autopsy: No
Father's Surname: Fairbank
Time of Death: 11:50 PM
Marital Status: Married
Hispanic Origin: Non Hispanic
Place of Death: Nursing Home
Years of Schooling: 16
Certifier: Physician
Referred to Coroner: No
Method of Disposition: Cremation
Mother's Surname: Tegtmeier
Race: White
Birth Place: Cleveland, Cuyahoga County, Ohio
Residence: Ohio
Age: 86

17. KARL FERDINAND[4] TEGTMEIER *(KARL FERDINAND[3], JOHANN FRIEDRICH[2], TEGTMEIER[1])* was born August 30, 1883 in Berea, Cuyahoga Co. OH, and died April 9, 1956 in Cuyahoga Co., OH. He married (1) LENA LENTHE ABT 1907, daughter of ADOLPH LENTHE and MINNIE EHLERT. She was born ABT 1883 in Ohio, and died Bef. 1926 in Cuyahoga Co, Ohio. He married (2) ROSE KOVALIK married after 1930. She died June 19, 1947 in Cleveland, Cuyahoga, Ohio.

(He goes from "Karl" to "Ferd" to "Fred" during 30 years of census)

Notes for Karl Ferdinand Tegtmeier:
1900 U.S. Census • Ohio • Cuyahoga • Other Townships • ED# 222—page 8 (next door)
Tegtmeier, Ferd, head, farmer, age 52, married 18 years, Feb 1848, immigrated 1862, 38 years ago, farmer; Fredrica age 41, April 1859, married 18 years, had 4 children, 3 survive, born in Germany, both parents born in Germany; immigrated 1870, 30 years ago; **CARL****, son age 16, born August 1883 in Ohio, at school; Frieda, age 15, Jan 1885, born in Ohio; Fred age 10, son, born May 1890 in Ohio (Three Tegtmeier families living next to each other: ** Temeyer, P____; Henry Tegtmeir, and Ferd Tegtmeier)

1910 Census
Carl Tegtmeier
Age in 1910: 26
Estimated Birth Year: 1883
Birthplace: Ohio
Home in 1910: MIDDLEBURG TWP, CUYAHOGA, Ohio
1910, next door to Mrs. Fredrica Tegtmeiere, (mother):

1910 U.S. Census • Ohio • Cuyahoga • Other Townships • ED# 23
Tegtmeier, Carl age 26, works at a factory, Lena age 24; both born in Ohio.

OBITUARY Id#: 0752231
Name: Tegtmeier, Carl
(Karl Ferdinand Tegtmeier has used the name Carl, Ferd and Fred in various census.)
Date: Apr 11 1956
Source: Cleveland Press; Cleveland Necrology File, Reel #161.
Notes: Tegtmeier, Carl, late residence, 4247 W. 35th St., beloved father of Celia Hickok, Adelbert, Nina Bartel, Norma Pernoja, Rose Biller, and grandfather, brother of Fred and Erma Behner. Friends received at Corrigan's Funeral Home, Lorain Ave. at W. 148th St., where services will be held Thursday, Apr. 12, at 2:30 p. m. Interment Sunset Memorial Park Cemetery.

Notes for Lena Lenthe:
OBITUARY Id#: 0203307
Name: Lenthe, Adolph (this shows that Lena had already died, and Rose is not there yet)
Date: Aug. 17, 1926
Source: Cemetery record; Cleveland Necrology File, Reel #050.
Notes: Lenthe-Adolph, beloved husband of Minnie (nee Ehlert), father of the late Lena Tegtmeier** and Mrs. Ella Walford, grandfather of Adelbert, Nina and Norma Tegtmeier, and Virginia and Ellenore Walford. Funeral Tuesday, Aug. 17, from the late residence, 4193 W. 150th street, formerly Harrington road, at 2:30 p. m. Friends invited. 1926. Age 66. Alger Cemetery Cleveland, Ohio.

Notes for Rose Kovalik: (second wife)
OBITUARY Id#: 0357901
Name: Tegtmeier, Rose
Date: Jun 19 1947
Source: Source unknown; Cleveland Necrology File, Reel #079.
Notes: Tegtmeier, Rose (nee Kovalik), beloved wife of Carl; dear mother of Celia Hickok and Rose Biller, and grandmother; sister of Caroline Kadlubak and Anna Mirowsky. Friends received at Corrigan's Funeral Home, Lorain Ave. at W. 148th St., Until 10 A. M. Saturday, then at Emanuel Evangelical Reformed Church, 4515 W. 130th St., where services will be held at 1:30 p. m. Interment Sunset Memorial Park.

More About Rose Kovalik:
Burial: Sunset Memorial Park

Children of Karl Tegtmeier and Lena Lenthe are:

i. Adelbert E.[5] Tegtmeier, b. June 1913, Ohio; d. December 17, 1991, Ohio.

Notes for Adelbert E. Tegtmeier:
1930 Census: 1930 United States Federal Census > Ohio > Cuyahoga > Chagrin Falls > District 553
Fredricka J. Tegtmeier, age 71, widow; Frieda, daughter, age 44; Fred, son age 39, farmer (head of the household)—Karl Ferdinand Tegtmeier becomes known as "Fred"; Erna, daugh-

ter age 26; Adelbert, son age 16; Nina, pend daughter age 15; Norma pend daughter age 15;

ADELBERT E. TEGTMEIER
Gender: Male
Date of Death: December 17, 1991
Birth Date: June, 1913
Volume: 088485
Certificate: 28766
Father's Surname: TEGTMEIER
Time of Death: 02:48 pm
Marital Status: Widowed
Hispanic Origin: Non-Hispanic
Place of Death:
Years of Schooling: Elementary or Secondary
Race: White
Birth Place: Ohio
Residence: Ohio
Age: 78 Years

ii. NINA TEGTMEIER, b. ABT 1915; m. XXX BARTEL.

Notes for NINA TEGTMEIER:
1930 Census: 1930 United States Federal Census > Ohio > Cuyahoga > Chagrin Falls > District 553
Fredricka J. age 71, widow; Frieda, daughter, age 44; Fred, son age 39, farmer (supports household); Erna, daughter age 26; Adelbert, son age 16; Nina, pend daughter age 15; Norma pend daughter age 15;

Nina and her twin sister are living with their father and grandmother. Karl's first wife died before 1926 (as listed in Adolph Lenths obituary) and Rose is also gone.

Nina & Norma are twins.

iii. NORMA TEGTMEIER, b. ABT 1915, Ohio; m. XXX PERNOJA.

Children of KARL TEGTMEIER and ROSE KOVALIK are:

iv. CELIA[5] TEGTMEIER, b. after 1926; m. xxx HICKOK.

v. ROSE TEGTMEIER, b. after 1926; m. xxx BILLER.

18. ERMA MARIA[4] TEGTMEIER *(KARL FERDINAND[3], JOHANN FRIEDRICH[2], TEGTMEIER[1])* was born March 25, 1904 in Berea, Cuyahoga Co. OH, and died February 16, 1977 in Medina Co. Ohio. She married ELMER BEHNER December 2, 1930. He was born ABT 1904.

Notes for ERMA MARIA TEGTMEIER:
1910 U.S. Census • Ohio • Cuyahoga • Other Townships • ED# 23
Tegtmeier, Mrs. Fredrica, head, age 51, widowed, born in Germany, 5 children, 4 survive; Frieda, daughter age 35 born in Ohio; Fred age 19, general farm, Irma age 6**. (Note "Irma")

Social Security Info:
Erma Behner
Born: 25 Mar 1904
Last Benefit: 44017 Berea, Cuyahoga, Ohio, United States of America
Died: Feb 1977
State (Year) SSN issued: Ohio (1952–1953)
Erma M Behner
Gender: Female
Date of Death: 16 February 1977
Volume: 22820
Certificate: 021062
Autopsy: Unknown
Marital Status: Widowed
Place of Death:, Medina County
Certifier: Physician
Race: White
Residence: Berea, Cuyahoga County
Age: 72 Years (born about 1903)

Notes for ELMER BEHNER:
SEARCHING FOR Mr. Behner and Erma:

1930 United States Federal Census > Ohio > Cuyahoga > Cleveland (Districts 501–533) > District 505
Behner, Albert S, age 33; Erma age 32; Paul 11; Dorothy 9, Jack age 6; Doris Allen, grandmother age 81.

Earle L Behner
Gender: Male
Date of Death: 04 August 1971
Volume: 20578
Certificate: 061391
Autopsy: No Autopsy
Marital Status: Married
Place of Death:, Medina County
Certifier: Physician
Race: White
Residence:, Medina County
Age: 73 Years

Child of Erma Tegtmeier and Elmer Behner is:

i. Glenn[5] Behner, b. August 18, 1937, Berea, Cuyahoga Co. OH; d. January 29, 1999, Brookpark, Cuyahoga Co. OH.

Notes for Glenn Behner:
GLENN ARTHUR BEHNER
Gender: Male
Date of Death: January 29, 1999
Birth Date: August 18, 1937
Volume: 31815
Certificate: 001685
Autopsy: N
Father's Surname: BEHNER
Time of Death: 11:50 PM
Marital Status: divorced
Hispanic Origin: Not Hispanic
Place of Death: nursing home
Years of Schooling: 10
Certifier: Physician
Branch of Service:
Method of Disposition: Burial

Mother's Surname: TEGTMEIER **
Race: White
Birth Place: BEREA, CUYAHOGA, Ohio
Residence: BROOK PARK, CUYAHOGA, Ohio

19. WILLIAM H.[4] PULS *(ADELINE LOUISE[3] TEGTMEIER, JOHANN FRIEDRICH[2], TEGTMEIER[1])* was born January 1884 in Cuyahoga Co, Ohio, and died April 18, 1943 in Berea, Cuyahoga Co.,Ohio. He married ANNA PARKER. She was born ABT 1885, and died September 9, 1963 in Cuyahoga Co, Ohio.

Notes for WILLIAM H. PULS:
1900 U.S. Census • Ohio • Cuyahoga • Other Townships • ED# 222—page 13
Puls, William age 43, born Nov 1856 in Ohio, farmer, both parents from Germany. married 17 years, Adeline, wife, age age 37, Aug 1862 born in Ohio, 6 children, 3 survive; William age 15, Jan 1884; Elsie age 11, Dec 1888; Leonard age 4, June 1895.

OBITUARY Id#: 0285696
Name: Puls, William H.
Date: Apr 18 1943
Source: Source unknown; Cleveland Necrology File, Reel #066.
Notes: Puls: William H., beloved husband of Anna, father of Mrs. Leah Svat, Mrs. LaVern Woddups, Thelma and William; brother of Leonard, Mrs. Elsie Rohde and Mrs. Elva Rohde; now at the Davis Funeral Chapel (successor to Emil C. Haag), 50 E. Bridge st., Berea; services from St. Paul's Lutheran Church, Monday, April 19, at 2:30.

Notes for ANNA PARKER:
OBITUARY Id#: 0682241
Name: Puls, Anna
Date: Sep 9 1963
Source: Plain Dealer; Cleveland Necrology File, Reel #147.
Notes: Puls. Anna Puls (nee Parker), beloved wife of the late William H., mother of Leah Svat. LaVerne Waddups, Thelma Phillips, William D., and grandmother, sister of Hazel Fine, Agnes Morley, Polly McGue, Lillie Morley, John and the late Reuben, passed away Sunday. Friends may call After 7 P.M. Monday, And From 2–4 And 7–9 P.M. Tuesday, at the Baker Funeral Home, Berea, where services will be held Wednesday, Sept. 11, at 1:30 p.m.

Children of WILLIAM PULS and ANNA PARKER are:

i. LEAH[5] PULS, b. ABT 1900; m. xxx SVAT; b. ABT 1900.

Notes for LEAH PULS:
Id#: 0285696
Name: Puls, William H.
Date: Apr 18 1943
Source: Source unknown; Cleveland Necrology File, Reel #066.
Notes: Puls: William H., beloved husband of Anna, father of Mrs. Leah Svat, Mrs. LaVern Woddups, Thelma and William; brother of Leonard, Mrs. Elsie Rohde and Mrs. Elva Rohde; now at the Davis Funeral Chapel (successor to Emil C. Haag), 50 E. Bridge st., Berea; services from St. Paul's Lutheran Church, Monday, April 19, at 2:30.

ii. LAVERNE PULS, b. ABT 1902; m. xxx WODDUPS.

Notes for LAVERNE PULS:
OBITUARY Id#: 0285696
Name: Puls, William H.
Date: Apr 18 1943
Source: Source unknown; Cleveland Necrology File, Reel #066.
Notes: Puls: William H., beloved husband of Anna, father of Mrs. Leah Svat, Mrs. LaVern Woddups, Thelma and William; brother of Leonard, Mrs. Elsie Rohde and Mrs. Elva Rohde; now at the Davis Funeral Chapel (successor to Emil C. Haag), 50 E. Bridge st., Berea; services from St. Paul's Lutheran Church, Monday, April 19, at 2:30.

iii. THELMA PULS, b. ABT 1904; m. xxx PHILLIPS.

Notes for THELMA PULS:
Id#: 0682241
Name: Puls, Anna
Date: Sep 9 1963
Source: Plain Dealer; Cleveland Necrology File, Reel #147.

Notes: Puls. Anna Puls (nee Parker), beloved wife of the late William H., mother of Leah Svat. LaVerne Waddups, Thelma Phillips **, William D., and grandmother, sister of Hazel Fine, Agnes Morley, Polly McGue, Lillie Morley, John and the late Reuben, passed away Sunday. Friends may call After 7 P.M. Monday, And From 2–4 And 7–9 P.M. Tuesday, at the Baker Funeral Home, Berea, where services will be held Wednesday, Sept. 11, at 1:30 p.m.

iv. WILLIAM PULS, b. ABT 1906.

20. LEONARD[4] PULS *(ADELINE LOUISE[3] TEGTMEIER, JOHANN FRIEDRICH[2], TEGTMEIER[1])* was born June 1895 in Cuyahoga Co, Ohio, and died October 4, 1957 in Berea, Cuyahoga Co.,Ohio. He married ETHEL L. PINCOMBE. She was born ABT 1896 in Ohio, and died March 3, 1956 in Berea, Cuyahoga Co.,Ohio.

Notes for LEONARD PULS:
1900 U.S. Census • Ohio • Cuyahoga • Other Townships • ED# 222—page 13
Puls, William age 43, born Nov 1856 in Ohio, farmer, both parents from Germany. married 17 years, Adeline, wife, age age 37, Aug 1862 born in Ohio, 6 children, 3 survive; William age 15, Jan 1884; Elsie age 11, Dec 1888; Leonard age 4, June 1895.

Id#: 0285697
Name: Puls, William W.
Date: June 19, 1926
Source: Cemetery record; Cleveland Necrology File, Reel #066.
Notes: Puls-William W., beloved husband of the late Adeline, father of William H. Puls, Mrs. Elsie Rohde, Mrs. Elva Rohde of Brook Park, O., and Leonard Puls of Berea, O., and brother of Charles Puls of Cleveland, O., at his home on Hummel road, age 69 years. Funeral from his late residence, Saturday, June 19, at 2:30 p. m. 1926. St. Pauls' Cemetery Berea, Ohio.

Id#: 0682237
Name: Puls, Leonard F.
Date: Oct 4 1957
Source: Cleveland Press; Cleveland Necrology File, Reel #147.

Notes: Puls, Leonard F., beloved husband of the late Ethel L. (nee Pincombe), father of Carol J. Keck, Arlene A. Byers, Myrtle J. Malone, and grandfather, brother of Elsie and Elva Robde and the late William, passed away Wednesday. Friends may call at the Baker Funeral Home, Berea, where services will be held Saturday, Oct. 5, at 1:30 p. m.

Notes for Ethel L. Pincombe:
Id#: 0682235
Name: Puls, Ethel L.
Date: Mar 3 1956
Source: Cleveland Press; Cleveland Necrology File, Reel #147.
Notes: Puls, Ethel L. (nee Pincombe), beloved wife of Leonard, mother of Carol Jean Keck, Arlene A. Byers, Myrtle J. Malone, and grandmother, sister of Ella Olsen, William, Walter and the late Silas, Arthur and Alvin, passed away Friday. Friends may call After 7 P. M. at the Baker Funeral Home, Berea, where services will be held Monday, Mar. 5, at 1:30 p. m.

Children of Leonard Puls and Ethel Pincombe are:

i. Carol Jean[5] Puls, b. ABT 1915; m. xxx Keck.

Notes for Carol Jean Puls: She married a Mr. Keck
Id#: 0682237
Name: Puls, Leonard F.
Date: Oct 4 1957
Source: Cleveland Press; Cleveland Necrology File, Reel #147.
Notes: Puls, Leonard F., beloved husband of the late Ethel L. (nee Pincombe), father of Carol J. Keck, Arlene A. Byers, Myrtle J. Malone, and grandfather, brother of Elsie and Elva Robde and the late William, passed away Wednesday. Friends may call at the Baker Funeral Home, Berea, where services will be held Saturday, Oct. 5, at 1:30 p. m.

ii. Arlene Puls, b. ABT 1917; m. xxx Byers; b. ABT 1915.

Notes for Arlene Puls: she married a Mr. xxx Byers.
Id#: 0682237
Name: Puls, Leonard F.
Date: Oct 4 1957

Source: Cleveland Press; Cleveland Necrology File, Reel #147. Notes: Puls, Leonard F., beloved husband of the late Ethel L. (nee Pincombe), father of Carol J. Keck, Arlene A. Byers, Myrtle J. Malone, and grandfather, brother of Elsie and Elva Robde and the late William, passed away Wednesday. Friends may call at the Baker Funeral Home, Berea, where services will be held Saturday, Oct. 5, at 1:30 p. m.

iii. MYRTLE PULS, b. ABT 1919; m. XXX MALONE.

Notes for MYRTLE PULS:
Id#: 0682237
Name: Puls, Leonard F.
Date: Oct 4 1957
Source: Cleveland Press; Cleveland Necrology File, Reel #147.
Notes: Puls, Leonard F., beloved husband of the late Ethel L. (nee Pincombe), father of Carol J. Keck, Arlene A. Byers, Myrtle J. Malone, and grandfather, brother of Elsie and Elva Robde and the late William, passed away Wednesday. Friends may call at the Baker Funeral Home, Berea, where services will be held Saturday, Oct. 5, at 1:30 p. m.

Generation No. 4

21. ALMETA BERTHA CHRISTINE[5] AHLEMAN *(HULDA LOUISE MARIA[4] TEGTMEIER, JOHANN HEINRICH[3], JOHANN FRIEDRICH[2], TEGTMEIER[1])* was born January 26, 1901 in Riga Twp, Riga, MI, and died November 15, 1979. She married JOHN BERNARD MEIER February 14, 1922 in Toledo, OH. He was born June 2, 1887 in Toledo, OH, and died June 1, 1969.

Notes for ALMETA BERTHA CHRISTINE AHLEMAN:
1920 Census • Michigan • Lenawee • Riga
Ernest Ahleman, age 51, born in Michigan, farmer; Hulda age 46, born in Ohio; Arthur age 23; Almeta age 18; Eloise (SP?) age 16; Walter age 12; Paul 2 and 7/12months; children all born in Michigan.

The Meiers Family
Left to right:
Lester Meier and his wife Mary (Klebold),,
Cousin Lucille Tegtmeier
John Meier
Sitting, Lucene Meier Pyers
And Doris Meier Hille
Photo circ. 2007, courtesy of Les Meier.

More About JOHN BERNARD MEIER:
Burial: Fort Meigs Cemetery, Perrysburg, OH

Children of ALMETA AHLEMAN and JOHN MEIER are:

41. i. John Arthur[6] Meier, b. December 25, 1922, Curtice, OH.
42. ii. Lucene Elsie Meier, b. November 15, 1924, Curtice, OH.
43. iii. Doris Hulda Meier, b. October 22, 1925, Curtice, OH.
44. iv. Lester Bernard Meier, b. January 7, 1931, Curtice, OH.

22. ELSIE EMMA HULDA[5] AHLEMAN *(HULDA LOUISE MARIA[4] TEGTMEIER, JOHANN HEINRICH[3], JOHANN FRIEDRICH[2], TEGTMEIER[1])* was born April 20, 1903 in Riga Twp., Riga MI, and died May 15, 1994. She married ELWIN C. MARKS August 6, 1924 in Blissfield, MI. He was born August 20, 1898 in Blissfield, MI, and died November 1, 1997 in Clayton, MI.

Notes for ELSIE EMMA HULDA AHLEMAN:
1920 Census • Michigan • Lenawee • Riga
Ernest Ahleman, age 51, born in Michigan, farmer; Hulda age 46, born in Ohio; Arthur age 23; Almeta age 18; Eloise (SP?) age 16; Walter age 12; Paul 2 and 7/12months; children all born in Michigan.

More About Elsie Emma Hulda Ahleman:
Burial: Dover Center Cemetery, Clayton MI Section C
More About Elwin C. Marks:
Burial: Cover Center Cemetery, Clayton MISection C

Children of Elsie Ahleman and Elwin Marks are:

45.	i.	Leola May[6] Marks, b. October 12, 1925, Henry Co., OH.
46.	ii.	William Carl Elwin Marks, b. March 1, 1930, Monroe Co., MI.
47.	iii.	Herbert Bernard Marks, b. March 31, 1936, Deerfield, MI.
48.	iv.	Stanley Arthur Marks, b. January 23, 1940, Deerfield, MI.

23. Walter Adolph[5] Ahleman *(Hulda Louise Maria[4] Tegtmeier, Johann Heinrich[3], Johann Friedrich[2], Tegtmeier[1])* was born January 16, 1907 in Riga Twn, Riga, MI, and died February 17, 1959 in Napolean, Henry Co.,. He married Ethel M. Strayer December 26, 1929. She was born September 10, 1906 in Grand Rapids, OH, and died April 17, 1996.

Notes for Walter Adolph Ahleman:
1920 Census • Michigan • Lenawee • Riga
Ernest Ahleman, age 51, born in Michigan, farmer; Hulda age 46, born in Ohio; Arthur age 23; Almeta age 18; Eloise (SP?) age 16; Walter age 12; Paul 2 and 7/12months; children all born in Michigan.

1930 United States Federal Census > Ohio > Henry > Washington > District 25
Walter R Ahleman, head, age 21, born in MI, famrer; Ethel, wife, age 21 born in Ohio, teacher, publci school; Ernest age 61, farmer, 24 when he first was married; Hulda, age 56, 19 when first married; Paul E. Brother, age 13 born in MI.

WALTER A AHLEMAN
Gender: Male
Date of Death: February 18, 1959
Volume: 15687
Certificate: 11528
Marital Status: Married

Place of Death: Napoleon, Henry County
Race: White
Residence:, Henry County
Age: 52

Walter Ahleman
Born: 16 Jan 1907
Died: Feb 1959
State (Year) SSN issued: Ohio (Before 1951)

More About WALTER ADOLPH AHLEMAN:
Burial: HeathCemetery, Henry Co., Wash. Twp, Liberty Ctr, OH
Occupation: 1930, Farmer/Washington, Henry, OH

Children of WALTER AHLEMAN and ETHEL STRAYER are:

49. i. Florence Elsie[6] Ahleman, b. November 30, 1930, Henry Co., Liberty Center, OH.
50. ii. Donald Ernest Ahleman, b. March 4, 1934, Liberty Center, Henry Co., OH.

24. PAUL ERNEST[5] AHLEMAN *(HULDA LOUISE MARIA[4] TEGTMEIER, JOHANN HEINRICH[3], JOHANN FRIEDRICH[2], TEGTMEIER[1])* was born April 6, 1917 in Riga Twn, Riga, MI. He married (1) LOLA E. HUFF November 9, 1941. She was born August 10, 1908 in Toledo, OH, and died April 17, 1954 in Henry Co., OH. He married (2) PAULINE SNAPP December 25, 1958 in England. She was born September 30, 1929 in Maryland.

Notes for PAUL ERNEST AHLEMAN:
1930 United States Federal Census > Ohio > Henry > Washington > District 25
Walter R Ahleman, head, age 21, born in MI, famer; Ethel, wife, age 21 born in Ohio, teacher, public school; Ernst age 61, farmer, 24 when he first was married; Hulda, age 56, 19 when first married; Paul E. Brother, age 13 born in MI.

More About LOLA E. HUFF:
Burial: Heath Cemetery, Henry Coi, Wash Twn Liberty Center OH

Children of PAUL AHLEMAN and LOLA HUFF are:

51. i. Damaris Anne[6] Ahleman, b. June 10, 1944, Lowrey Air Force Base, CO.

ii. LARRY ERNEST AHLEMAN, b. March 22, 1943, Lincoln, NE.

25. RUTH[5] TEGTMEIER *(HENRY WILLIAM CARL[4], JOHANN HEINRICH[3], JOHANN FRIEDRICH[2], TEGTMEIER[1])* was born ABT 1913 in Ohio. She married FRANCIS P. DAVIDSON, son of SAMUEL DAVIDSON and JEANNETTE PAYN. He was born July 9, 1908 in Cuyahoga Co., OH, and died March 5, 1996 in Richfield, Summit, Ohio.

Notes for RUTH TEGTMEIER:
1920 Census; Brookpark, Cuyahoga, OHIO
William Brandes, head, age 75, born in Ohio, Cristina, wife, age 78 born in Breman, Germany; Henry Tegtmeier, age 45, son in law; Augusta age 40 born in Ohio; Ruth ** age 7 born in Ohio, granddaughter; Oscar age 6 grandson, born in Ohio;

Need to find where the children are....
Ruth A. Davidson
Last Residence: 85204 Mesa, Maricopa, Arizona, United States of America
Born: 16 May 1913
Died: 21 Oct 1994
State (Year) SSN issued: Ohio (Before 1951)

Ruth Davidson
Last Residence: 45410 Dayton, Montgomery, Ohio, United States of America
Born: 1 Jun 1913
Died: Dec 1981
State (Year) SSN issued: Ohio (Before 1951)

Ruth M. Davidson
Last Residence: 44135 Cleveland, Cuyahoga, Ohio, United States of America
Born: 7 Apr 1915
Died: Mar 1995
State (Year) SSN issued: Ohio (Before 1951)

Notes for FRANCIS P. DAVIDSON:
1930 United States Federal Census > Ohio > Cuyahoga > Parma Heights > District 693
Samuel, head age 52, carpenter, born in Ohio; Jeannette age 49, born in Missouri; Francis P, ** son, 21; Mary E. 19; Alan W. 18; Samuel K 12; Donald 13, Roberta, daughter 8—all children born in Ohio.

Francis P. Davidson
Last Residence: 44286 Richfield, Summit, Ohio, United States of America
Born: 9 Jul 1908
Died: 5 Mar 1996
State (Year) SSN issued: Ohio (Before 1951)

Children of RUTH TEGTMEIER and FRANCIS DAVIDSON are:
52. i. Nancy[6] Davidson, b. ABT 1935.
ii. RICHARD DAVIDSON, b. ABT 1936.
iii. SUSAN DAVIDSON, b. ABT 1938; m. XXX HAHN.

Notes for SUSAN DAVIDSON:
OBITUARY Id#: 0752230
Name: Tegtmeier, Augusta C.
Date: Apr 4 1967
Source: Plain Dealer; Cleveland Necrology File, Reel #161.
Notes: Tegtmeier. Augusta C. Tegtmeier, age 88, beloved wife of the late Henry, dear mother of Ruth Davidson and Oscar, grandmother of Nancy Jones, Richard Davidson and Susan Hahn, great-grandmother of Elizabeth Jones, passed away Sunday. Funeral services will be held Wednesday, April 5, at 1:30 p.m. at Baker Funeral Home, Berea. Family suggests contributions be made to Immanuel United Church of Christ Building Fund, 4511 W. 130th St. Visiting Hours 3–5 And 7–9 P.M. Tuesday.

26. EDWIN A.[5] SCRIVENS *(LUCIE ADELINE JULIANNA[4] TEGTMEIER, JOHANN HEINRICH[3], JOHANN FRIEDRICH[2], TEGTMEIER[1])* was born January 24, 1899 in Ohio, and died July 1976 in Cleveland, OH. He married CLARA HANSEN, daughter of HANS HANSEN and MARIAN. She was born ABT 1900 in Ohio.

Notes for Edwin A. Scrivens:
1920 U.S. Census • Ohio • Cuyahoga • Middleburg • ED# 556
William R Scrivens, age 49, born in Ohio; Lucy J age 42 born in Ohio; Edwin H **, son age 20; William A age 18; Florence age 16; Clayton age 15; all born in Ohio.

1930 United States Federal Census > Ohio > Cuyahoga > Middleburg Heights > District 671
Edwin H Scrivens**, age 31, first married when he was 28, electician in a body shop, born in Ohio; Clara H., age 29, first married when she was 27, born in Ohio, she is a trained nurse. No children listed.
(Charles J. Taylor, age 32, born in Ohio living next door—possible brother to Clara Taylor; On other side, William Scrivens, age 28, single, farmer)

Notes for Clara Hansen:
Id#: 0715243
Name: Scrivens, Clara H.
Date: Feb 3 1958
Source: Cleveland Press; Cleveland Necrology File, Reel #154.
Notes: Scrivens, Clara H. (nee Hansen), beloved wife of Edwin, H., mother of Mary Lou Prechtel, and grandmother, daughter of Hans and Marian, sister of Ellen A. Serivens and Laura H. Hossteld, passed away Friday. Friends may call at the Baker Funeral Home, Berea, where services will be held Tuesday, Feb. 4, at 2 p. m. In lieu of flowers contributions may be made to the Clara Scrivens Memorial Fund of Community Hospital.

Child of Edwin Scrivens and Clara Hansen is:

i. Mary Lou[6] Scrivens, b. Aft. 1930; m. xxx Prechtel; b. ABT 1930.

27. Florence Julia[5] Scrivens *(Lucie Adeline Julianna[4] Tegtmeier, Johann Heinrich[3], Johann Friedrich[2], Tegtmeier[1])* was born January 21, 1903 in Berea, Cuyahoga Co. OH, and died May 4, 1993 in Ohio. She married Lloyd William Schultz, son of William Schultz and Elizabeth Glebb. He was born October 18, 1899 in Ohio, and died July 30, 1979 in Ohio.

Notes for FLORENCE JULIA SCRIVENS:
1920 U.S. Census • Ohio • Cuyahoga • Middleburg • ED# 556
William R Scrivens, age 49, born in Ohio; Lucy J age 42 born in Ohio; Edwin H, son age 20; William A age 18; Florence age 16; Clayton age 15; all born in Ohio.

1930 United States Federal Census > Ohio > Cuyahoga > Middleburg Heights > District 671
Lloyd W. Schultz, age 30, garage mechanic, born in Ohio, parents born in Ohio; Florence J, age 27, born in Ohio. No children listed.

Florence J Schultz
Gender: Female
Date of Death: 04 May 1993
Birth Date: 21 January 1903
Volume: 29404
Certificate: 037957
Autopsy: No
Father's Surname: Scrivens
Time of Death: 4:20 PM
Marital Status: Widowed
Hispanic Origin: Non Hispanic
Place of Death: Nursing Home
Years of Schooling: 99
Certifier: Physician
Referred to Coroner: No
Mother's Surname: Tegtmeier
Race: White
Birth Place: Berea, Cuyahoga County, Ohio
Residence: Ohio
Age: 90

Notes for LLOYD WILLIAM SCHULTZ:
1910 U.S. Census • Ohio • Cuyahoga • Cleveland • ED# 326
William Schultz, age 37, married 14 years, wire works, born in Ohio, parents both German; Matilda, age (hard to say, maybe 30) married 14 years, born in Germany; Lloyd age 10, born in Ohio.

1920 U.S. Census • Ohio • Cuyahoga • Cleveland • ED# 106
William A Schultz, age 45, born in Ohio, foreman, janitor; Elizabeth wife, age 42, born in Ohio; parents born in Ohio; Lloyd W. age 20, born in Ohio; toolmaker, machinist; Paul J. age 12, born in Ohio.

Lloyd W Schultz
Gender: Male
Date of Death: 30 July 1979
Birth Date: 19 October 1899
Volume: 23728
Certificate: 050572
Autopsy: 9
Marital Status: Married
Hispanic Origin: German
Place of Death: Medina, Medina County
Certifier: Physician
Race: White
Birth Place: Ohio
Residence: Medina County
Age: 79 Years

More About LLOYD WILLIAM SCHULTZ:
Occupation: 1920, Toolmaker/Cuyahoga Co/Ohio

Child of FLORENCE SCRIVENS and LLOYD SCHULTZ is:
53. i. William L.[6] Schultz, b. August 2, 1931, Berea, Cuyahoga, OH.

28. WILLIAM A.[5] SCRIVENS *(LUCIE ADELINE JULIANNA[4] TEGTMEIER, JOHANN HEINRICH[3], JOHANN FRIEDRICH[2], TEGTMEIER[1])* was born April 30, 1901 in Cuyahoga Co., OH, and died July 6, 1997 in Cleveland, OH. He married CLARETTA R. KONZEN Aft. 1930, daughter of JACOB KONZEN and OLIVIA YATES. She was born ABT 1907 in Ohio, and died October 24, 1960 in Cleveland, Cuyahoga Co., Ohio.

Notes for William A. Scrivens:
1920 U.S. Census • Ohio • Cuyahoga • Middleburg • ED# 556
William R Scrivens**, age 49, born in Ohio; Lucy J age 42 born in Ohio; Edwin H, son age 20; William A age 18; Florence age 16; Clayton age 15; all born in Ohio.

1930 United States Federal Census > Ohio > Cuyahoga > Middleburg Heights > District 671
Edwin H Scrivens, age 31, first married when he was 28, electician in a body shop, born in Ohio; Clara H., age 29, first married when she was 27, born in Ohio, she is a trained nurse. No children listed. (Charles J. Taylor, age 32, born in Ohio living next door—possible brother to Clara Taylor; On other side, WILLIAM Scrivens **, age 28, single, farmer)

Individual: Scrivens, William
Issued in: Ohio
Birth date: Apr 30, 1901
Death date: Jul 6, 1997
ZIP Code of last known residence: 44130
Primary location associated with this ZIP Code: Cleveland, Ohio

William Arthur Scrivens
Gender: Male
Date of Death: 06 July 1997
Birth Date: 30 April 1901
Volume: 31206
Certificate: 062303
Autopsy: No
Father's Surname: Scrivens
Time of Death: 11:11 AM
Marital Status: Widowed
Place of Death: Residence
Years of Schooling: 13
Certifier: Physician
Referred to Coroner: Yes
Method of Disposition: Burial
Mother's Surname: Tegtmeier

Race: White
Birth Place: Cuyahoga County, Ohio
Residence: Ohio
Age: 96

More About William A. Scrivens:
Event 4: Last residence ZIP: 44130
Occupation: Issued in: Ohio

Notes for Claretta R. Konzen:
1930 United States Federal Census > Ohio > Cuyahoga > Middleburg Heights > District 671
Jacob Konzen, age 54, born in Ohio, he is a huckster, vegetables; father born in Germany, mother born in Germany; Olivia age 52 born in New Jersey, father born in England, mother born in North Ireland; Claretta, age 23, born in Ohio; Elnora, age 18; Alverna, age 14; George Yates, son-in-law, age 52. This household is right next door to William, Edwin & Clara Scrivens

Id#: 0715244
Name: Scrivens, Claretta R. (Konzen)
Date: Oct 24 1960
Source: Cleveland Press; Cleveland Necrology File, Reel #154.
Notes: Scrivens, Claretta R. (Konzen), late residence, 15873 Sheldon Rd., beloved wife of William A., dear mother of Jay D. and Peter A., and grandmother, daughter of the late Jacob and Olivia (Yates), sister of Alverna Botch, Eleanor Konzen and the late Marie Diebold. Friends received at Corrigan's Funeral Home, Lorain Ave. at W. 148th St. Funeral mass Tuesday, Oct. 25, St. Bartholomew Church, 14875 E. Bagley Rd., at 10:30 a. m.

Children of William Scrivens and Claretta Konzen are:

i. Peter A.[6] Scrivens, b. ABT 1934.
ii. Jay D. Scrivens, b. ABT 1933.

29. Leland J.[5] Smith *(Christina Dorothea Emilie[4] Tegtmeier, Johann Heinrich[3], Johann Friedrich[2], Tegtmeier[1])* was born ABT 1910 in Ohio, and died 1972 in Brookpark, Ohio. He married Alice Allen. She was born ABT 1910 in Ohio.

Notes for LELAND J. SMITH:
Home in 1920: Ohio • Cuyahoga • Brook Park
ED# 518
1920 Census: Julius C. Smith, age 40, born in Ohio, farmer, father born in Ohio, mother born in Germany; Christina age 39, both parents born in Germany; Leland J. age 10; Bertha age 7; all born in Ohio;

1930 United States Federal Census > Ohio >
Cuyahoga > Chagrin Falls > District 553
Smith, Julius, head, age 50, Christina, wife, age 48; Leland son age 20; Julia Tegtmeier, mother in law, age 82, widowed; Bertha Smith, age 46, sister.

More About LELAND J. SMITH:
Event 3: Residence code: Ohio
Event 4: Last residence ZIP: 43110
Occupation: Issued in: Ohio

Child of LELAND SMITH and ALICE ALLEN is:
54. i. Glen A.[6] Smith, b. ABT 1938, Cleveland, Cuyahoga Co., OH.

30. LORETTA MATTIE[5] TEGTMEIER *(WILLIAM CARL[4], JOHANN HEINRICH[3], JOHANN FRIEDRICH[2], TEGTMEIER[1])* was born August 26, 1911. She married PAUL FRANKLIN BERRY June 15, 1935. He was born 26 Apr 1910, and died 07 May 1998.

Loretta Tegtmeier, born 09/26/1911, graduated from Berea High School the spring I was born! She did housework at some VIP homes, then became a typist. A quiet person, I got to know her better when I stayed with her to help clean and can fruit in summer. She grew house plans for their new homes, enjoyed soap operas (Guiding Light, etc.) and singing along with Bing (Crosby) in her lovely voice. She chose nice Avon gifts to give our brothers at Christmas. She ALWAYS baked my favorite elderberry pie when we came for a visit from North Dakota! She married Paul Berry, a rail road foreman from West Salem and they had David and Karen.

—Lois Tegtmeier Hinrichs

Tegtmeier Weddings: Lorretta & Paul Berry (upper left); George Allen & Ruth Davidson, and Leland Smith and Alice Allen. 1935. Photo courtesy of Stephanie Berry-Estep.

1930 Census 1930 United States Federal Census > Ohio > Cuyahoga > Chagrin Falls > District 553
Tegtmeier, William, head age 46, farmer, married at age 26, born in Ohio; Anna, wife, age 42, married at age 22, born in Germany; Loretta M age 18, stenographer at a garage; Raymond J age 17; Julia W age 15; Alice L age 13; Henry A age 12; William Jr. age 10; Harold E. is 9'; Richard E. is 6; Lois R. age 2.

After retiring, Paul and Loretta drove to Cape Coral, Florida to their winter house. He never stopped working, and once was repairing the roof after the age of 80 when he slipped and fell off. He was OK, bruised, but never stopped doing chores. He and Loretta had a lovely winter home on the water in Cape Coral, Florida.

Paul Franklin Berry
Gender: Male
Date of Death: 07 May 1998
Birth Date: 26 April 1910
Volume: 31539
Certificate: 037960
Autopsy: No
Father's Surname: Berry
Time of Death: 11:37 PM
Marital Status: Married
Hispanic Origin: Non Hispanic
Place of Death: Hospital/Inpatient
Years of Schooling: 12
Certifier: Physician
Referred to Coroner: No
Method of Disposition: Burial
Mother's Surname: Rockenfelder
Race: White
Birth Place: Wayne County, Ohio
Residence: Ohio
Age: 88

Children of LORETTA TEGTMEIER and PAUL BERRY are:
55. i. David Paul[7] Berry, b. 01 Oct 1936, Lodi, Ohio.
56. ii. Karen Diane Berry, b. 22 Mar 1942, West Salem, Ohio.

31. RAYMOND JULIUS[5] TEGTMEIER *(WILLIAM CARL[4], JOHANN HEINRICH[3], JOHANN FRIEDRICH[2], TEGTMEIER[1])* was born December 7, 1912 in Brookpark, OH, and died September 1982 in Wayne County, Ohio. He married LAURA ANNA MINICHBAUER. She was born August 1, 1916 in Cleveland, Cuyahoga County, Ohio, and died October 10, 1995 in Wayne County, Ohio.

Notes for RAYMOND JULIUS TEGTMEIER:
Raymond was born December 7, 1912, later Pearl Harbor Day. He had asthma as a young boy. Mother said he had to harness horses before he could reach their backs. He was the first of our family to graduate at Congress High School after we moved to a larger farm between Burbank and Congress. All of our brothers worked hard on the farm. Ray later worked in Cleveland at Alcoa, and came back to manage the farm when Dad was not able. Ray also

Loretta Tegtmeier (left) circ 1912.

Bottom left: Raymond Tegtmeier and sister Loretta. It was not uncommon for boys to be dressed as girls. It Was a way of protecting them and hiding their gender.

Bottom right: Paul Berry and Loretta Tegtmeier, wedding day, June 1935.

Photos courtesy of Stephanie Berry-Estep.

became a master welder at Deibold, Wooster, making safes. He married Laura Minichbauer from Cleveland. They had three children: Donna, Sharon and Dan. Ray died September 8, 1982, three weeks before Mother. Laura died October 11. 1995.

—*Lois Tegtmeier Hinrichs.*

1930 Census 1930 United States Federal Census > Ohio > Cuyahoga > Chagrin Falls > District 553
Tegtmeier, William, head age 46, farmer, married at age 26, born in Ohio; Anna, wife, age 42, married at age 22, born in Germany; Loretta M age 18, stenographer at a garage; Raymond J age 17; Julia W age age 15; Alice L age 13; Henry A age 12; William Jr. age 10; Harold E. is 9; Richard E. is 6; Lois R. age 2.
Social Security issued by the Railroad Board
Birth date: Dec 7, 1912
Death date: Sep 1982
Burbank, Ohio

Raymond Tegtmeier and his wife Laura lived on the farm that Ray grew up in the valley by Killbuck Creek near Burbank, OH. Little Granny stayed with them. ("Little"—she must have been about 110 pounds soaking wet, but strong? She tossed my sister over the couch when she was about 65 years old!) Laura's mother also stayed with them. She would stare out the window and rock in her chair for hours. Both grandmothers had rooms downstairs where it was warm. The rest of the family stayed upstairs. My sister, Shirley, remembers when they didn't have a bathroom, and you had to go out side behind the porch to the out house. Not bad in the spring and summer, but the winter stroll had to be awful. They had about 300 acres and rotated crops of field corn, soy beans or wheat, and raised cattle, pigs and sheep. The woods were full of beautiful hardwoods of walnut, poplar, pine, among others. Ray tended the farm, but also held a job in Cleveland. Ed Taylor Senior made 4 wood inlaid card tables from the wood from the farm: black walnut, hickory, ash and poplar.

—Sandra Taylor Bell

More About Raymond Julius Tegtmeier:
Event 3: Residence code: Ohio
Event 4: Last residence ZIP: 44214
Occupation: Social Security Issued: Railroad Board

Notes for Laura Anna Minichbauer:
Laura Tegtmeier died on October 10, 1995. Born August 1, 1916, Tegtmeier was 79 years old and lived in Wooster, OH.

Laura Anna Tegtmeier
Gender: Female
Date of Death: 10 October 1995
Birth Date: 01 August 1916
Volume: 30431
Certificate: 084524
Autopsy: No
Social Security
Father's Surname: Minichbauer
Time of Death: 8:25 PM
Marital Status: Widowed
Hispanic Origin: Non Hispanic
Place of Death: Nursing Home
Years of Schooling: 12
Certifier: Physician
Referred to Coroner: No
Method of Disposition: Burial
Mother's Surname: Reitz
Race: White
Birth Place: Cleveland, Cuyahoga County, Ohio
Residence: Ohio
Age: 79

More About LAURA ANNA MINICHBAUER:
Education: Social Security #: 297-64-2272
Event 4: Last residence ZIP: 44691
Occupation: Issued in: Ohio

Children of RAYMOND TEGTMEIER and LAURA MINICHBAUER are:
57. i. Donna Mae[7] Tegtmeier, b. 01 Sep 1944.
58. ii. Sharon Lee Tegtmeier, b. 04 Jan 1947.
59. iii. Daniel Howard Tegtmeier, b. 23 Sep 1957.

32. ALICE HENRIETTA[5] TEGTMEIER *(WILLIAM CARL[4], JOHANN HEINRICH[3], JOHANN FRIEDRICH[2], TEGTMEIER[1])* was born May 28, 1916 in Brookpark, Ohio. She married (1) EDWARD WILLIAM TAYLOR July 2, 1940 in Buffalo, NY, son of GEORGE TAYLOR and MAYME TRAUTMAN. He was born August 1, 1914 in New York, and died January 22, 1967 in Jost Van Dyke, US Virgin Islands. She married (2) John Goralsky ABT 1973. He was born in Coalport, PA, and died in Cleveland, OH.

Notes for Alice Henrietta Tegtmeier:

Notes from sister, Alice Tegtmeier Taylor

Looking back, a long time ago, the year was 1916. I was born, the third girl. We had five brothers, and eventually 2 other sisters. We lived in Brookpark on a small farm outside of Cleveland, Ohio. (Years later Ford Motor Company built a huge plant and Brookpark was no longer farmland, but became bedroom communities for the workers at the plant.) We all helped. Nearly all the food we ate was grown on the farm. Wheat was traded for flour. My grandmother owned the farm and had a gas well installed so we were very comfortable even though the winters were cold. My grandfather died of asthma when my mother was 14 years old. She always had to work hard.

I remember it was an exciting day when electricity was installed. We came home from school, and Mom had the lights on all over the house. That was really exciting. I remember many trips when John Hopkins Airport was built. We ended with 9 children. We rarely played at other children's homes. Mom insisted that other children come to our house, so no one got into trouble. However, having a large yard we played baseball nearly every evening, other children sharing the fun. We churned our own butter from sour cream.

Christmas Eve we always went to church at St. Paul's Lutheran Church on Front Street in Berea. We took part in the service—each one of us having two weeks to learn our part and walk up in front of the congregation and recite. We usually wore a pair of new shoes (part of our Christmas gifts) I remember how excited we were. We would come home, and there in the living room, my mother had completely trimmed the Christmas tree, complete with lit candles that sparkled, reflecting colors from the tinsel and the ornaments. I have wonderful memories of all of us singing every Christmas carol Christmas Day. Our tree had real candles which were lit. Each of us loved to sing and Christmas was the best time of the year.

I had a sister "Julia" who evidently was a favorite of the teachers. Once or twice a year my mother would invite the teacher to stay with us over night. Miss Sype always brought several games. After the evening meal we would gather around the table and Miss Sype would introduce us to a new game. We were always on our best behavior. My mother was the most patient person I ever

Alice Henrietta Tegtmeier Taylor

Married to Ed Taylor 1940

Children: Shirley, Jim, Sandy and Eddy
Photo circ 1955.

knew. My dad was always in the field working very hard. In the summer we would take turns carrying a bucket of water to wherever he happened to be plowing or raking. I wondered how he could stand being out in the hot sun.

The time came when he couldn't pay the taxes on the farm. Two of the men who checked the gas well from time to time, heard of a farm for sale that was very reasonable in Wayne County. We moved to this farm outside of Wooster, Ohio. I remember the owners name, Mr. & Mrs. Myers. It was there where we lived until I graduated from high school, the old farmhouse near Killbuck River in the valley.

Marie was a dear friend and neighbor in Cleveland, and I stayed with Marie Offenburg after I graduated from high school, and got a job taking care of two boys. Mom gave me $ 6.00 and a few pennies to get a start. I also stayed with Mrs. Foster, and with the money I earned, I signed up for a secretarial course at Cleveland College. Then I went with Western Auto as a secretary. Mrs. Foster let me stay with her. I bought a full length beaver coat (looking very luxurious for about $ 100. I saw an ad in the paper for a third girl to help pay rent, and I answered the ad. The apartment was in Cleveland. Ed Taylor lived with two other men on the second floor, and we girls had an apartment on the third floor. We were married July 27, 1940 in New York.

In the fall Pop would set aside a time to butcher a cow. I remember an Aunt and Uncle coming to help. It was a different experience. As the meat was being cooked, we had special dishes cooking and the aroma was wonderful. The skin was sent away to be tanned and we would love sitting on the soft hide. The meat was cooked, then canned.

We all loved to play baseball, and with that many brothers and kids, we could always have a game after school in the yard. Mom would enjoy having our friends there, and the evenings were long in the summer months, and we could play nearly until 10:00 at night while it was still light out.

'I remember Mama' was a radio show that we listened to every time it was on radio, probably once a week.

I remember gathering around a lamp for light at the kitchen table doing school work with 5 other siblings. I used to love scooping the cream off the milk, and I used this on my face in the morning. It would feel so good on my face. When a new house was being built we found wood was shaved which we put together which ended up in beautiful curls. Oh, how cute we looked with curls. Every winter we built forts with our shovels. We had fierce wars until we decided to go indoors and warm up. My brothers have all died but we girls who are left remember a wonderful childhood.

—Alice Tegtmeier Taylor

Notes regarding Alice from her sister, Lois Tegtmeier Hinricks

Alice was born My 28, 1916. She loved making doll clothes and playing dolls with her best friend, Marie Offenberg. She and Dick demonstrated an artistic talents early in life. She continued to paint and take classes in Florida and many of her works grace our homes.

When we moved to the Killbuck Creek farm, Ali tried to tame the weeds and hillside across the little stream in front of our house. She hoed and dug out the earth to make a little pond, surrounding it with "rolling stones" and water plants. The weeds grew back and our brothers just laughed. (We'd fix them if we had a second chance today!)

Nobody said "no" if we were told to hoe the corn … or tie up grape or tomato vines, but Ali did it right to protect her delicate white skin by slathering on thick cram from the top of the crock in the pantry and donning a wide brimmed garden hat, covering her smooth, creamy arms with a long-sleeved man's shirt, before she tripped lightly out the back shed door into the field. I can see Kathryn Hepburn joining her and having a hilarious time together! Oh, for a second round of living and growing up on the farm! What fund we'd make it … Even so, she, Ali, brightened the scene and saw the lighter side of life. What hysterical laughs Mother, Ali and I would sometimes go into when things got too serious, just to lighten the load and … survive!

After high school, Ali (Alice) fled to the City, took shorthand classes and got a nice job with Western Auto "downtown" Cleveland. Along with sticks of gum, she slipped in her letters home, then came French doors to brighten the living room, new linoleum for the dining room, and soon her Prince Charming met her at the Board House and they 'shoved off to near Buffalo to live and prosper. Then they came back to Cleveland to finish their dream. Alice and Ed Taylor had four children: Shirley, Eddie, Jim and Sandy. Ed died shortly after retiring and Ali makes her home with Shirley in Bradenton, Florida.

—Lois Tegtmeier Hinrichs

***

She often joked about meeting her first husband, Ed Taylor. He always joked that she fell down the stairs at a boarding house one day and he caught her. She never completely denied that story, and I believe they actually met at an apartment.

She asked Pat & Mary Scrivens to bring Mom and Pop up for the wedding in New York, Aunt Mat and Uncle Henry from Toledo.

She loved to paint, and was quite an artist. She painted huge flowers on the walls on Cedar Point Road in Berea, Ohio in 1950. She painted quite a few murals on walls in many different homes, and was quite an accomplished artist and still paints in 2004. If she didn't have a family, I'm sure she would have put all of her efforts into being a full time artist which she loves every chance she can get.

—Sandra Taylor Bell, daughter

Notes for Edward William Taylor:
Social Security record:
Edward Taylor Sr.
Born: 1 Aug 1914
Died: Jan 1967
State (Year) SSN issued: Ohio (Before 1951)

June 1940, their first shopping list: On a piece of brown paper from the bag of their first grocery list: 3, 12, 30, 5, 25, 5, 20 = $ 1.15 for groceries. (budgeting on pennies)

EDWARD WILLIAM TAYLOR, son of George Edgar Taylor and Mayme Trautman of Buffalo, New York, was born August 1, 1914 in New York. He began working with National Cash Register Company. They trained him in Cleveland, transferred him to Maryland, and then stationed him in Albany, NY. Alice and Ed had their first 2 children in New York where Ed decided to quite National Cash Register and start his own business with a Hardware

Store in Albany, "Taylor and Son" with room above where they could live. Ed was close to his family, but Alice was very homesick for her family back in Cleveland. So Ed sold the business and moved to Berea, Ohio, and bought a house on Cedar Point Road, bought some land to build a hardware store and a grocery store. He worked the hardware store and rented out the other shop. As time went on he added more shops, a restaurant, a dry cleaners, a beauty salon, a glass shop (window glass), barber shop, and it turned into a little shopping center. He planned to retire when he was 45, collecting the rents from the shops after retirement. It was a good plan, and he did retire when he was 45.

His sister, Miriam and her husband, Dick, talked Ed and Alice into a trip to the Virgin Islands. Ed fell in love with it, especially a little British Island with the whitest of sand called Jost Van Dyke. It was about 5 miles away by boat from St. Thomas. But quiet, serene, no electricity, and he loved it. He bought 7 acres from the Caldwoods who lived on the island, hired a young man name Philly Caldwood (later became well known as "Foxy") to be his captain, and began building a house out of sweat, sea water and cement. He and Alice would travel down to the islands, visit Caneel Bay, play chess, and take fabulous pictures of the islands. He hired those living on the island to help build the house, brought in a generator for a little electricity, and brought in a kerosene refrigerator. He brought cement in and laid the foundation to the little church in Great Harbor. His place was on White Bay. The Queen's Highway was a little goat path that stretched over the hill to Great Harbor.

The island itself was beautiful—on one side the whitest sand, and what was left of an old fort with cannon still in the water, and the greatest reef and blue water. Sandy and Jim would spend hours snorkling. The other side of the island was sheer cliff, jutting sharply down into the Atlantic Ocean.

In 1963 Ed and Alice brought the 2 younger kids with them. Of course "Spunky" the boat got them over to the island, but then promptly died, so they had to get it repaired. While trying to rebuild and clean the engine. They learned how to climb the coconut trees to get the coconuts, make coconut bread with a little flour. Picked up cattle dung (usually filled with red ants) to use for the garden—only cactus and century plants would grow. Too much sand and rock. Mancheneal trees were everywhere. If you stand under a mancheneal tree when it rains, the sap is like acid, and burns.

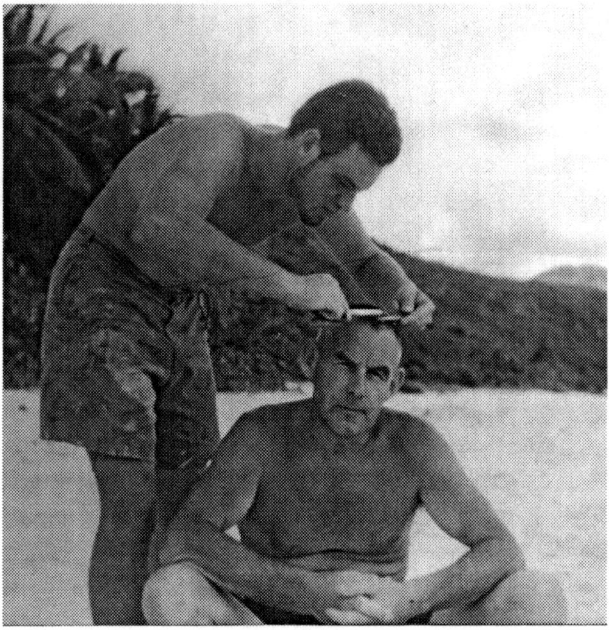

Ed Taylor Jr. giving his Dad, Ed Taylor, Sr. a hair cut with a tin snip on Jost Van Dyke, British Virgin Islands. They were building a retirement house on White Bay. circ. 1963

Ed's health was failing, and he decided to sell the island property, but wanted to show his daughter and her husband the island since they had never been there. Once arrived, Ed was cleaning the house and getting everything stocked up, working on the cistern and up the hill. That night before going to bed, he showed Shirley & Gene where the money was "just in case", then shaved before going to bed. Philly Caldwood (Foxy) came down to visit, and he and Ed talked late into the night. Ed died in his sleep that night on the island he loved.

The coffin was lost on the trip back to the states. It turned up in Chicago in a few days. Embalming methods were crude at best in the islands, but the body had to be identified, and it was my sister, Shirley who was asked to identify the body. She had nightmares for years afterward, and doesn't remember the funeral.

—Sandra Taylor Bell

Id#: 0751511
Name: Taylor, Edward W.
Date: Jan 31 1967
Source: Plain Dealer; Cleveland Necrology File, Reel #161.
Notes: Taylor. Edward W. Taylor, beloved husband of Alice, dear father of Shirley Barr, Edward, Jr., James and Sandra and grandfather of Jeffrey and Kathy, brother of Marion Boebel, passed away Thursday in the Virgin Islands. Friends may call at The Baker Funeral Home, Berea, From 7–9 P.M. Monday. Services private. Please omit flowers. Donations may be made to the Heart Fund or St. Paul's Lutheran Church Building Fund.

More About EDWARD WILLIAM TAYLOR:
Burial: Middleburgh Hts, Cuyahoga Co., OH

Children of ALICE TEGTMEIER and EDWARD TAYLOR are:

60.	i.	Shirley Ann[7] Taylor, b. 11 Oct 1941, Scranton, PA.
61.	ii.	Edward William Taylor, b. 11 Jan 1944, Alden, NY.
62.	iii.	James Robert Taylor, b. 22 Mar 1949, Berea, Ohio.
63.	iv.	Sandra Mina Taylor, b. 17 Mar 1950, Berea, Ohio.

33. HENRY ADOLPH[5] TEGTMEIER *(WILLIAM CARL[4], JOHANN HEINRICH[3], JOHANN FRIEDRICH[2], TEGTMEIER[1])* was born March 19, 1918 in Ohio, and died December 9, 1992 in Fairfield Glade, TN. He married HARRIETT BARENDT May 28, 1945. She was born January 9, 1923 in Cleveland, Cuyahoga Co., OH.

Notes for HENRY ADOLPH TEGTMEIER:
I have a riddle: Henry was born a day after me, yet was older. How could that be? Henry was born March 19, 1918—during World War I. Our family had stopped talking German around the table ANYWHERE in deference to neighbors and friends who might think we were supporting the Germans. Henry and Bill had learned enough conversational German by then that helped considerably in structuring sentences later in college classes.

When Henry was little, he did his own "show and tell". He came running in to show everyone new ducklings, squeezing the neck of one in each fist! (Obviously, the ducklings survive.) In high school when a girl came in her car to take him for a ride, he headed out the back door to shoot crows in the woods. Once as I was walking to the house from the bar, he called to me to come back, turn around and walk backwards up the barn bank. (I usually did a I was told.) I did. Then he said, "Turn around." He had propped up a snake with wire! You can guess where I went, screaming. But then, he could be serious as a Pastor. After Seminary and a year of internship at San Antonio, Texas, he and Harriet went to Longview, TX where he served a congregation several years, then moved back to Ohio. They retired to Fairfield Glade (near Crossville) Tennessee where they enjoyed helping start and finish one more Church. Henry married Harriet Barendt from Cleveland. They had four children: Miriam, Paul, Joan and Joel.

—Lois Tegtmeier Hinrichs

Social Security Issued in: Ohio
Birth date: Mar 19, 1918
Death date: Dec 9, 1992
ZIP Code of last known residence: 38555
Primary location associated with this ZIP Code: Crossville, Tennessee (officially recorded by Social Security) actually Fairfield Glade, TN)

Henry Tegtmeier loved golf, and after his death, Christ Lutheran in Tennessee still has golf tournaments and a dinner in his honor (2004)

—Alice Tegtmeier Taylor.

More About Henry Adolph Tegtmeier:
Education: Social Security issued in Ohio
Event 4: Last residence ZIP: 38555

Children of Henry Tegtmeier and Harriett Barendt are:
64. i. Miriam Ann[7] Tegtmeier, b. 08 Apr 1946.
65. ii. Joan Charlotte Tegtmeier, b. 07 Aug 1947.
66. iii. Paul Tegtmeier, b. 03 Aug 1948.
67. iv. Joel Tegtmeier, b. 13 Aug 1959.

34. William Edward[5] Tegtmeier *(William Carl[4], Johann Heinrich[3], Johann Friedrich[2], Tegtmeier[1])* was born March 6, 1920 in Brookpark, Ohio, and died July 24, 2000 in Savannah, OH. He married Lois Genvieve Westlund June 15, 1946, daughter of Emil Westlund and Sigrid. She was born December 31, 1922 in Youngstown, Ohio.

Henry & Hariette Tegtmeier and family, Miriam, Paul, Joan, Joel, Harriett and Henry. Photo circ. 1970.

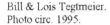

Bill & Lois Tegtmeier. Photo circ. 1995.

Notes from Lois Tegtmeier Hinricks

Bill and Harold, little 'tow-heads', one year apart. Sometimes they were called the "Katzenjamer Kids". Billy loved to stand on his head. But when he started stuttering, our parents made him quit. Later, his chores were feeding and milking the cows. Sometimes he showed my how he gave the cats a drink! Billy worked on the Railroad a couple of summers to make more money for college. After graduating from Capital University with a BA degree in education, he enlisted in the Navy and served in the Pacific during World War II. He taught and coached in High School in Ansonia and Savannah, Ohio until retirement. He married Lois Westlund from Youngstown, Ohio. They had four children; Linda, Terry, Tim and Todd. bill was born March 6, 1920. He died July 24, 2002.

—Lois Tegtmeier Hinrichs

William Tegtmeier died on July 24, 2000. Born March 6, 1920, Tegtmeier was 80 years old and lived in Savannah, OH. (Prostate cancer.)

Source: Social Security Administration
Name: WILLIAM E TEGTMEIER
Gender: Male
Date of Death: July 24, 2000
Birth Date: March 6, 1920; Volume: 32458
Certificate: 052856; Autopsy: N
Father's Surname: TEGTMEIER
Time of Death: 11:45 AM
Marital Status: married
Hispanic Origin: German
Place of Death: residence
Years of Schooling: 17
Certifier: Physician
Branch of Service: NAVY
Method of Disposition: Burial
Mother's Surname: PAPENHAGEN
Race: White
Birth Place: BROOK PARK, CUYAHOGA, Ohio
Residence: ASHLAND, Ohio
Age: 80 years

Historical Newspapers > Mansfield News Journal (Mansfield, Ohio) > 1958 > March > 25
COACH OF THE YEAR: Bill Tegtmeier, whose protégés placed second in the ACL race copped their sixth consecutive Ashland County tourney title was named "Coach of the Year" by the players finishing 17 votes ahead of his nearest competitor, Ellsworth Cox of Hayesville...."

Notes for Lois Genvieve Westlund:
Lois G Westlund
Age: 7 years
Estimated birth year: 1922
Relation to Head-of-house: Daughter
Home in 1930: Youngstown, Mahoning, Ohio

1930 Census
Emil Westlund, head, age 42; born in Wisconsin, parents born in Sweden; Sigrid, wife age 35, born in Minnesota, parents born in Sweden; Lois G., daughter, born in Ohio, age 7.

More About LOIS GENVIEVE WESTLUND:
Occupation: Teacher

Children of WILLIAM TEGTMEIER and LOIS WESTLUND are:

68. i. Linda Jean[6] Tegtmeier, b. August 24, 1947, Youngstown, OH, North Side Hospital.
69. ii. Terry Tegtmeier, b. ABT 1949.
70. iii. Timothy Tegtmeier, b. September 15, 1955.
iv. TODD ALAN TEGTMEIER, b. February 19, 1962; m. WENDY FLOYD, December 19, 1993.

35. HAROLD WILLIAM[5] TEGTMEIER *(WILLIAM CARL[4], JOHANN HEINRICH[3], JOHANN FRIEDRICH[2], TEGTMEIER[1])* was born March 2, 1921 in Brookpark, Ohio, and died May 18, 2003 in West Salem, Wayne, Ohio. He married LUCILLE CLARISSA HERMAN March 2, 1943 in Jackson Presbyterian Church, Creston, Ohio. She was born September 12, 1922 in Hermanville, Creston, Ohio.

Notes for HAROLD WILLIAM TEGTMEIER:
Harold W. Tegtmeier
Social Security
Last Residence: 44287 West Salem, Wayne, Ohio, United States of America
Born: 2 Mar 1921
Died: 18 May 2003

Notes from Lucile Shumaker Tegtmeier

Harold William Tegtmeier, the seventh of the nine children of William and Anna Papenhagen Tegtmeier, was born March 2, 1921 in Brookpark, Ohio. In 1930, the family moved to a farm they purchased in Congress Township, Wayne County, West Salem, Ohio, near Killbuck Creek. Harold graduated from Congress High School in 1939. He worked for several years in factories but his heart was really in open spaces, watching things grow and farming. So he became a full-time farmer working for other farmers. Adam Pamer was a Canaan Lutheran Church friend of Harold's and was interested in Eleanor

Herman of nearby Creston whom he later married. Adam introduced Harold to Eleanor's sister, Lucille, and they soon became a twosome.

Lucille, the third of five children of Howard and Hazel Shumaker Herman was born on the family farm at Hermanville (Creston) September 12, 1922. She graduated from Creston High School in 1940, attended Wooster Business College; and worked as a secretary at the Akron Brass Company in Wooster for three years.

Lucille fell in love with Harold as he was an intelligent, young, good Christian farmer with an outgoing personality. Also good looking. Harold gave her an engagement ring for her 21st birthday in 1943, and they were married six months later on Harold's 23rd birthday in a very small wedding in her church, Jackson Presbyterian Church, Creston, Ohio.

For their honeymoon they traveled by bus to sister Alice and Edward Taylor's home at Alden, New York. They visited Niagara Falls, too. While Alice and Lucille were shopping one day, Harold was left in charge of little Shirley and Eddie. Eddie got the egg carton out of the "frig" and broke the eggs on the floor. Harold learned a lot from his first babysitting job!

Harold and Lucille started housekeeping and farming on the Joe Irvin farm several miles northwest of Congress Village, Ohio. Harold soon taught Lucille how to drive the car so she could go to two for parts. This got hectic at times but today she is glad she can drive. After one year, they moved to the Naftzger farm near Wooster where they farmed for the next twelve years.

Their four children were all born in the Lodi Hospital while the family lived near Wooster.

All four children graduated from the local Northwestern High School. The three boys all served in the armed forces as did our future son-in-law. Jim, Don and Randy are all farmers while David is a part-time farmer as he works at Ashland University. Barbara and family have lived in the Toledo area for years but her brothers all live within a mile from the old homestead.

The four children all married and they and their spouses have provided us with nine grandchildren and six great grandchildren. This month, July 2004, Barb

Lucille and Harold Tegtmeier
Wedding 1921 (left)

(Below)
Celebrating their 50th wedding anniversary

(left) Children: Barbara, Jim holding David, and Donald.

and Jim Kramer and David and Rita are going to Alaska to celebrate their silver wedding anniversaries, 2004.

Much has happened over the years. We started farming one small farm with an old tractor and milking eight cows and no electric. The boys now farm about a thousand acres and use many big tractors and equipment. They also have about 65 milk-cows and raise all the calves. We miss the electric when it goes off for a short time! Corn, soybeans, wheat, alfalfa and pumpkins are grown. In 1958, Harold and Lucille bought their first farm. In 1970 they bought an adjoining farm and made several purchases since. All three sons have bought land too.

Harold was always interested in his church, community, farming, and working. He was a Congress Township Trustee for 38 years and on the Wayne Soil and Water Board for 20 years. Tegtmeier Farms received the Goodyear Cooperator award in 1998. Harold was honored as the Daily Record Citizen of the Year in 1990. He helped organize the Town and Country Fire District and served as its first president. He served on the West Salem Equity Board, Farm Bureau, church offices, and the Northwestern Puritan Cub where he enjoyed participating in their annual musicals. He built a replica of the old kid-wagon he had ridden to school years before and with his Belgian horses he enjoyed being in many parades over the years.

Harold and Lucille enjoyed 59 years of married life. They were very busy but happy years most of the time. They did take vacation some years. They celebrated their 50th anniversary on a cruise to the Panama Canal with about sixteen other Tegtmeiers and friends.

The last of 2002 Harold was diagnosed with pancreatic cancer and he died May 18, 2003. After a large attendance at the viewing and funeral, he was buried in the Canaan Lutheran Church cemetery near his parents and sister Julia. He had lived a full and good life. His friends, and especially his family really miss him but realize he is enjoying heaven!

—Lucille Tegtmeier, July 2004

Harold took an early interest in farming: the soil, animals, trees, seedtime and harvest, weather ... all aspects ... always to try new ways, improvement sand being a good steward. He especially liked horses, built an authentic "kid wagon" (like all of us except Loretta, rode to school earlier.) He hitched his Belgian team to it and gave many rides for young and old, at county fairs and special events. He also built a two-seat sleigh, upholstered for snowy, winter rides.

Once, when Dad was hospitalized, Harold took a second-hand tractor apart with parts everywhere. Mother said, "If you ever get that back together to run again ..." He did! How he would have enjoyed the Tegtmeier reunion hosted by his son and family, David & Rita, August 15, 2004. He died May 18, 2003.

—Lois Tegtmeier Hinrichs
CONGRESS TWP, OHIO

Kid Wagon

As schools progressed from the one-room country schools to centralized schools in the early nineteen hundreds, and pupils could not walk the distance to school, it became necessary for the school boards to furnish KID WAGONS and local farms would bid on a contract at auction to supply a team of horses and a disciplinarian (driver). KID WAGONS had two long rows of seats and could haul about 26 kids. Pupils got on and off through the rear door. In stormy weather the front doors were slid tight together and hooked, and the side curtains were snapped down tight. It was too dark to read as there were only windows at each end of the wagon. In Winter the frozen mud, with embedded hoof prints, set up a rhythm which could shake your teeth loose and the horses would come to the school with icicles hanging from their noses. I recall one of the drivers stopping and putting sharp calks on the front feet shoes on the team so they could negotiate the freezing rain on the road.

I started school at Brookpark by riding a KID WAGON)or bobsled when there was a lot of snow.) After our family moved to Congress township in 1930, I rode a Kid Wagon from Killbuck Valley to Congress. There were six or seven Kid Wagons that converged at the Congress School about the same P.M. time each school day.

My father bid our route one year, with my oldest brother being the disciplinarian and boarding the horses in the Mowrey barn in Congress during the school day. Walter Johnson adn son Leroy had the route some years and sometimes used four horses to pull the Kid Wagon from the foot of the Big Hill to Congress during the winter when other vehicles could not negotiate the now State Road # 604. It was then a township road and brush would brush both sides of the wagon at various places along the road. A record low was set on eyear when teh bid on that route was $ 29.00 a month.

One recent article reported a school board bought three Kid Wagons in 1915 for a total of $ 435.00 and in 1989 purchased new school buses for $ 43,000. each. Kid Wagons disappeared about 1935 due to motorized buses and improved roads. I finally decided to get busy and build one so my grandchildren could see one. I also bought a team of Belgian Horses and had enjoyed being in parades since 1990.

—Harold Tegtmeier, West Salem, Ohio

Above: Lucille & Harold Tegtmeier celebrating their 50th Anniversary with children an grandchildren.

Below: Business card of Harold Tegtmeier for the Kid Wagon. Photos courtesy of Lucill Tegtmeier.

Notes for LUCILLE CLARISSA HERMAN:
The kid wagon played a big part in Harold's life. He went to school riding in one in Brookpark, Ohio and also in Congress. He built one—a duplicate—and had it in many parades over the years with his horses. (This year—2004—the boys had it in just 2 parades on Sunday giving rides.) His tombstone ha a picture of the kid wagon on it.

Children of HAROLD TEGTMEIER and LUCILLE HERMAN are:

71. i. James Herman[6] Tegtmeier, b. February 14, 1945, Lodi Hospital, near Wooster, Ohio.
72. ii. Donald Phillip Tegtmeier, b. November 14, 1948, Lodi Hospital, near Wooster, Ohio.
73. iii. Barbara Lucille Tegtmeier, b. December 15, 1952, Lodi Hospital, near Wooster, Ohio.
74. iv. David Harold Tegtmeier, b. September 15, 1954, Lodi Hospital, near Wooster, Ohio.

36. RICHARD ELMER[5] TEGTMEIER *(WILLIAM CARL[4], JOHANN HEINRICH[3], JOHANN FRIEDRICH[2], TEGTMEIER[1])* was born January 3, 1924 in Berea,Cuyahoga Co.OH, and died October 17, 1995 in Crossville, TN. He married SANDY LOUISE KESTNER September 29, 1951 in Ashland, Ashland Co. OH, daughter of FREDERICK KESTNER and ADELAIDE FAIR. She was born September 26, 1933 in Ashland, Ashland Co., OH.

Notes for RICHARD ELMER TEGTMEIER:
Richard, "Dick" was our family entrepreneuer. He tested his business savvy hiring me to pick pickles he sol at great profit. Dick and Sandy owned and managed a summer resort with cabins and boating equipment at Houghton Lake, Michigan for many years. Then they moved back to Ohio and Dick got into the building business. He co-owned and managed a roller rink, managed the Wooster college golf course, built and sold houses, and was contrctor forthe new Canaan Lutheran Church. Joining Henry and Harriet in retirement at Fairfield Glade, TN, he and Sandy enjoyed many more rounds of golf. Dick married Sandy Kestner, Ashland, Ohio. They had three children: Doug, Debbie and Dean.

—Lois Tegtmeier Hinrichs

Birth date: Jan 3, 1924
Death date: Oct 17, 1995
ZIP Code of last known residence: 38555
Primary location associated with this ZIP Code: Crossville, Tennessee (for record according to Social Security)—Actually Fairfield Glade, TN.

Richard Tegtmeier died on October 17, 1995. Born January 3, 1924, Tegtmeier was 71 years old and lived in Fairfield Glade, TN.

More About RICHARD ELMER TEGTMEIER:
Education: Social Security #: 277-22-4930
Ethnicity/Relig.: Lutheran
Event 4: Last residence ZIP: 38555
Occupation: Issued in: Ohio

More About SANDY LOUISE KESTNER:
Education: 1938, Christened, Aurora, IL
Ethnicity/Relig.: Lutheran

More About RICHARD TEGTMEIER and SANDY KESTNER:
Marriage: 29 Sep 1951, Ashland, Ashland Co. OH

Children of RICHARD TEGTMEIER and SANDY KESTNER are:
75. i. Douglas Richard[7] Tegtmeier, b. 06 Dec 1952, Wooster, Montgomery Co., OH.
76. ii. Debra Louise Tegtmeier, b. 09 Jan 1955, Wooster, Wayne Co. OH.
77. iii. Dean Edward Tegtmeier, b. 02 Mar 1957, Ashland, Ashland Co., OH.

37. LOIS RUTH[5] TEGTMEIER *(WILLIAM CARL[4], JOHANN HEINRICH[3], JOHANN FRIEDRICH[2], TEGTMEIER[1])* was born March 18, 1928 in maybe Brookpark, OH. She married PETER CORNELIUS HINRICHS June 3, 1950 in W. Canaan, Wayne Co., Ohio at Canaan Lutheran Church, son of PETER HINRICHS and EMMA GROTH. He was born October 23, 1925 in Arlington, Kingsbury, SD, and died July 31, 1994 in Dickinson, Stark Co. ND.

Some of Dick & Sandy's descendents: Back row: Debra Tegtmeir Miller, her brother Dean, Debra's son, Jonatha, and her husband , Terry Miller. Front Row, Dean's children, Sara and Shawn.

Notes for Lois Ruth Tegtmeier:
Born at home. Christened April 22, 1928, sponsors: Ruth Tegtmeier an Leland Smith Confirmed 6/01/1941 at Canaan Lutheran

As the last child of nine, my version of our family saga is from my recollection! Each of us would probably write about events the others wouldn't even know or think noteworthy. I conclude with the following thoughts.

Many of our family and friends from Berea visited us in Killbuck Valley over the years. Most came unannounc3d, sometimes by car loads to spend Sunday with us. Often they would be opening picnic baskets, setting out food and drink when we came home from Church. We were invited to be their guests. Potato chips, store bread, bananas—food that rarely was on our table. (I didn't appreciate the bread mother baked twice a week, in a wood heated oven until years later.)

One lady exclaimed to Mother, "Ann, you've got heaven on earth here on your farm." Mothe4 later remarked to me, "She should know what work is the rest of the week!"

Aunts and uncles and cousins were important as we grew up. They came to our high school graduations. Most lived close enough to visit often.

My brothers said vacation for them began when school started in the fall. After long, hot days of field work, they cooled off in the "swimming hole" in Killbuck Creek with other neighbor boys. Then we lit the coal oil lamp, gathered around the kitchen table for Scripture reading and the Lord's prayer. The house grew quiet. A cricket would chirp in the house, frogs croaked in the little creek across the road, and a wipper-will sang as we drifted into sleep.

Some Sunday afternoons in summer, Dad and I would take chairs in the yard and sing hymns by memory. When he smoked a cigar, it reminded me of company. He died after a short illness April 10, Easter Sunday, 1955 at 73 years old.

Mother wanted to be a school teacher. Her children believed she taught us daily lessons for life! She spent her last years with Loretta in Florida during winters, and with us in North Dakota during summers, busy with needlework and reading. She lived to be 93, enjoying life to the fullest. She died in Dickinson, September 30 1982 and was buried in Canaan Cemetery.

—Lois Tegtmeier Hinrichs

Notes for Peter Cornelius Hinrichs:
Married June 03, 1950, Rev. P. A. Hinrichs, officiant. (father)

Reverend Peter C. Hinrichs, Pastor of St. John Lutheran Church in Dickinson, North Dakota for 30 years, was a strong supporter of life-long learning and was instrumental in starting Comm University. Pastor Hinrichs served on the North Dakota State Board of Higher Education. He was also on the Board of Directors at Augsburg Publishing House. As well, "Pete" was a key player relative to the Great Plains Institute of Theology and Presented many conferences. Pastor Pete taught many youth and adult classes, including courses in theology and psychology as part of the curriculum at Dickinson state University. He also served as a lecturer at Warburg Theological Seminary in Dubuque, Iowa.

While on the Board of Augsburg Publishing House, he wrote many theological book reviews.

—courtesy of Lois Hinricks

Lois (Tegtmeier) and the Rev'd Pete Hinrichs

July 2004 Yellowstone Cabin
"The Shepherd's Fold"
Back Row: Mark, Michelle, Luke, Ben, Steve and Debbie
Front Row: Rachel, Loey (Lois Tegtmeier), Steven

Lois Tegtmeier Hinrichs with he grandchildren
Christmas 2003
Back Row: Andrew, Rachael
Center: Benjamin
Front: Lois and Luke

Children of Lois Tegtmeier and Peter Hinrichs are:

78. i. Mark Peter[6] Hinricks, b. October 30, 1951, Redfield, SD.

79. ii. Steven Heye Hinricks, b. January 23, 1954, Redfield, Spink Co, SD.

38. Howard J.[6] Tegtmeier *(Gustav Adolph[5], Johann Heinrich[4], Johann Friedrich[3], Unknown[2], Unknown Unknown[1])* was born ABT 1913 in Ohio.

Notes for Howard J. Tegtmeier:
1930 Brook Park, Cuyahoga, Ohio
Adolph G Tegtmeier, age 48, first married when he was 28, machinst in the auto factory (probably Ford Motor Company headquartered in Brookpark at that time; wife Alma, age 37, first married when she was 18; Howard J age 17. (I Don't see Dale …)

39. William L.[5] Teckmyer *(Fred C.[4], Friedrich Wilhelm[3] Tegtmeier, Johann Friedrich[2], Tegtmeier[1])* was born June 17, 1912 in Ohio, and died February 1978 in Cleveland, Cuyahoga, Ohio. He married Jane Arters. She was born August 14, 1915, and died February 1986 in Cleveland, Cuyahoga, Ohio.

Notes for William L. Teckmyer:
1930 Census Lakewood Cuyahoga Ohio
Teckmyer, Fred C. head, rail road, owns own home, 48 years old; married when he was 29, born in Ohio father from Germany, mother from Michigan; secretary for Steel company, $ 10,000 per year; Marion L. wife, age 41, born in Ohio, father from Ohio, mother from Canada; age 22 when first married; William L 17, son, Fred C., Jr. 16; Isabel M. age 11, children all born in Ohio.

William Teckmyer
Last Residence: 44121 Cleveland, Cuyahoga, Ohio, United States of America
Born: 17 Jun 1912
Died: Feb 1978
State (Year) SSN issued: Ohio (Before 1951)

Jane Teckmyer (Possible wife??)
Last Residence: 44124 Cleveland, Cuyahoga, Ohio, United States of America
Born: 14 Aug 1915
Died: Feb 1986
State (Year) SSN issued: Ohio (Before 1951)

Notes for JANE ARTERS:
Jane A Teckmyer
Gender: 2
Date of Death: 08 February 1986
Birth Date: 14 August 1915
Volume: 26348
Certificate: 008984
Autopsy: Yes—Used for certification
Marital Status: Widowed
Hispanic Origin: British, Scotch-Irish, Welsh, Scottish
Place of Death: Lyndhurst, Cuyahoga County
Certifier: Coroner
Race: White
Birth Place: Ohio
Residence: Lyndhurst, Cuyahoga County
Age: 70 Years

Child of WILLIAM TECKMYER and JANE ARTERS is:

i. WILLIAM L.[6] JR., TECKMYER, b. December 29, 1943, Cleveland, Cuyahoga Co., Ohio; d. December 21, 1998.

Notes for WILLIAM L. JR., TECKMYER:
William Lowe Teckmyer JR
Gender: Male
Date of Death: 21 December 1998
Birth Date: 29 December 1943
Volume: 31800
Certificate: 103175
Autopsy: No
Father's Surname: Teckmyer
Time of Death: 4:04 PM
Marital Status: Divorced
Hispanic Origin: Non Hispanic
Place of Death: Hospital/Inpatient
Years of Schooling: 16
Certifier: Physician
Referred to Coroner: No
Method of Disposition: Cremation
Mother's Surname: Arters

Race: White
Birth Place: Cleveland, Cuyahoga County, Ohio
Residence: Ohio
Age: 54

40. Victor C.^{5} Pfizenmayer *(Madeline^{4} Tegtmeier, Friedrich Wilhelm^{3}, Johann Friedrich^{2}, Tegtmeier^{1})*

Children of Victor C. Pfizenmayer are:

i. Victor C.^{6} Pfizenmayer.
ii. Thomas David Pfizenmayer.

Generation No. 5

41. John Arthur^{7} Meier *(Almeta Bertha Christine^{6} Ahleman, Hulda Louise Maria^{5} Tegtmeier, Johann Heinrich^{4}, Johann Friedrich^{3}, Unknown^{2}, Unknown Unknown^{1})* was born 25 Dec 1922 in Curtice, OH. He married

The Meiers Siblings
Upper left: Lester & Mary Meier (wife)
Upper right: John Meier
Lower left: Doris Meier Hille
Lower Right: Lucene Meier Pyers
Photo circ 2007, courtesy of Les Meier.

DORIS JANE METZKER 10 Nov 1944. She was born 17 Jun 1923 in Toledo, OH, and died 09 Jan 2003 in Bellville, OH.

More About JOHN MEIER and DORIS METZKER:
Marriage: 10 Nov 1944

Children of JOHN MEIER and DORIS METZKER are:
80. i. Ronald Arthur[8] Meier, b. 21 Feb 1946, Toledo, OH.
81. ii. Richard Allen Meier, b. 06 Mar 1949, Toledo, OH; d. 18 Jun 2000.
82. iii. Beverly Ann Meier, b. 16 Aug 1954, Perrysburg, OH.

42. LUCENE ELSIE[6] MEIER *(ALMETA BERTHA CHRISTINE[5] AHLEMAN, HULDA LOUISE MARIA[4] TEGTMEIER, JOHANN HEINRICH[3], JOHANN FRIEDRICH[2], TEGTMEIER[1])* was born November 15, 1924 in Curtice, OH. She married VICTOR JUNIOR PYERS October 2, 1954. He was born December 15, 1919 in Lime City, OH, and died June 17, 1993 in Fort Meigs Cemetery, Perrysburg, OH. Child of LUCENE MEIER and VICTOR PYERS is:

Child of VICTOR PYERS and LUCENE MEIER:
i. DEAN HALE[7] PYERS, b. August 7, 1962, Toledo, OH.

43. DORIS HULDA[7] MEIER *(ALMETA BERTHA CHRISTINE[6] AHLEMAN, HULDA LOUISE MARIA[5] TEGTMEIER, JOHANN HEINRICH[4], JOHANN FRIEDRICH[3], UNKNOWN[2], UNKNOWN UNKNOWN[1])* was born 22 Oct 1925 in Curtice, OH. She married DALE HERMAN HILLE 11 Dec 1948 in Toledo, OH. He was born 14 Aug 1924 in Wood Do., Bowling Green, OH.

More About DALE HILLE and DORIS MEIER:
Marriage: 11 Dec 1948, Toledo, OH

Children of DORIS MEIER and DALE HILLE are:
83. i. Karen Rae[8] Hille, b. 21 Apr 1951, Perrysburg, OH.
ii. DENNIS KAY HILLE, b. 08 Apr 1953, Bowling Green, OH.
84. iii. Karlyn Sue Hille, b. 19 Jul 1955, Bowling Green, OH.

44. LESTER BERNARD[6] MEIER *(ALMETA BERTHA CHRISTINE[5] AHLEMAN, HULDA LOUISE MARIA[4] TEGTMEIER, JOHANN HEINRICH[3], JOHANN FRIEDRICH[2], TEGTMEIER[1])* was born January 7, 1931 in Curtice, OH. He married MARY LOU KLEBOLD April 23, 1950. She was born June 4, 1932 in Columbus, OH.

Children of LESTER MEIER and MARY KLEBOLD are:

85. i. Linda Christine[8] Meier, b. 25 Apr 1951, Toledo, OH.
86. ii. Eileen Kay Meier, b. 19 Oct 1952, Bowling Green, OH.
87. iii. Cynthia Ann Meier, b. 06 Apr 1956, Toledo, OH.
88. iv. Laureen Marie Meier, b. 31 May 1958, Bowling Green, OH.

45. LEOLA MAY[6] MARKS *(ELSIE EMMA HULDA[5] AHLEMAN, HULDA LOUISE MARIA[4] TEGTMEIER, JOHANN HEINRICH[3], JOHANN FRIEDRICH[2], TEGTMEIER[1])* was born October 12, 1925 in Henry Co., OH. She married WESLEY ALGER HUNT June 25, 1960. He was born October 4, 1928 in Franklyn Twp., MI.

Child of LEOLA MARKS and WESLEY HUNT is:

89. i. Karen Jane[7] Hunt, b. February 11, 1962, Adrian, MI.

46. WILLIAM CARL ELWIN[6] MARKS *(ELSIE EMMA HULDA[5] AHLEMAN, HULDA LOUISE MARIA[4] TEGTMEIER, JOHANN HEINRICH[3], JOHANN FRIEDRICH[2], TEGTMEIER[1])* was born March 1, 1930 in Monroe Co., MI. He married MILDRED IRENE EMERY May 25, 1951. She was born January 3, 1933 in Adrian, MI.

Children of WILLIAM MARKS and MILDRED EMERY are:

90. i. Nancy Kay[7] Marks, b. December 12, 1957, Adrian, MI.
91. ii. Judy Lyn Marks, b. June 4, 1960, Adrian, MI.
92. iii. Wendy Lee Marks, b. July 25, 1964, Adrian, MI.

47. HERBERT BERNARD[6] MARKS *(ELSIE EMMA HULDA[5] AHLEMAN, HULDA LOUISE MARIA[4] TEGTMEIER, JOHANN HEINRICH[3], JOHANN FRIEDRICH[2], TEGTMEIER[1])* was born March 31, 1936 in Deerfield, MI. He married JANICE GIBSON April 27, 1957. She was born May 12, 1936 in Toledo, OH.

Children of HERBERT MARKS and JANICE GIBSON are:

i. TODD BERNARD[7] MARKS, b. November 29, 1957, Hudson, MI; m. TERRY ASHDOWN, August 14, 1982; b. March 16, 1958, Pierre, S. Dakota.

ii. Gregg Herbert Marks, b. January 18, 1960, Mt. Clemens, MI; m. Dana Lynne Caruthers, August 12, 1995; b. June 17, 1962, Denver, CO.

93. iii. Scott Edward Marks, b. May 18, 1964, Lansing, MI.

48. Stanley Arthur[6] Marks *(Elsie Emma Hulda[5] Ahleman, Hulda Louise Maria[4] Tegtmeier, Johann Heinrich[3], Johann Friedrich[2], Tegtmeier[1])* was born January 23, 1940 in Deerfield, MI. He married Judith Katherine Backman June 21, 1980. She was born October 11, 1946 in Fresno, CA.

Children of Stanley Marks and Judith Backman are:

i. Travis Stanley[7] Marks, b. September 5, 1981, Fresno, CA.

ii. Troy William Marks, b. December 31, 1989, Fresno, CA.

49. Florence Elsie[6] Ahleman *(Walter Adolph5, Hulda Louise Maria4 Tegtmeier, Johann Heinrich3, Johann Friedrich2, Tegtmeier[1])* was born November 30, 1930 in Henry Co., Liberty Center, OH. She married Richard F. Henning August 4, 1950. He was born October 30, 1929 in Napoleon, OH.

Children of Florence Ahleman and Richard Henning are:

i. Chari Lynn[7] Henning, b. November 29, 1953, Henry Co., OH; d. July 6, 1959.

More About Chari Lynn Henning:
Burial: Heath Cemetery, Henry Co., Wash. Twp, Liberty Ctr, OH

94. ii. Debra Kay Henning, b. October 16, 1956, Napoleon, OH.

95. iii. Lori Jean Henning, b. October 7, 1959, Wauseon, OH.

50. Donald Ernest[6] Ahleman *(Walter Adolph[5], Hulda Louise Maria[4] Tegtmeier, Johann Heinrich[3], Johann Friedrich[2], Tegtmeier[1])* was born March 4, 1934 in Liberty Center, Henry Co., OH. He married Marilyn Lou Stevens November 14, 1967. She was born July 3, 1934 in Holgate, OH.

Children of Donald Ahleman and Marilyn Stevens are:

96. i. Shelly Joanne[7] Ahleman, b. August 5, 1967, Toledo, OH.

ii. David John Ahleman, b. October 16, 1969, Toledo, OH.

51. Damaris Anne[6] Ahleman *(Paul Ernest[5], Hulda Louise Maria[4] Tegtmeier, Johann Heinrich[3], Johann Friedrich[2], Tegtmeier[1])* was born June 10, 1944 in Lowrey Air Force Base, CO. She married Ronald Bromley August 31, 1968. He was born January 6, 1940 in CA.

Children of Damaris Ahleman and Ronald Bromley are:

i. Robert Paul[7] Bromley, b. October 7, 1971, Boise, ID.

ii. Maria Ann Bromley, b. June 8, 1973, Boise, ID.

52. Nancy[6] Davidson *(Ruth[5] Tegtmeier, Henry William Carl[4], Johann Heinrich[3], Johann Friedrich[2], Tegtmeier[1])* was born ABT 1935. She married xxx Jones.

Notes for Nancy Davidson:
OBITUARY Id#: 0752230
Name: Tegtmeier, Augusta C.
Date: Apr 4 1967
Source: Plain Dealer; Cleveland Necrology File, Reel #161.
Notes: Tegtmeier. Augusta C. Tegtmeier, age 88, beloved wife of the late Henry, dear mother of Ruth Davidson and Oscar, grandmother of Nancy Jones, Richard Davidson and Susan Hahn, great-grandmother of Elizabeth Jones, passed away Sunday. Funeral services will be held Wednesday, April 5, at 1:30 p.m. at Baker Funeral Home, Berea. Family suggests contributions be made to Immanuel United Church of Christ Building Fund, 4511 W. 130th St. Visiting Hours 3–5 And 7–9 P.M. Tuesday.

Child of Nancy Davidson and xxx Jones is:

i. Elizabeth[7] Jones, b. Bef. 1967, Ohio.

Notes for Elizabeth Jones:
OBITUARY Id#: 0752230
Name: Tegtmeier, Augusta C.
Date: Apr 4 1967
Source: Plain Dealer; Cleveland Necrology File, Reel #161.
Notes: Tegtmeier. Augusta C. Tegtmeier, age 88, beloved wife of the late Henry, dear mother of Ruth Davidson and Oscar, grandmother of Nancy Jones, Richard Davidson and Susan Hahn, great-grandmother of Elizabeth Jones***, passed away Sunday. Funeral services will be held Wednesday, April 5, at

1:30 p.m. at Baker Funeral Home, Berea. Family suggests contributions be made to Immanuel United Church of Christ Building Fund, 4511 W. 130th St. Visiting Hours 3–5 And 7–9 P.M. Tuesday.

53. WILLIAM L.[6] SCHULTZ *(FLORENCE JULIA[5] SCRIVENS, LUCIE ADELINE JULIANNA[4] TEGTMEIER, JOHANN HEINRICH[3], JOHANN FRIEDRICH[2], TEGTMEIER[1])* was born August 2, 1931 in Berea, Cuyahoga, OH. He married DOLORES ANN HINES October 18, 1952 in St Matthew Lutheran Church, Medina, OH. She was born December 2, 1934.

Notes for WILLIAM L. SCHULTZ:

William L. Schultz and family: Back row: Tim, Cynthia, David, Connie, James
Front Row: Dolores and Bill Schultz. Courtesy of Bill Schultz, Medina, Ohio

Children of WILLIAM SCHULTZ and DOLORES HINES are:

- i. JAMES WILLIAM[7] SCHULTZ, b. May 5, 1953; m. GLORIA J. DYKE, September 22, 1982.
- ii. DAVID ALAN SCHULTZ, b. April 7, 1956; m. RHONDA HUGHES, April 22, 1989.
- iii. CONNIE ANN SCHULTZ, b. July 21, 1954; m. Andrew Adams, May 19, 1978.
- iv. CYNTHIA SUE SCHULTZ, b. January 7, 1958; m. DENNIS BALLIET, July 19, 1979.
- v. TIMOTHY BEN SCHULTZ, b. March 18, 1960.

54. GLEN A.[6] SMITH *(LELAND J.[5], CHRISTINA DOROTHEA EMILIE[4] TEGTMEIER, JOHANN HEINRICH[3], JOHANN FRIEDRICH[2], TEGTMEIER[1])* was born ABT 1938 in Cleveland, Cuyahoga Co., OH. He married CAROL.

Notes for GLEN A. SMITH:
Glen was a fine auto mechanic, had his own business in Berea, Ohio.

Children of GLEN SMITH and CAROL are:

- i. CARIA[7] SMITH.
- ii. CINDY SMITH.
- iii. GREGORY SMITH.

55. DAVID[6] PAUL BERRY *(LORETTA MATTIE[5] TEGTMEIER, WILLIAM CARL[4], JOHANN HEINRICH[3], JOHANN FRIEDRICH[2], TEGTMEIER[1])* was born 01 Oct 1936 in Lodi, Ohio. He married BEVERLY ANN COOPER 09 Jun 1957. She was born 03 Aug 1939.

Children of DAVID BERRY and BEVERLY COOPER are:

- i. Wesley David[8] Berry, b. 15 Oct 1958, Ashland, Ohio; m. SUSAN ANNETTE FRAZIER, 14 Nov 1987; b. 02 Jul 1958.

  More About WESLEY BERRY and SUSAN FRAZIER:
  Marriage: 14 Nov 1987

97. ii. TAMALA ANNE BERRY, b. 08 Nov 1961.
98. iii. Stephanie Renee Berry, b. 07 Mar 1969.

56. Karen Diane^{7} Berry *(Loretta Mattie^{6} Tegtmeier, William Carl^{5}, Johann Heinrich^{4}, Johann Friedrich^{3}, Unknown^{2}, Unknown Unknown^{1})* was born 22 Mar 1942 in West Salem, Ohio. She married Don Boyer. He was born ABT 1940.

Notes for Don Boyer:
Don Boyer and his wife moved near Denver, CO, and began a business where they cut, harvest and treat the aspen wood, shave it very fine, and make lampshades out of the wood. (Am not positive that all the children were born in Colorado, but will correct if need be.)

Children of Karen Berry and Don Boyer are:

i. Bryan^{8} Boyer, b. ABT 1962, Denver, CO.
ii. Bradley Boyer, b. ABT 1963, Denver, CO.
iii. Lisa Boyer, b. ABT 1964, Denver, CO.

57. Donna Mae^{6} Tegtmeier *(Raymond Julius^{5}, William Carl^{4}, Johann Heinrich^{3}, Johann Friedrich^{2}, Tegtmeier^{1})* was born September 1, 1944. She married William Schemrich December 7, 1962. He was born ABT 1928.

Children of Donna Tegtmeier and William Schemrich are:

i. Ronnie^{7} Schemrich, b. ABT 1958.
ii. Dale Schemrich, b. ABT 1959.
iii. Shawn Schemrich, b. ABT 1960.

58. Sharon Lee^{6} Tegtmeier *(Raymond Julius^{5}, William Carl^{4}, Johann Heinrich^{3}, Johann Friedrich^{2}, Tegtmeier^{1})* was born January 4, 1947. She married Gary Erro May 16, 1967. He was born ABT 1947.

Children of Sharon Tegtmeier and Gary Erro are:

i. Jody Ann^{7} Erro.
ii. Amanda Marie Erro.

59. Daniel Howard^{6} Tegtmeier *(Raymond Julius^{5}, William Carl^{4}, Johann Heinrich^{3}, Johann Friedrich^{2}, Tegtmeier^{1})* was born September 23, 1957. He married Beth Ann Bougher May 5, 1978. She was born January 14, 1959.

Dan and Beth Tegtmeier , Sarah and Ethan, 2004.

Children of Daniel Tegtmeier and Beth Bougher are:

i. Ethan Daniel[7] Tegtmeier, b. January 26, 1990.

ii. Sarah Christine Tegtmeier, b. May 16, 1993.

60. Shirley Ann[6] Taylor *(Alice Henrietta[5] Tegtmeier, William Carl[4], Johann Heinrich[3], Johann Friedrich[2], Tegtmeier[1])* was born October 11, 1941 in Scranton, PA. She married Eugene Barr June 1, 1963 in Berea, Ohio, son of George Barr and Rena DaviS. He was born November 13, 1935 in West Virginia.

Notes for Shirley Ann Taylor:

Shirley attended Berea High School, Berea, Ohio, the same school her mother (Alice Tegtmeyer) attended years earlier. She graduated fro Capital University, BSN 1963 and Ohio State University MSN 1977. She was Assistant Professor at Ohio University in nUrsing in Zanesville, Ohio. After having 3 children, and living in Thornville, Ohio, she divorced in November of 1985. Moving to Bradenton, Florida she became Director of Nursing at Manatee Palms Hospital

Left: Some of Alice Tegtmeier's descendents, daughter Shirley and Gene Barr, children Jeff, Kathy and Angela, circ. 1975.

Bottom
Ed Taylor, and nieces Kathy & Angie Barr.

in 1997, retired and cared for her mother, Alice Tegtmeier. Her favorite things: Enjoying sunsets on the ocean in Bradenton, Florida since the early 1987.

More About SHIRLEY ANN TAYLOR:
Divorced: 1985

Notes for EUGENE BARR:
Divorced 1985
Living in Thornville, Ohio as of 2004 with his second wife.

Children of SHIRLEY TAYLOR and EUGENE BARR are:

94. i. Jeffrey^{7} Eugene Barr, b. December 3, 1963, Zanesville, Ohio.
95. ii. Kathy Anne Barr, b. December 4, 1965, Zanesville, OH.
96. iii. Angela Lynn Barr, b. October 7, 1969, Zainesville, Ohio.

61. EDWARD WILLIAM^{6} TAYLOR *(ALICE HENRIETTA^{5} TEGTMEIER, WILLIAM CARL^{4}, JOHANN HEINRICH^{3}, JOHANN FRIEDRICH^{2}, TEGTMEIER^{1})* was born January 11, 1943 in Alden, NY. He married NANCY UNTEZUBER. She was born May 3, 1948.

Notes for EDWARD WILLIAM TAYLOR:
Born at home in Alden NY.
Divorced.
2004: Currently living in Medina, Ohio

Children of EDWARD TAYLOR and NANCY UNTEZUBER are:

i. CRAIG EDWARD[7] TAYLOR, b. September 7, 1962; m. DEBRA "CRICKET" JONES, April 23, 1999, Christ the King Lutheran, Twinsburg, OH.

Notes for CRAIG EDWARD TAYLOR:
1962. Lived in Berea, Ohio

102. ii. CHRISTINE JEAN TAYLOR, b. November 1974.

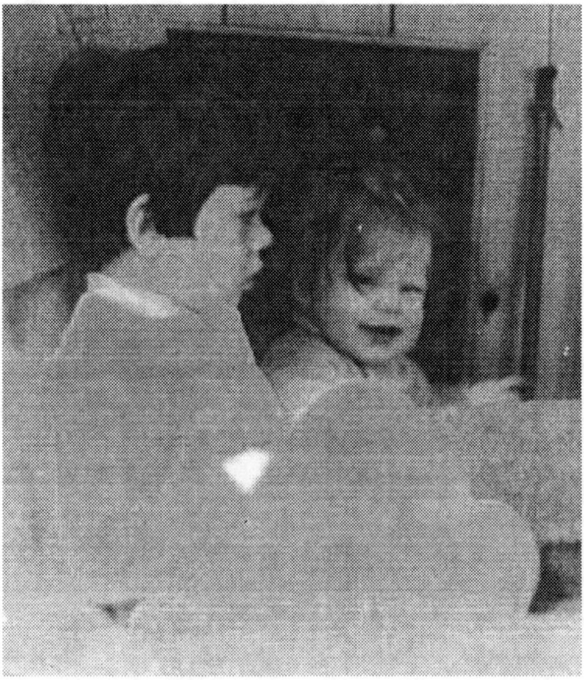

Craig and Christine Taylor
Photo circ 1975, courtesy of Sandra Taylor Bell

62. James Robert^{6} Taylor *(Alice Henrietta^{5} Tegtmeier, William Carl^{4}, Johann Heinrich^{3}, Johann Friedrich^{2}, Tegtmeier^{1})* was born March 22, 1949 in Berea, Ohio. He married (1) Margie Moore August 28, 1971 in Newfoundland, Canada. She was born May 1, 1950 in Newfoundland, Canada. He married (2) Nancy ABT 1998. Divorced: ABT 1997

Notes for Margie Moore:
Margie was born in Newfoundland. She and Jim met and married their when Jim was stationed in the Argentia at the Naval Base. He had an opportunity to work with McDonald's Restaurant after he was discharged in Bradenton, Florida through a friend in the Navy. Margie is a Nurse working in Sarasota. They were divorced some years ago. Jim currently is working in Georgia and maintaining a hunting property.
Margie Farwell, a/k/a/Margie Taylor a/k/a/Margie Moore married to Bill Farwell
3129 Novus court
Sarasota Florida 34237
941 366 9276

Children of James Taylor and Margie Moore are:

i. Shane Edward^{7} Taylor, b. August 1, 1978.
ii. Chasta Taylor, b. March 21, 1981.

63. Sandra Mina^{6} Taylor *(Alice Henrietta^{5} Tegtmeier, William Carl^{4}, Johann Heinrich^{3}, Johann Friedrich^{2}, Tegtmeier^{1})* was born March 17, 1950 in Berea, Ohio. She married Peter Graham Bell June 3, 1984 in Pine Shores Presb. Church, Sarasota, Fl, son of Hal Bell and Jane Kluepfel. He was born August 29, 1937 in Wauseon, Ohio and died September 2, 2006.

Notes for Peter Graham Bell:
Peter grew up in Wauseon, Ohio. He joined the Air Force for 7 years and was traveled to China and Greenland, then Charleston, South Carolina. He met and married Nancy Clark and they had a son, Peter Graham Bell, Jr.—who they called PJ. PJ was killed in a motorcycle accident. Peter Sr worked with National Airlines which was sold to Pan American Airlines, which went bankrupt in 1990. He currently works the night shift at the US Post Office in Miami, Florida.

Left: James Robert Taylor
Son of Alice Tegtmeier and Ed Taylor
Circ. 1967.

Sandra Taylor and Pete Bell
Married June 3, 1984.
Heather,
Alice Tegtmeier Taylor
And Josh Bell
Circ 2002

Below, Sandy & Pete Bell circ 1990.

Sandra graduated from Cuyahoga Community College AA Journalism 1970, and Syracuse University, NY 1972 BS Public Communications. Pete met Sandra Taylor in Sarasota, Florida where she was working with Pine Shores Presbyterian Church. They commuted from Miami toSarasota for over a year each weekend (about 4.5 hour drive 1 way) before they married June 3, 1984. They had Heather, born in Sarasota, Florida, and Joshua Bell born in Miami.

In 1992 and Hurricane Andrew hit the house, a category 5 hurricane. Though shuttered, all the windows and doors blew out, though much of the stone roof remained. Everything was ruined, broken wood everywhere. All the glass was broken, furniture wet, and the wallpaper was even torn apart. The 30' top brace of our screened in pool had torpedoed over the house and crashed through our neighbors front window(and shutters) opening their house to the wind. But we, who didn't think we'd survive the night, huddled in the hallway with mattresses and the dog were happy just to see the morning—what we lost didn't seem to matter as much as we were alive. Neighbors who had left their homes, and came back to find the damage, left the area for good and moved back north.

I remember Joshua (about 5 years old) sweeping water into a dustpan to help clean up. Everyone left the area, no lights—you could really see the stars at night for the first time as there were no city lights to dim out their twinkle. The National Guard soon was marching up the road, keeping guard. They pitched their tents 2 blocks away, and invited us to eat with them. I remember Pete's step daughter, Cindy, sending a care package via US Mail—socks, a can opener, some cans, and a bottle of wine. It was wonderful to see that mail truck—no one had mail delivered for weeks, and here he was coming with news from the outside! And the bottle of wine didn't hurt. Those socks really felt good on wet, swollen feet!

The kids had gone out and picked up pots from the street, we built a fire in the back yard and could cook. The refrigerator had blown into the kitchen sink, and there were no cupboard doors, let alone some of the stuff that use to reside in the cupboards.

I don't remember how long it took us to dig out, Knocked the rest of the broken glass from the windshield of the VW so we could find stuff—like replacement doors, windows. But it took days for the roads to be clear enough to get out. I remember getting cards and checks from some of the cousins, and that was so much appreciated. I know remember if I thanked everyone—I am so sorry if I didn't. It helped us to rebuild.

—Sandra Bell

Children of SANDRA TAYLOR and PETER BELL are:

i. HEATHER LYNNE[7] BELL, b. September 30, 1984, Sarasota, FL.

Notes for HEATHER LYNNE BELL:
Heather was born in Sarasota, Florida. Florida has Magnet Schools in their public school system, and she tried out and got into the School of Arts program in downtown Miami. It meant nearly an hour drive to school, and an hour back, plus classes started earlier and let out later. She graduated 11th in her class and was offered several scholarships. Heather then enrolled the at Kansas City Art Institute.

ii. JOSHUA TAYLOR BELL, b. October 13, 1986, Miami, FL.

Notes for JOSHUA TAYLOR BELL:
Joshua Bell was born in Miami, Florida and currently attends Coral Reef Magnet School, school of Agriculture with a class of 700. In the summer of 2003 he participated in the REAP program at Kentucky State University for 6 weeks.

64. MIRIAM ANN[7] TEGTMEIER *(HENRY ADOLPH[6], WILLIAM CARL[5], JOHANN HEINRICH[4], JOHANN FRIEDRICH[3], UNKNOWN[2], UNKNOWN UNKNOWN[1])* was born 08 Apr 1946. She married PAUL CAMPER. He was born ABT 1937.

Children of MIRIAM TEGTMEIER and PAUL CAMPER are:

i. NICOLE[8] CAMPER.

ii. NATHAN CAMPER, m. DIANNE.

65. JOAN CHARLOTTE[6] TEGTMEIER *(HENRY ADOLPH[5], WILLIAM CARL[4], JOHANN HEINRICH[3], JOHANN FRIEDRICH[2], TEGTMEIER[1])* was born August 7, 1947. She married TOM TRUMAN June 13, 1970. He was born July 21, 1946.

Children of JOAN TEGTMEIER and TOM TRUMAN are:

- i. TOM[7] TRUMAN, b. September 14, 1972.
- ii. JACOB TRUMAN, b. September 13, 1974.
- iii. ASHLEY TRUMAN, b. April 20, 1976.
- iv. DAVID TRUMAN, b. September 12, 1978.

66. PAUL[6] TEGTMEIER *(HENRY ADOLPH[5], WILLIAM CARL[4], JOHANN HEINRICH[3], JOHANN FRIEDRICH[2], TEGTMEIER[1])* was born August 3, 1948. He married SANDRA RICE November 4, 1972. She was born July 19, 1953.

Children of PAUL TEGTMEIER and SANDRA RICE are:

- i. JAMIE[7] TEGTMEIER, b. April 25, 1975.
- ii. JEREMY TEGTMEIER, b. March 30, 1976.
- iii. JERROD TEGTMEIER, b. October 22, 1984.

67. JOEL[6] TEGTMEIER *(HENRY ADOLPH[5], WILLIAM CARL[4], JOHANN HEINRICH[3], JOHANN FRIEDRICH[2], TEGTMEIER[1])* was born August 13, 1959. He married TAMMIE October 20, 1978. She was born July 30, 1959.

Children of JOEL TEGTMEIER and TAMMIE are:

- i. ANGELA[7] TEGTMEIER, b. April 19, 1979.
- ii. MATTHEW TEGTMEIER, b. February 3, 1981.

68. LINDA JEAN[7] TEGTMEIER *(WILLIAM EDWARD[6], WILLIAM CARL[5], JOHANN HEINRICH[4], JOHANN FRIEDRICH[3], UNKNOWN[2], UNKNOWN UNKNOWN[1])* was born 24 Aug 1947 in Youngstown, OH, North Side Hospital. She married LARRY GENE FENTON 19 Dec 1992 in Germantown, OH, son of WALDO FENTON and SARA BELL. He was born 02 Mar 1947 in Mansfield, OH.

More About LARRY FENTON and LINDA TEGTMEIER:
Marriage: 19 Dec 1992, Germantown, OH

Children of LINDA TEGTMEIER and LARRY FENTON are:

107. i. Shawn Michael[8] Fenton, b. 19 Jan 1968, Columbus, OH.
108. ii. Amy Krista Fenton, b. 15 May 1971, Pittsburgh, PA.

69. TERRY[7] TEGTMEIER *(WILLIAM EDWARD[6], WILLIAM CARL[5], JOHANN HEINRICH[4], JOHANN FRIEDRICH[3], UNKNOWN[2], UNKNOWN UNKNOWN[1])* was born 25 Sep 1949 in Bolivar, Oh. He married BRENDA G. TEGTMEIER. She was born 08 Mar 1949.

Children of Terry Tegtmeier and Brenda Tegtmeier are:

i. Matthew R.[8] Tegtmeier, b. 27 Jun 1980.

ii. Jennifer L. Tegtmeier, b. 12 Dec 1976; m. Paul R. Roley; b. 12 Nov 1976.

70. Timothy[6] Tegtmeier *(William Edward[5], William Carl[4], Johann Heinrich[3], Johann Friedrich[2], Tegtmeier[1])* was born September 15, 1955. He married Pam Honaker June 15, 1977.

Notes for Timothy Tegtmeier:
WOOSTER, Ohio—Timothy W. Tegtmeier, controller at The College of Wooster, has been named treasurer of the College, effective July 1 (2002)

"I am pleased that Tim has accepted the treasurer's responsibility," said William Snoddy, Wooster's vice president for finance and business. "He is a proven associate who will serve the College well in this official capacity."

Tegtmeier has been Wooster's controller since joining the College in 1983. As treasurer, he will assume the duties of chief accounting officer and fiscal agent for the College. A member of the Wooster staff since 1959, Snoddy has held the positions of both treasurer and vice president for finance and business for the past 18 years. Snoddy will continue to serve as vice president.

A native of Ashland County, Tegtmeier grew-up in Bailey Lakes and graduated from Crestview High School in 1974. He is a 1978 graduate of Capital University, where he earned a bachelor of arts degree in business administration.

Prior to joining Wooster's staff, Tegtmeier was employed as a certified public accountant in the Canton office of the Ernst & Ernst accounting firm for about five years.

Tegtmeier belongs to two professional organizations, the Ohio Association of College and University Business Officers and the National Association of College and University Business Officers. A member of the board of the Wooster chapter of the American Red Cross, he also belongs to the Wooster Kiwanis Club and is treasurer of the Canaan Lutheran Church. (Website August 2002)

Children of Timothy Tegtmeier and Pam Honaker are:

i. Christine[7] Tegtmeier.

ii. Jonathan Tegtmeier.

71. James Herman[6] Tegtmeier *(Harold William[5], William Carl[4], Johann Heinrich[3], Johann Friedrich[2], Tegtmeier[1])* was born February 14, 1945 in Lodi Hospital, near Wooster, Ohio. He married Jeanne Marie Gresser June 20, 1965. She was born ABT 1945.

Notes for James Herman Tegtmeier:
From Lucille Shumaker Tegtmeier
James Herman Tegtmeier was Harold and Lucille's little sweetheart as he was born on Valentine Day, February 14, 1945. The hospital was quarantined the next day due to scarlet fever. For the next days, Harold climbed the outside fire escape and talked to Lucille and got to see his son through the window! After ten days the new dad took his wife and son to her folk's home for a couple of weeks. World War II was in progress and all young men were being drafted into the army. Early one morning when little Jimmy was two weeks old, his dad left on a bus with about 40 other draftees. That evening, Lucille was quite surprised, but overjoyed, when a bus stopped and Harold came into the house. It seemed that Uncle Sam decided that Lucille and son needed Harold more than he did!

And now for a few interesting events. Little Jimmy, Donnie and David all ran away from home when they were three years old o so in search of their dad but luckily they were found. Guess Barbara was more of a home-body!

Jim, when 12, got badly hurt in a farm accident when he got tangled with a tractor power take-off and spent several weeks in the hospital.

Children of James Tegtmeier and Jeanne Gresser are:

109. i. Molly Marie[8] Tegtmeier, b. 24 May 1971.

110. ii. Randy James Tegtmeier, b. 24 Mar 1975.

72. Donald Phillip[6] Tegtmeier *(Harold William[5], William Carl[4], Johann Heinrich[3], Johann Friedrich[2], Tegtmeier[1])* was born November 14, 1948 in Lodi Hospital, near Wooster, Ohio. He married Neva Nestor October 20, 1984. She was born ABT 1948.

Notes for Donald Phillip Tegtmeier:
Donald Phillip Tegtmeier was born on November 14, 1948, the same day that Prince Charles was born. The "Phillip" was given in honor of the royal family but that baby was not named for several weeks or maybe the new little Tegtmeier would have been named Donald Charles. Of course, the second was to be a girl, but the parents were quite happy with another healthy little boy.

Donnie spent time in the hospital, too when he was only two. His Uncle Richard Tegtmeier had open house at his new Wooster Skateland which the Tegtmeiers attended. Going home afterwards, little Donnie unwrapped his candy bar and opened the back door to throw the paper out. Unfortunately, he went out the door too! His parents were scared but were happy he was crying when his parents got to him. The doctor said the Lord had been with us. Donnie had scratches, bruises, and a concussion but got home in a couple of weeks. His heavy snowsuit helped to protect him.

Don broke his leg while playing soccer when in high school. It was a hard time for him with pain and getting around.

More About Donald Tegtmeier and Neva Nestor:
Marriage: 20 Oct 1984

Children of Donald Tegtmeier and Neva Nestor are:
- i. Adam Donald[8] Tegtmeier, b. 17 Jun 1986.
- ii. Heidi Rose Tegtmeier, b. 12 Apr 1989.

73. Barbara Lucille[6] Tegtmeier *(Harold William[5], William Carl[4], Johann Heinrich[3], Johann Friedrich[2], Tegtmeier[1])* was born December 15, 1952 in Lodi Hospital, near Wooster, Ohio. She married James Kramer June 8, 1979. He was born June 6, 1950.

Notes for Barbara Lucille Tegtmeier:
Barbara Lucille Tegtmeier, born December 15, 1952, a special Christmas gift to her parents that year—Lucille Tegtmeier

Barbara had an emergency operation when her appendix erupted.

Notes for JAMES KRAMER:
2004: Barbara & Jim and Barbara's Brother, David and his wife Rita went to Alaska to celebrate their 25th wedding anniversaries in June.

Children of BARBARA TEGTMEIER and JAMES KRAMER are:
111. i. William[8] Kramer, b. 05 Jan 1974.
ii. MATTHEW JAMES KRAMER, b. 29 Sep 1982.

74. DAVID HAROLD[6] TEGTMEIER *(HAROLD WILLIAM[5], WILLIAM CARL[4], JOHANN HEINRICH[3], JOHANN FRIEDRICH[2], TEGTMEIER[1])* was born September 15, 1954 in Lodi Hospital, near Wooster, Ohio. He married RITA KAY KAMP June 24, 1979, daughter of NORMAN KAMP and ARLENE RASTETTER. She was born February 25, 1959 in Ashland, OH.

Notes for DAVID HAROLD TEGTMEIER:
One time David broke his arm when he fell off his pony.

Children of DAVID TEGTMEIER and RITA KAMP are:
i. LUKE DAVID[7] TEGTMEIER, b. May 11, 1983.
ii. JILL ARLENE TEGTMEIER, b. October 29, 1985.
iii. MARK DAVID TEGTMEIER, b. April 25, 1990.

75. DOUGLAS RICHARD[6] TEGTMEIER *(RICHARD ELMER[5], WILLIAM CARL[4], JOHANN HEINRICH[3], JOHANN FRIEDRICH[2], TEGTMEIER[1])* was born December 6, 1952 in Wooster, Montgomery Co., OH. He married SUZANNE GULYAS August 14, 1976 in Centerville, Montgomery Co., OH. She was born January 9, 1954 in Dayton, OH.

Children of DOUGLAS TEGTMEIER and SUZANNE GULYAS are:
i. JEFF[7] TEGTMEIER, b. December 22, 1982, Columbus, Ohio.
ii. RYAN TEGTMEIER, b. October 11, 1984, Columbus, Ohio.

76. DEBRA LOUISE[6] TEGTMEIER *(RICHARD ELMER[5], WILLIAM CARL[4], JOHANN HEINRICH[3], JOHANN FRIEDRICH[2], TEGTMEIER[1])* was born January 9, 1955 in Wooster, Wayne Co. OH. She married TERRY MILLER July 6, 1974 in Wooster, Wayne Co., OH. He was born November 5, 1952.

Children of DEBRA TEGTMEIER and TERRY MILLER are:

i. JEREMIAH[8] MILLER, b. 20 Jun 1978.

ii. JONATHAN PAUL MILLER, b. 24 Aug 1979; m. REBEKAH WRIGHT, 10 Aug 2002, Wooster, Wayne Co. Ohio.

More About JONATHAN MILLER and REBEKAH WRIGHT:
Marriage: 10 Aug 2002, Wooster, Wayne Co. Ohio

77. DEAN EDWARD[6] TEGTMEIER *(RICHARD ELMER[5], WILLIAM CARL[4], JOHANN HEINRICH[3], JOHANN FRIEDRICH[2], TEGTMEIER[1])* was born March 2, 1957 in Ashland, Ashland Co., OH. He married MICHELE HAYNES June 21, 1980 in Toronto, Canada. She was born August 15, 1957 in Toronto, Ohio.

(see photo of Dean and his sister Debra previous page. Below Dean are Shawn and sara.)

Children of DEAN TEGTMEIER and MICHELE HAYNES are:

i. CELESTE[7] TEGTMEIER, b. ABT 1982.

ii. SHAWN TEGTMEIER, b. ABT 1984; m. MICHELLE.

iii. SARA TEGTMEIER, b. ABT 1986.

78. MARK PETER[6] HINRICHS *(LOIS RUTH[5] TEGTMEIER, WILLIAM CARL[4], JOHANN HEINRICH[3], JOHANN FRIEDRICH[2], TEGTMEIER[1])* was born October 30, 1951 in Redfield, SD. He married SANDRA KAE LANDGREBE December 26, 1976, daughter of MORTIMER LANDGREBE and ARLENE WEEKS. She was born April 16, 1952 in Bismarck, ND.

Children of MARK HINRICHS and SANDRA LANDGREBE are:

i. LUCAS ALEXANDER[7] HINRICHS, b. March 19, 1982, Dickinson, Stark, ND.

Baptized 05/23/1982

ii. RACHEL ELIZABETH HINRICHS, b. October 16, 1987, Dickinson, Stark, ND.

Notes for RACHEL ELIZABETH HINRICHS:
Baptized 12/29/1985

St. John Lutheran Church, Dickinson ND by grandfather Peter Hinrichs, officiant

79. Steven Heye[6] Hinrichs *(Lois Ruth[5] Tegtmeier, William Carl[4], Johann Heinrich[3], Johann Friedrich[2], Tegtmeier[1])* was born January 23, 1954 in Redfield, Spink Co, SD. He married Deborah Martin May 2, 1981 in Dickinson, Stark, ND, daughter of Norman Martin and Winnifred Dwyer. She was born August 10, 1949 in Bismarck, Burleigh, ND.

Notes for Steven Heye Hinrichs:
Baptized 2/10/1954 in Redfield, SD; Sponsors: Henry & Harriet Tegtmeier, and Heye-Doris Hinrichs

More About Steven Heye Hinrichs:
Education: Dr. of Pathology. Professor
Residence: Omaha, NE

Children of Steven Hinrichs and Deborah Martin are:

i. Benjamin Heye[7] Hinricks, b. November 29, 1983, Sacramento, CA.

Notes for Benjamin Heye Hinrichs:
Baptized, St. John Lutheran Church, 2/5/1984, Dickinson, Stark, ND

ii. Andrew Peter Hinrichs, b. March 30, 1988.

Generation No. 6

80. Ronald Arthur[7] Meier *(John Arthur[6], Almeta Bertha Christine[5] Ahleman, Hulda Louise Maria[4] Tegtmeier, Johann Heinrich[3], Johann Friedrich[2], Tegtmeier[1])* was born February 21, 1946 in Toledo, OH. He married Janice Marie Williams July 14, 1968. She was born March 29, 1946 in Toledo, OH.

Children of Ronald Meier and Janice Williams are:

i. David John[8] Meier, b. August 24, 1971, Toledo, OH.

ii. Mark Arthur Meier, b. August 24, 1971, Toledo, OH.

81. Richard Allen[7] Meier *(John Arthur[6], Almeta Bertha Christine[5] Ahleman, Hulda Louise Maria[4] Tegtmeier, Johann Heinrich[3], Johann Friedrich[2], Tegtmeier[1])* was born March 6, 1949 in Toledo, OH, and died June 18, 2000. He married Sally Helen Kolasinaki January 23, 1981. She was born December 2, 1958 in Toledo, OH.

More About Richard Allen Meier:
Burial: Bellville Cemetery, Dowling, OH

Children of Richard Meier and Sally Kolasinaki are:

- i. James Andrew[8] Meier, b. January 17, 1982, Toledo, OH.
- ii. Paul Jacob Meier, b. May 17, 1984, Toledo, OH.
- iii. William Joseph Meier, b. October 20, 1985, Toledo, OH.
- iv. Elizabeth Jane Meier, b. August 20, 1987, Toledo, OH.

82. Beverly Ann[7] Meier *(John Arthur[6], Almeta Bertha Christine[5] Ahleman, Hulda Louise Maria[4] Tegtmeier, Johann Heinrich[3], Johann Friedrich[2], Tegtmeier[1])* was born August 16, 1954 in Perrysburg, OH. She married Allyn Kent Euler August 17, 1974. He was born October 8, 1945 in Bowling Green, OH.

Children of Beverly Meier and Allyn Euler are:

- i. Abel W.[8] Euler, b. September 12, 1976, Bowling Green, OH.
- ii. Jason Allyn Euler, b. April 2, 1981, Bowling Green, OH.

83. Karen Rae[7] Hille *(Doris Hulda[6] Meier, Almeta Bertha Christine[5] Ahleman, Hulda Louise Maria[4] Tegtmeier, Johann Heinrich[3], Johann Friedrich[2], Tegtmeier[1])* was born April 21, 1951 in Perrysburg, OH. She married William Kristopher Roman September 22, 1973. He was born October 15, 1949 in Canton, OH.

Children of Karen Hille and William Roman are:

- i. Sarah Elizabeth[8] Roman, b. July 9, 1978, Columbus, OH.
- ii. Meghan Grier Roman, b. October 26, 1982, Columbus, OH.

84. Karlyn Sue[7] Hille *(Doris Hulda[6] Meier, Almeta Bertha Christine[5] Ahleman, Hulda Louise Maria[4] Tegtmeier, Johann Heinrich[3], Johann*

FRIEDRICH[2], *TEGTMEIER*[1]*)* was born July 19, 1955 in Bowling Green, OH. She married TERRY LEE STAMPER June 28, 1980. He was born March 9, 1956 in Grayson, KY.

Child of KARLYN HILLE and TERRY STAMPER is:

i. AARON CHRISTOPHER[8] STAMPER, b. June 25, 1981, Stamford, CT.

85. LINDA CHRISTINE[7] MEIER *(LESTER BERNARD*[6]*, ALMETA BERTHA CHRISTINE*[5] *AHLEMAN, HULDA LOUISE MARIA*[4] *TEGTMEIER, JOHANN HEINRICH*[3]*, JOHANN FRIEDRICH*[2]*, TEGTMEIER*[1]*)* was born April 25, 1951 in Toledo, OH. She married JACK RICHARD SIMMONS December 29, 1969. He was born February 5, 1949 in Toledo, OH.

Children of LINDA MEIER and JACK SIMMONS are:

112. i. Katherine Kramer[9] Simmons, b. 15 Jun 1970, Bowling Green, OH.
113. ii. Sarah Jane Simmons, b. 12 Aug 1973, Toledo, OH.
iii. MEGAN MEIER SIMMONS, b. 22 Jun 1983, Toledo, OH.
iv. ABIGAIL CHRISTINE SIMMONS, b. 06 Nov 1986, Toledo, OH.

86. EILEEN KAY[8] MEIER *(LESTER BERNARD*[7]*, ALMETA BERTHA CHRISTINE*[6] *AHLEMAN, HULDA LOUISE MARIA*[5] *TEGTMEIER, JOHANN HEINRICH*[4]*, JOHANN FRIEDRICH*[3]*, UNKNOWN*[2]*, UNKNOWN UNKNOWN*[1]*)* was born 19 Oct 1952 in Bowling Green, OH. She married BARTON THOMAS STAMPER 02 Oct 1971 in Black Hawk, CO. He was born 21 Aug 1949 in Denver, CO.

More About BARTON STAMPER and EILEEN MEIER:
Marriage: 02 Oct 1971, Black Hawk, CO

Children of EILEEN MEIER and BARTON STAMPER are:

114. i. Joshua Noel Thomas[9] Stamper, b. 27 Sep 1972, Denver, CO.
115. ii. Benjamin Jacob Stamper, b. 11 Apr 1975, Denver, CO.

87. CYNTHIA ANN[8] MEIER *(LESTER BERNARD*[7]*, ALMETA BERTHA CHRISTINE*[6] *AHLEMAN, HULDA LOUISE MARIA*[5] *TEGTMEIER, JOHANN HEINRICH*[4]*, JOHANN FRIEDRICH*[3]*, UNKNOWN*[2]*, UNKNOWN UNKNOWN*[1]*)* was born 06 Apr 1956 in Toledo, OH. She married (1) ROBERT EUGENE THOMPSON 06 Sep 1974. He was born

16 Apr 1950 in Denver, CO. She married (2) GARY ALLYN DINGMAN 05 May 1995. He was born 10 Jun 1957 in Longmont, CO.

More About ROBERT THOMPSON and CYNTHIA MEIER:
Marriage: 06 Sep 1974

More About GARY DINGMAN and CYNTHIA MEIER:
Marriage: 05 May 1995

Children of CYNTHIA MEIER and ROBERT THOMPSON are:
116. i. Andrew Scott[9] Thompson, b. 07 Aug 1977, Denver, CO.
117. ii. Ian Robert Thompson, b. 05 Oct 1979, Denver, CO.

Child of CYNTHIA MEIER and GARY DINGMAN is:
iii. JUSTIN CODY[9] DINGMAN, b. 18 Jun 1997, Denver, CO.

88. LAUREEN MARIE[8] MEIER *(LESTER BERNARD[7], ALMETA BERTHA CHRISTINE[6] AHLEMAN, HULDA LOUISE MARIA[5] TEGTMEIER, JOHANN HEINRICH[4], JOHANN FRIEDRICH[3], UNKNOWN[2], UNKNOWN UNKNOWN[1])* was born 31 May 1958 in Bowling Green, OH. She married DOUGLAS CHARLES BAUER 24 Jun 1984 in Denver, CO. He was born 23 Mar 1956 in Denver, CO.

More About DOUGLAS BAUER and LAUREEN MEIER:
Marriage: 24 Jun 1984, Denver, CO

Children of LAUREEN MEIER and DOUGLAS BAUER are:
i. SCOTT RYAN[9] BAUER, b. 10 Aug 1987, San Francisco, CA.
ii. WILLIAM TAYLOR BAUER, b. 08 Sep 1990, San Francisco, CA.

89. KAREN JANE[8] HUNT *(LEOLA MAY[7] MARKS, ELSIE EMMA HULDA[6] AHLEMAN, HULDA LOUISE MARIA[5] TEGTMEIER, JOHANN HEINRICH[4], JOHANN FRIEDRICH[3], UNKNOWN[2], UNKNOWN UNKNOWN[1])* was born 11 Feb 1962 in Adrian,MI. She married DANIEL GEORGE SHONER 10 May 1986. He was born 21 Feb 1959 in Ypsilanti, MI.

More About DANIEL SHONER and KAREN HUNT:
Marriage: 10 May 1986

Children of KAREN HUNT and DANIEL SHONER are:

i. MICHAEL W.[9] SHONER, b. 05 May 1992; d. 17 Sep 1992, Saline Mi.
ii. JENNA MARIE SHONER, b. 26 Jan 1994, Saline, MI.
iii. RACHEL NICOLE SHONER, b. 21 Dec 1995, Ann Arbor, MI; d. 30 Sep 1996.

90. NANCY KAY[8] MARKS *(WILLIAM CARL ELWIN[7], ELSIE EMMA HULDA[6] AHLEMAN, HULDA LOUISE MARIA[5] TEGTMEIER, JOHANN HEINRICH[4], JOHANN FRIEDRICH[3], UNKNOWN[2], UNKNOWN UNKNOWN[1])* was born 12 Dec 1957 in Adrian, MI. She married LEONARD J. BEAUBIEN 18 Dec 1980. He was born 29 Nov 1958 in Adrian, MI.

More About LEONARD BEAUBIEN and NANCY MARKS:
Marriage: 18 Dec 1980

Children of NANCY MARKS and LEONARD BEAUBIEN are:

i. CHRISTOPHER J.[9] BEAUBIEN, b. 31 Aug 1982, Adrian, MI.
ii. AUDREY KAY BEAUBIEN, b. 18 Aug 1985.

91. JUDY LYN[8] MARKS *(WILLIAM CARL ELWIN[7], ELSIE EMMA HULDA[6] AHLEMAN, HULDA LOUISE MARIA[5] TEGTMEIER, JOHANN HEINRICH[4], JOHANN FRIEDRICH[3], UNKNOWN[2], UNKNOWN UNKNOWN[1])* was born 04 Jun 1960 in Adrian, MI. She married CRAIG SCHNEIDERBUER 20 Oct 1984. He was born 17 Jun 1955 in Toledo, OH.

More About CRAIG SCHNEIDERBUER and JUDY MARKS:
Marriage: 20 Oct 1984

Children of JUDY MARKS and CRAIG SCHNEIDERBUER are:

i. ERIC STEPHEN[9] SCHNEIDERBUER, b. 29 Jul 1988, Toledo, OH.
ii. EMILY LYN SCHNEIDERBUER, b. 09 Jan 1991, Toledo, OH.

92. WENDY LEE[8] MARKS *(WILLIAM CARL ELWIN[7], ELSIE EMMA HULDA[6] AHLEMAN, HULDA LOUISE MARIA[5] TEGTMEIER, JOHANN HEINRICH[4], JOHANN FRIEDRICH[3], UNKNOWN[2], UNKNOWN UNKNOWN[1])* was born 25 Jul 1964 in Adrian, MI. She married BENTLEY JOHN LASER 18 Jun 1988 in First United Methodist Church, Adrian, MI. He was born 01 Dec 1958 in Wauseon, OH.

More About Bentley Laser and Wendy Marks:
Marriage: 18 Jun 1988, First United Methodist Church, Adrian, MI

Children of Wendy Marks and Bentley Laser are:

- i. Bently John Ii[9] Laser, b. 29 Mar 1991, Toledo, OH.
- ii. Holly Jeanne Laser, b. 19 Nov 1992, Grayling, MI.
- iii. Shelby Lee Laser, b. 16 Oct 1996, Toledo, OH.

93. Scott Edward[8] Marks *(Herbert Bernard[7], Elsie Emma Hulda[6] Ahleman, Hulda Louise Maria[5] Tegtmeier, Johann Heinrich[4], Johann Friedrich[3], Unknown[2], Unknown Unknown[1])* was born 18 May 1964 in Lansing, MI. He married Marie Colleen Shupick 07 Jun 1986. She was born 15 Oct 1965 in Eagle Butte, S. Dakota.

More About Scott Marks and Marie Shupick:
Marriage: 07 Jun 1986

Children of Scott Marks and Marie Shupick are:

- i. Jaycee Marie[9] Marks, b. 03 Dec 1991, Elgin, IL.
- ii. Trevor Scott E. Marks, b. 14 Jan 1994, Elgin, IL.

94. Debra Kay[8] Henning *(Florence Elsie[7] Ahleman, Walter Adolph[6], Hulda Louise Maria[5] Tegtmeier, Johann Heinrich[4], Johann Friedrich[3], Unknown[2], Unknown Unknown[1])* was born 16 Oct 1956 in Napoleon, OH. She married Joey Donald Bergstedt 12 Jul 1980. He was born 12 Jul 1959 in Napoleon, OH.

More About Joey Bergstedt and Debra Henning:
Marriage: 12 Jul 1980

Children of Debra Henning and Joey Bergstedt are:

- i. Jennifer Elizabeth[9] Bergstedt, b. 09 Jun 1984, Wauseon, OH.
- ii. Jessica Elyse Bergstedt, b. 19 Apr 1985, Wauseon, OH.
- iii. Alyssa Kathleen Bergstedt, b. 07 Nov 1991, Wauseon, OH.

95. Lori Jean[8] Henning *(Florence Elsie[7] Ahleman, Walter Adolph[6], Hulda Louise Maria[5] Tegtmeier, Johann Heinrich[4], Johann Friedrich[3], Unknown[2],*

Unknown Unknown[1]*)* was born 07 Oct 1959 in Wauseon, OH. She married Alfred Coey 14 Oct 1978. He was born 27 Sep 1956 in Wauseon, OH.

More About Alfred Coey and Lori Henning:
Marriage: 14 Oct 1978

Children of Lori Henning and Alfred Coey are:

i. Jason Tyler[9] Coey, b. 26 Mar 1980, Wauseon, OH.
ii. Jacob Lee Coey, b. 12 May 1990, Wauseon, OH.

96. Shelly Joanne[8] Ahleman *(Donald Ernest*[7]*, Walter Adolph*[6]*, Hulda Louise Maria*[5] *Tegtmeier, Johann Heinrich*[4]*, Johann Friedrich*[3]*, Unknown*[2]*, Unknown Unknown*[1]*)* was born 05 Aug 1967 in Toledo, OH. She married Rodney Richard Parsell 02 Aug 1992. He was born 24 Apr 1968 in Unionville, MI.

More About Rodney Parsell and Shelly Ahleman:
Marriage: 02 Aug 1992

Child of Shelly Ahleman and Rodney Parsell is:

i. Lucas Prescott[9] Parsell, b. 15 Jul 1994, Napoleon, OH.

97. Tamala Anne[8] Berry *(David Paul*[7]*, Loretta Mattie*[6] *Tegtmeier, William Carl*[5]*, Johann Heinrich*[4]*, Johann Friedrich*[3]*, Unknown*[2]*, Unknown Unknown*[1]*)* was born 08 Nov 1961. She married (1) Daniel Staley ABT 1975. She married (2) Ernie Mcclenahan ABT 1977. She married (3) Paul J. Bailey ABT 1979. She married (4) Robert Allen Ballou 20 Jul 1996. He was born 26 Jan 1969.

More About Robert Ballou and Tamala Berry:
Marriage: 20 Jul 1996

Children of Tamala Berry and Paul Bailey are:

i. Timothy Adam[9] Bailey, b. 12 Dec 1980.
ii. Priscilla Joy Bailey, b. 20 Dec 1984, Medina, Ohio; m. Christopher Allen Sigler, 15 May 2004; b. 08 Jun 1972.

More About CHRISTOPHER SIGLER and PRISCILLA BAILEY:
Marriage: 15 May 2004

iii. JUSTINE NICOLE BAILEY, b. 16 Dec 1986.
iv. ANDREW PAUL BAILEY, b. 08 Sep 1989.

98. STEPHANIE RENEE[8] BERRY *(DAVID PAUL[7], LORETTA MATTIE[6] TEGTMEIER, WILLIAM CARL[5], JOHANN HEINRICH[4], JOHANN FRIEDRICH[3], UNKNOWN[2], UNKNOWN UNKNOWN[1])* was born 07 Mar 1969. She married VONDON TIMOTHY ESTEP 09 Apr 1988. He was born 13 Jun 1960.

More About VONDON ESTEP and STEPHANIE BERRY:
Marriage: 09 Apr 1988

Children of STEPHANIE BERRY and VONDON ESTEP are:
i. VONDON TIMOTHY[9] ESTEP II, b. 16 Mar 1993.
ii. TRISTAN SAMUEL ESTEP, b. 13 Dec 2000.

99. JEFFREY[8] BARR *(SHIRLEY ANN[7] TAYLOR, ALICE HENRIETTA[6] TEGTMEIER, WILLIAM CARL[5], JOHANN HEINRICH[4], JOHANN FRIEDRICH[3], UNKNOWN[2], UNKNOWN UNKNOWN[1])* was born 03 Dec 1963 in Zanesville, Ohio. He married M. CHRISTINA SIDWELL 20 Feb 1993 in Columbus, Ohio.

Notes for JEFFREY BARR:
Surgery while yet an infant.

Stephanie Berry-Estep
circ 2004

Notes for M. Christina Sidwell:
Sister died of Leukemia 2001.

More About Jeffrey Barr and M. Sidwell:
Marriage: 20 Feb 1993, Columbus, Ohio

Children of Jeffrey Barr and M. Sidwell are:

i. Blake[9] Barr, b. 04 Jul 1996.

ii. Blair Barr, b. 14 Feb 2001.

100. Kathy Anne[8] Barr *(Shirley Ann[7] Taylor, Alice Henrietta[6] Tegtmeier, William Carl[5], Johann Heinrich[4], Johann Friedrich[3], Unknown[2], Unknown Unknown[1])* was born 04 Dec 1965 in Zanesville, OH. She married Richard Skillman 03 Jan 1998 in Grace Lutheran, Thornville, OH, son of Leroy Skillman and Betty.

Wedding invitation: reception following ceremony at Elks lodge in Newark. Planned honeymoon on voyage from Miami, Florida. Invited everyone to join them a year in advance so everyone could plan on joining festivities.

Kathy was named after her mother's roomate in college.

More About Richard Skillman and Kathy Barr:
Marriage: 03 Jan 1998, Grace Lutheran, Thornville, OH
Kathy was named after her mother's friend in college, Kathy Boebel.

Child of Kathy Barr and Richard Skillman is:

i. Spencer[8] Skillman, b. October 4, 1997.

101. Angela Lynn[8] Barr *(Shirley Ann[7] Taylor, Alice Henrietta[6] Tegtmeier, William Carl[5], Johann Heinrich[4], Johann Friedrich[3], Unknown[2], Unknown Unknown[1])* was born 07 Oct 1969 in Zainesville, Ohio. She married Alan Gresh.

Notes for Angela Lynn Barr:
Intestinal problems. Surgery while still an infant.
Divorced.

Angela Barr Gresh,
Alec and Allison

Richard and Kathy Barr Skillman
Spencer and Keeli

Children of ANGELA BARR and ALAN GRESH are:

i. ALLISON NICOLE[9] GRESH, b. 27 Jul 2001.

ii. ALEC CONNER GRESH, b. 18 Jun 2004.

102. CHRISTINE JEAN[8] TAYLOR *(EDWARD WILLIAM[7], ALICE HENRIETTA[6] TEGTMEIER, WILLIAM CARL[5], JOHANN HEINRICH[4], JOHANN FRIEDRICH[3], UNKNOWN[2], UNKNOWN UNKNOWN[1])* was born Nov 1974. She married BRIAN LEE SLONE 18 Jul 1998 in Christ the King Lutheran, Twinsburg, OH.

More About BRIAN SLONE and CHRISTINE TAYLOR:
Marriage: 18 Jul 1998, Christ the King Lutheran, Twinsburg, OH

Children of CHRISTINE TAYLOR and BRIAN SLONE are:
i. ABIGAIL[9] SLONE, b. 1997.
ii. VICTORIA SLONE, b. 2002.

103. TOM[8] TRUMAN *(JOAN CHARLOTTE[7] TEGTMEIER, HENRY ADOLPH[6], WILLIAM CARL[5], JOHANN HEINRICH[4], JOHANN FRIEDRICH[3], UNKNOWN[2], UNKNOWN UNKNOWN[1])* was born 14 Sep 1972.

Children of TOM TRUMAN are:
i. GRACE[9] TRUMAN.
ii. ALEX TRUMAN.
iii. ABIGAIL TRUMAN.
iv. JONATHAN TRUMAN.

104. JACOB[8] TRUMAN *(JOAN CHARLOTTE[7] TEGTMEIER, HENRY ADOLPH[6], WILLIAM CARL[5], JOHANN HEINRICH[4], JOHANN FRIEDRICH[3], UNKNOWN[2], UNKNOWN UNKNOWN[1])* was born 13 Sep 1974. He married MAGGIE.

Children of JACOB TRUMAN and MAGGIE are:
i. JACOB[9] TRUMAN.
ii. PAIGE TRUMAN.
iii. KAITLYN TRUMAN.

105. JAMIE[8] TEGTMEIER *(PAUL[7], HENRY ADOLPH[6], WILLIAM CARL[5], JOHANN HEINRICH[4], JOHANN FRIEDRICH[3], UNKNOWN[2], UNKNOWN UNKNOWN[1])* was born 25 Apr 1975. She married RICHARD HARTLEY.

Child of JAMIE TEGTMEIER and RICHARD HARTLEY is:
i. THADDEUS[9] HARTLEY.

106. JEREMY[8] TEGTMEIER *(PAUL[7], HENRY ADOLPH[6], WILLIAM CARL[5], JOHANN HEINRICH[4], JOHANN FRIEDRICH[3], UNKNOWN[2], UNKNOWN UNKNOWN[1])* was born 30 Mar 1976. He married TIFFANY SINDERYELD.

Children of JEREMY TEGTMEIER and TIFFANY SINDERYELD are:
118. i. Angel a[9] Tegt meier.
ii. MATTHEW TEGTMEIER, m. ALICE.

107. SHAWN MICHAEL[8] FENTON *(LINDA JEAN[7] TEGTMEIER, WILLIAM EDWARD[6], WILLIAM CARL[5], JOHANN HEINRICH[4], JOHANN FRIEDRICH[3], UNKNOWN[2], UNKNOWN UNKNOWN[1])* was born 19 Jan 1968 in Columbus, OH. He married SHARON ANN MYERS 19 Dec 1992 in Germantown, OH, daughter of ROBERT MYERS and CAROL ASKINS. She was born 30 Apr 1969 in Dayton, OH.

More About SHAWN FENTON and SHARON MYERS:
Marriage: 19 Dec 1992, Germantown, OH

Children of SHAWN FENTON and SHARON MYERS are:
i. AMANDA MICHELLE[9] FENTON, b. 04 Jan 2001, Dayton, OH.

Notes for AMANDA MICHELLE FENTON:
Christened 27 May 2001, Germantown, OH

ii. RACHEL ELIZABETH FENTON, b. 21 Mar 2004, Kettering, OH.

108. AMY KRISTA[8] FENTON *(LINDA JEAN[7] TEGTMEIER, WILLIAM EDWARD[6], WILLIAM CARL[5], JOHANN HEINRICH[4], JOHANN FRIEDRICH[3], UNKNOWN[2], UNKNOWN UNKNOWN[1])* was born 15 May 1971 in Pittsburgh, PA. She married PAUL DAVID KENNEDY 10 Sep 1994 in Columbus, OH, son of JOHN KENNEDY and EILEEN JOHNSON. He was born 02 Oct 1970.

More About PAUL KENNEDY and AMY FENTON:
Marriage: 10 Sep 1994, Columbus, OH

Child of AMY FENTON and PAUL KENNEDY is:
i. JACK WILLIAM[9] KENNEDY, b. 05 Jan 2003, Mt. Carmel West Hosp'l, Columbus, OH.

Amy Fenton, Paul Kennedy holding Jack Kennedy, Shawn Fenton holding Amanda Fenton, Sharon Meier Fenton holding the baby , Rachel Fenton.

109. MOLLY MARIE[8] TEGTMEIER *(JAMES HERMAN[7], HAROLD WILLIAM[6], WILLIAM CARL[5], JOHANN HEINRICH[4], JOHANN FRIEDRICH[3], UNKNOWN[2], UNKNOWN UNKNOWN[1])* was born 24 May 1971. She married BRAD STULL. He was born ABT 1971.

Children of MOLLY TEGTMEIER and BRAD STULL are:

i. KATIE MARIE[9] STULL, b. 09 Jun 1999.

ii. RILEY ANN STULL, b. 06 Jun 2003.

110. RANDY JAMES[8] TEGTMEIER *(JAMES HERMAN[7], HAROLD WILLIAM[6], WILLIAM CARL[5], JOHANN HEINRICH[4], JOHANN FRIEDRICH[3], UNKNOWN[2], UNKNOWN UNKNOWN[1])* was born 24 Mar 1975. He married HEATHER EUBANKS 07 Jul 1998.

More About RANDY TEGTMEIER and HEATHER EUBANKS:
Marriage: 07 Jul 1998

Children of Randy Tegtmeier and Heather Eubanks are:

i. Cody James[9] Tegtmeier, b. 10 Jul 2000.

ii. Brock Gilbert Tegtmeier, b. 17 Jun 2002.

111. William[8] Kramer *(Barbara Lucille7 Tegtmeier, Harold William6, William Carl5, Johann Heinrich4, Johann Friedrich3, Unknown2, Unknown Unknown[1])* was born 05 Jan 1974. He married Erin 20 Jun 1997. She was born ABT 1974.

More About William Kramer and Erin:
Marriage: 20 Jun 1997

Children of William Kramer and Erin are:

i. Madeline[9] Kramer, b. 16 Jan 1999.

ii. Grant Kramer, b. 10 Oct 2001.

Generation No. 7

112. Katherine Kramer[9] Simmons *(Linda Christine[8] Meier, Lester Bernard[7], Almeta Bertha Christine[6] Ahleman, Hulda Louise Maria[5] Tegtmeier, Johann Heinrich[4], Johann Friedrich[3], Unknown[2], Unknown Unknown[1])* was born 15 Jun 1970 in Bowling Green, OH. She married Steven Scott Kirsch 03 Sep 1991. He was born 28 Jan 1970 in South Bend, IN.

More About Steven Kirsch and Katherine Simmons:
Marriage: 03 Sep 1991

Child of Katherine Simmons and Steven Kirsch is:

i. Brian Scott[10] Kirsch, b. 04 Mar 1994, Beaufort, NC.

113. Sarah Jane[9] Simmons *(Linda Christine[8] Meier, Lester Bernard[7], Almeta Bertha Christine[6] Ahleman, Hulda Louise Maria[5] Tegtmeier, Johann Heinrich[4], Johann Friedrich[3], Unknown[2], Unknown Unknown[1])* was born 12 Aug 1973 in Toledo, OH. She married Michael Raymond Fishbaugh 14 Sep 1996. He was born 12 Feb 1971 in Toledo, OH.

More About MICHAEL FISHBAUGH and SARAH SIMMONS:
Marriage: 14 Sep 1996

Children of SARAH SIMMONS and MICHAEL FISHBAUGH are:

- i. KASEY JANE[10] FISHBAUGH, b. 23 Nov 1998, Columbus, Ohio.
- ii. JACK MICHAEL FISHBAUGH, b. 17 Jul 2000, Maumee, Ohio.
- iii. ALLISON JANE FISHBAUGH, b. 17 Jul 2003, Toledo, Ohio.

114. JOSHUA NOEL THOMAS[9] STAMPER *(EILEEN KAY[8] MEIER, LESTER BERNARD[7], ALMETA BERTHA CHRISTINE[6] AHLEMAN, HULDA LOUISE MARIA[5] TEGTMEIER, JOHANN HEINRICH[4], JOHANN FRIEDRICH[3], UNKNOWN[2], UNKNOWN UNKNOWN[1])* was born 27 Sep 1972 in Denver, CO. He married KORY LEA BEHNY 05 Aug 1995. She was born 01 Mar 1973 in Wheat Ridge, CO.

More About JOSHUA STAMPER and KORY BEHNY:
Marriage: 05 Aug 1995

Children of JOSHUA STAMPER and KORY BEHNY are:

- i. ANSA RACHEL[10] STAMPER, b. 11 Jun 1996, N. Hampton, MA.
- ii. HILJA KAY STAMPER, b. 11 Apr 1999, Hartford, CT.

115. BENJAMIN JACOB[9] STAMPER *(EILEEN KAY[8] MEIER, LESTER BERNARD[7], ALMETA BERTHA CHRISTINE[6] AHLEMAN, HULDA LOUISE MARIA[5] TEGTMEIER, JOHANN HEINRICH[4], JOHANN FRIEDRICH[3], UNKNOWN[2], UNKNOWN UNKNOWN[1])* was born 11 Apr 1975 in Denver, CO. He married VESPER IVY PORTER. She was born 12 Jan 1977 in Nuremburg, Germany.

Children of BENJAMIN STAMPER and VESPER PORTER are:

- i. ALBAN JACK COMFORT[10] STAMPER, b. 03 Feb 2003, West Orange, NJ.
- ii. ARDEN LILLE EVANGELINE STAMPER, b. 03 Oct 2005, West Orange, NJ.

116. Andrew Scott[9] Thompson *(Cynthia Ann[8] Meier, Lester Bernard[7], Almeta Bertha Christine[6] Ahleman, Hulda Louise Maria[5] Tegtmeier, Johann Heinrich[4], Johann Friedrich[3], Unknown[2], Unknown Unknown[1])* was born 07 Aug 1977 in Denver, CO. He married Erin Christine Geyser ABT 2005. She was born 24 Apr 1980 in Fairfield, CA.

More About Andrew Thompson and Erin Geyser:
Marriage: ABT 2005

Child of Andrew Thompson and Erin Geyser is:

i. Trevor Daniel[10] Thompson, b. 19 Aug 2006, Colorado Springs, CO.

117. Ian Robert[9] Thompson *(Cynthia Ann[8] Meier, Lester Bernard[7], Almeta Bertha Christine[6] Ahleman, Hulda Louise Maria[5] Tegtmeier, Johann Heinrich[4], Johann Friedrich[3], Unknown[2], Unknown Unknown[1])* was born 05 Oct 1979 in Denver, CO. He married Kristi Lea Sharp. She was born 12 Sep 1980 in Tuscon, AZ.

Child of Ian Thompson and Kristi Sharp is:

i. Keira Ashlea[10] Thompson, b. 27 Jul 2006, Denver, CO.

118. Angela[9] Tegtmeier *(Jeremy[8], Paul[7], Henry Adolph[6], William Carl[5], Johann Heinrich[4], Johann Friedrich[3], Unknown[2], Unknown Unknown[1])* She married Adam Rice.

Children of Angela Tegtmeier and Adam Rice are:

i. Jonah[10] Rice.
ii. Beth Rice.
iii. Amelia Grace Rice.

The Tegtmeier Reunion 2004 Back Row: Dave Berry, Shirley Taylor, Dan Tegtmeier, Miriam Tegtmeier, Linda Fenton, Jim Tegtmeier, Doug Tegtmeier, Peter Hindrichs; standing in front of back row: Joan Truman, Don Tegtmeier, Deb Miller; Kneeling in front of them: Paul Tegtmeier, Terry Tegtmeier, Barbara Kramer; Front Row: Karen Boyer, Ed Taylor, Joel Tegtmeier, Tim Tegtmeier and David Tegtmeier. *Courtesy photo*

Tegtmeier siblings circ. 1994
Loretta, Alice Bill, Dick and Lois.

Alice Taylor and Alice Smith Circ 2000.

Sisters Alice Taylor and Lois Hinrichs
Circ 2004

Stephanie Berry-Estep and her
Grandmother, Loretta Tegtmeier Berry.

Descendants of Joachim Christian Johann Papenhagen

1 Joachim Christian Johann Papenhagen b: 01 May 1836 in Mechlenburg, Germany d: 28 Dec 1906 in Ottowa Lake, Monroe Co, MI, son of Heinrich Papnehagen and Christina Nevers.
+Wilhelmina Marie Johanna Westendorf b: 13 May 1849 in Germany d: 05 Feb 1935 in Ottowa Lake, Monroe Co, MI, daughter of Daniel Johann Christian Westendorf.
... 2 Franz Wilhelm Johann Papenhagen b: 24 Nov 1872 in Germany d: 04 Oct 1931 in Defiance, Ohio
...... +Winifred Klinger b: 26 Sep 1872 in Ohio d: 02 Mar 1954
...... 3 Frank W. Papenhagen b: 20 Apr 1899 in Ohio d: Apr 1983 in Ft. Meyers, Beach Florida
.... +Marion D. b: 16 Jan 1901 in New York d: Sep 1990
.... 4 Boy Papenhagen b: ABT 1921
.... 4 Girl Papenhagen b: ABT 1923
...... 3 Edna Papenhagen b: ABT 1893 in Ohio
.... +Robert W. Emery b: ABT 1893 in Ohio
.... 4 Carolyn K. Emery b: ABT 1927 in Ohio
.... 4 Helen Edwards Emery b: ABT 1926 in Ohio
... 2 Marie Henriette Magdalene Guste Papenhagen b: 15 Jan 1879 in Germany d: 20 Oct 1959 in Toledo, Lucas, Ohio
...... +Albert W. Doering b: 12 Jan 1877 in Ohio d: 27 Jan 1952 in Toledo, Lucas, Ohio
...... 3 Helen I. Doering b: 02 Nov 1903 in Toledo, Ohio
.... +Elmer Swartz b: ABT 1902
.... 4 Boy Swartz b: ABT 1923
.... 4 Joanne Swartz b: ABT 1924
.... +Noppe
...... 3 Marie Doering b: 12 Dec 1904 in Toledo, Ohio d: 08 Jun 1999 in Toledo, Ohio
.... +Harold Ersig b: 09 Aug 1893 in St. Mary's, Ohio d: 04 Jan 1970 in Lucas Co, Ohio
.... 4 Dianne Ersig b: ABT 1925
.... 4 Dean Ersig b: ABT 1926

...... 3 Gertrude Doering b: 21 Jan 1907 in Toledo, Ohio d: 04 Feb 1997 in Whitehall, Trempealeau, Wisconsin
.... +Fred Mattka b: 28 Nov 1906 in Wisconsin d: 05 Feb 1988 in Western Springs, Cook, Illinois
.... 4 Meredith Mattka b: ABT 1940
.... 4 Billy Mattka b: 01 Feb 1941 d: 02 Apr 2004
.... 4 Jerry Mattka b: ABT 1943
...... 3 Thelma Doering b: ABT 1916 in Ohio
.... +Leonard Jacobs
.... 4 Elaine Jacobs
.... 4 Mary Jacobs
... 2 Herman Friedrick Johann Wilhelm Papenhagen b: 15 Jan 1875 in Germany d: 30 Sep 1952 in Toledo, Lucas, Ohio
...... +Louise H. Freeman b: 07 Jul 1876 in Ohio d: 18 Dec 1943
...... 3 Marie Papenhagen b: Aug 1899 in Ohio
.... +Jerry Ahrens b: ABT 1899
...... 3 Eloise Papenhagen b: ABT 1916 in Ohio
.... +Charles Quinn b: 09 Nov 1909 d: 19 Nov 1967
.... 4 Adopted Boy Quinn b: ABT 1936
...... 3 Arnold Papenhagen b: 11 Mar 1901 in Ohio d: 03 Feb 1982 in Perrysburg, Wood, Ohio
.... +Helen b: ABT 1901
.... 4 Ted Papenhagen b: ABT 1921
... 2 Paul Ludwig Friedrich Christian Papenhagen b: 15 Mar 1877 in Germany d: 21 Nov 1950 in Whiteford, Monroe, Michigan
...... +Emma Elg b: 28 Jun 1877 in Michigan d: 18 Nov 1943 in Whiteford, Monroe, Michigan
...... 3 Ethel S. Papenhagen b: 27 Oct 1901 in Michigan d: 29 Jan 1981 in Norvell, Jackson, Michigan
.... +Walter H. Komsteller b: 07 Dec 1901 in Monroe, Michigan d: 29 Oct 1973 in Norvell,Jackson, Michigan
.... 4 Loann Clare Komsteller b: 10 Dec 1932 in Los Angeles, CA
.... +Eugene B. Fairweather b: 08 Jun 1932
.............5 Michael B. Fairweather b: 23 Nov 1954
.... +Patty MaCrorie b: 02 Mar 1956
................6 Renee M. Fairweather b: 28 Aug 1979
................6 Rachel Fairweather b: 24 Dec 1982
................6 Randi M. Fairweather b: 08 Apr 1988
................6 Rikki L. Fairweather b: 15 May 1989
.............5 Linda Lee Fairweather b: 01 Jun 1956
.... +David Arnold b: ABT 1956
................6 Michele Lee Arnold b: 23 Oct 1978

................6 Bradley John Arnold b: 27 Mar 1984
..................*2nd Husband of Linda Lee Fairweather:
..................+Don Sharp b: ABT 1956
............5 Jean Marie Fairweather b: 11 Oct 1960
................+David West
................*2nd Husband of Jean Marie Fairweather:
................+Brian Miller
................*3rd Husband of Jean Marie Fairweather:
................+Doug Alas
................6 Candace Clare Fairweather Scully Alas b: 23 Nov 1985
................6 Emilio Mauricio Fairweather Alas Alas b: 06 Nov 1991
................6 James Alexander Alas b: 08 Oct 1993
.... 4 Neal Walter Komsteller b: 07 Dec 1934 in Streator, Illinois
............+Donna Jean Hayes b: 11 Jan 1933 d: 11 Jan 1996
............5 Kimberly Ann Komsteller b: 12 Dec 1955
................+Robert Schultz b: 28 Jul 1951
................6 Megan Lee Schultz b: 28 Jan 1975 d: 1975
................6 Misty Lynn Schultz b: 14 Sep 1977
..................+Allan B. Smith
..................7 Samantha Kay Smith b: 11 Feb 2001
..................7 Haley Ann Smith b: 03 Jul 2003
................6 Corey Robert Schultz b: 16 Dec 1981
................6 Casey Schultz b: 14 May 1985
............5 Jill Marie Komsteller b: 23 Jul 1959
................+Vern Proud
................*2nd Husband of Jill Marie Komsteller:
................+Marvin Quick b: 19 Mar 1955
................6 Lee Marvin Quick b: 11 Jul 1978
..................+Jennifer
..................*2nd Wife of Lee Marvin Quick:
..................+Lucy
..................7 Donavan Lee Quick b: Jan 2003
..................7 Breann Quick b: 2004
................6 Amber Marie Quick b: 18 May 1982
..................+Shawn Smith
................6 Ashley Lynn Quick b: 02 Oct 1985
..................7 Girl Quick b: Feb 2005
............5 Jeff Neal Komsteller b: 05 Jun 1961
................+Debbie Hall Heider b: 02 Jan 1956
................6 Michael Komsteller b: 16 May 1987
..................*2nd Wife of Neal Walter Komsteller:
..................+Mary Araujo Simons b: 20 Apr 1939

.... 4 Jane Lee Komsteller b: 18 Dec 1937 in Union City
.............+Donald D. Strange b: 12 Jun 1936
.............5 Melinda Lee Strange b: 28 Jan 1961 d: 28 Oct 1961
.............5 Bradley John Strange b: 18 Feb 1962
................+Terri Carlton b: 01 May 1964
................6 Lyndi Elizabeth Strange b: 03 Mar 1994
.............5 Brenda Lee Strange b: 12 Apr 1964
................+Jeff B. Potter b: 18 Aug 1960
................6 Jeff Dane Potter b: 05 Sep 1984
................6 Katie Lee Potter b: 01 Jul 1991
.............5 Lori Ann Strange b: 07 Jan 1969
................+Timothy Lyell b: 23 Jul 1968
................6 Brandon Baird Lyell b: 01 Jul 1996
................6 Brittany Lee Lyell b: 23 Jul 1998
...... 3 Norman Henry Papenhagen b: 05 May 1907 in Michigan d: 06 May 1995 in Michigan
.... +Doris Laverne Viers b: 15 Nov 1912
.... 4 Pauline Papenhagen b: 01 Sep 1933
.............+Marvin Fink
.............*2nd Husband of Pauline Papenhagen:
.............+Roger Wessendorf
.............5 Barbara Wessendorf b: 15 Nov 1952
................+Rex Wilcox
................6 Beth Marie Wilcox b: 04 May 1978
...................+Nate Garrelts
................6 Eva Brittany Wilcox b: 20 Feb 1988
.............5 Robert Wessendorf b: 02 Jul 1957
................+Sherry DeBoer
................*2nd Wife of Robert Wessendorf:
................+Jana Murphy
................*3rd Wife of Robert Wessendorf:
................+Janice DeFrancisco b: 30 Jun 1954
................6 Brandie Lynn Wessendorf b: 26 Nov 1974
...................+Robert Matheson
................6 Jennie Lee Wessendorf b: 02 Apr 1978
.............5 Bruce Wessendorf b: 21 Sep 1964
................*3rd Husband of Pauline Papenhagen:
................+Jim Leogrande
.... 4 Gerald Papenhagen b: 27 Nov 1936 d: 14 Dec 1951
.... 4 Gail Papenhagen b: ABT 1935
.............+Rita b: ABT 1935
.............5 Darlene Papenhagen b: ABT 1955
.............5 Kelly Papenhagen b: ABT 1957

. . . . 4 Susan Papenhagen b: ABT 1937
. . . .+Terri Aldrich b: ABT 1937
. . . . .5 Daniel Aldrich b: ABT 1957
. . . . .5 Tara Aldrich b: ABT 1960
. . . . *2nd Wife of Norman Henry Papenhagen:
. . . . +Angie b: 13 Jan
. . . . *3rd Wife of Norman Henry Papenhagen:
. . . . +Edna d: Sep 2004
. . . . . . 3 Doris Papenhagen b: 23 Jul 1914 in Ottawa Lake, Michigan
. . . . +Howard Never b: 15 Feb 1913 in Lucas, Toledo, Ohio d: 28 Apr 2000 in Sylvania, Lucas, Ohio
. . . . 4 Dathel Never b: 26 Nov 1938
. . . .+Robert Hilborn b: 18 Oct 1941
. . . . .5 Mark Robert Hilborn b: 01 Sep 1963
. . . . +Sandra b: ABT 1963
. . . . 6 Timothy Mark Hilborn b: 11 Apr 1989 in Minnesota
. . . . 6 Jenna Michelle Hilborn b: 28 Nov 1990 in Minnesota
. . . . .5 Scott Alan Hilborn b: 20 Nov 1965
. . . . +Shannon b: ABT 1965
. . . . 6 Kristen Eileen Hilborn b: 27 Feb 1993 in Brandon, Fl
. . . . 6 Trevor David Hilborn b: 17 Jun 1996 in Orlando, Fl
. . . . 6 Sheriana Genevieve Hilborn b: 15 May 1998 in Orlando, Fl
. . . . .5 Michael David Hilborn b: 16 Nov 1966
. . . . +Terri Sue Crunk b: 07 Aug 1967 in Woodburn, IN
. . . . *2nd Wife of Michael David Hilborn:
. . . . +Tracey Anne Clark b: 29 Aug 1968 in Fort Wayne, IN
. . . . 6 Aubrey Rachelle Hilborn b: 10 Sep 1998 in Ft. Wayne, IN
. . . . 4 Marian Bethany Never b: 14 Jul 1945
. . . .+Bill Decator
. . . . .5 [1] John H. Decator b: 05 Oct
. . . . +[2] Tamera b: ABT 1965
. . . . 6 Madison Decator b: 05 Jan 1994
. . . . 6 Marina Decator b: 19 Apr 1995
. . . . *2nd Wife of [1] John H. Decator:
. . . . +[3] Renee
. . . . 6 Brendan W. Decator b: 07 Jun 2005
. . . . .5 [4] Jonelle Decator b: 11 Oct
. . . . +[5] Billy Montes b: ABT 1965
. . . . 6 Alec Montes b: 09 Jul 1994
. . . . 6 Gabriel Montes b: 27 Dec 1995
. . . . *2nd Husband of Marian Bethany Never:
. . . . +Joseph Donofrio b: ABT 1945

.............5 [1] John H. Decator b: 05 Oct
................+[2] Tamera b: ABT 1965
................*2nd Wife of [1] John H. Decator:
................+[3] Renee
.............5 [4] Jonelle Decator b: 11 Oct
................+[5] Billy Montes b: ABT 1965
.... 4 Paul Grant Never b: 18 Nov 1941
.............+Joyce Philaum b: 17 Dec 1942
.............5 Keith Never b: 14 Jun 1965
.............5 Terri Never b: 03 May 1967
.............5 Laurie Never b: 19 Nov 1968
................+Greg Pieper b: 09 Feb 1960
................6 Alex Pieper b: 23 Mar 1992
.... 4 Rebecca Sue Never b: 12 Oct 1948
.............+George Carlson b: 30 Oct 1948
.............5 Todd Carlson b: ABT 1970
.............5 Lisa Carlson b: 26 Feb 1969
................+Tony Delong b: 13 Nov 1966
................6 Casey Delong b: 16 Jan 1989
................6 Samantha Delong b: 16 Jan 1989
.............5 Gina Carlson b: 15 Apr 1972
................+A. Jack Hooker
................*2nd Husband of Gina Carlson:
................+Paul Miller
.............5 Michael Carlson b: 20 Mar 1974
...... 3 Herbert Papenhagen b: 02 Nov 1908 in Michigan d: 05 Jul 1988 in Bradenton, Florida
.... +Linda Blome b: 20 Jun 1916
.... 4 David Herbert Papenhagen b: 12 Sep 1939
.............+Shirley Goetz b: ABT 1940
.............5 Dawn Papenhagen b: 29 Oct 1963
................+Joel Makzis b: ABT 1963
.............5 Christie Papenhagen b: 21 Jan 1967
................+Gary Childers b: ABT 1967
.............5 David Paul Papenhagen b: 22 Jun 1968
.... 4 Diann Papenhagen b: ABT 1940
.............+James Pavelka b: ABT 1940
.............5 Paula Pavelka b: ABT 1960
.............5 Steven Pavelka b: ABT 1962
.............5 Eric Pavelka b: ABT 1964
.... 4 Brian Papenhagen b: ABT 1942
.............+Vickie b: ABT 1943
.............5 Tracey Papenhagen b: ABT 1963

. . . . .5 Jodee Papenhagen b: ABT 1965
. . . . .5 Corey Papenhagen b: ABT 1966
. . . . *2nd Wife of Paul Ludwig Friedrich Christian Papenhagen:
. . . . +Inez Fowler b: 04 Apr 1889 d: 20 Mar 1945
. . . . *3rd Wife of Paul Ludwig Friedrich Christian Papenhagen:
. . . . +Mary Jacobs b: ABT 1889 d: 22 Mar 1964 in Toledo, Lucas, Ohio
. . . 2 Johanna Sophie Christine Friede Papenhagen b: 04 Dec 1880 in Germany d: Aft. 1930
. . . . . . +Charles W. Hacker b: ABT 1877 in Ohio d: 1944
. . . . . . 3 Harold Hacker b: ABT 1906 in Toledo, Ohio
. . . 2 Heinrich Conrad Jochen Papenhagen b: 20 Jan 1883 in Germany d: 05 Jan 1958 in Whiteford Twp., Monroe, Michigan
. . . . . . +Mattie Oelrich b: 19 Mar 1881 d: 30 Mar 1941
. . . . . . *2nd Wife of Heinrich Conrad Jochen Papenhagen:
. . . . . . +Ida b: in Michigan
. . . . . . *3rd Wife of Heinrich Conrad Jochen Papenhagen:
. . . . . . +Bertha
. . . 2 Bertha Henrietta Wilhelmine Papenhagen b: 16 Jun 1885 in Germany d: 07 Feb 1966 in Lucas Co, Ohio
. . . . . . +John C. Schumacher b: 27 Mar 1880 in Germany d: 05 Nov 1958 in Lucas Co., Ohio
. . . . . . 3 Elmer Schumacher b: 10 Jan 1912 in Michigan
. . . . +Eunice b: 09 Mar 1913 d: 05 Sep 1985
. . . . 4 Barbara Schumacher b: 09 Nov 1934
. . . . 4 James R. Schumacher b: 05 Sep 1945
. . . .+Karalene
. . . . .5 Laurie Schumacher
. . . . .5 Kenneth Schumacher
. . . . . . 3 Frank Schumacher b: ABT 1909 in Michigan
. . . . +Algie b: ABT 1909
. . . . 4 Larry Schumacher
. . . . 4 Tom Schumacher
. . . . 4 Cindy Schumacher
. . . . 4 Joan Schumacher
. . . . 4 John Jr. Schumacher
. . . . . . 3 Roy Schumacher b: 31 Jan 1921 in Michigan d: 12 Sep 1971
. . . . +Donna
. . . . 4 Richard Schumacher
. . . . 4 Robert Schumacher
. . . . 4 Susan Schumacher
. . . . 4 Ronald Schumacher
. . . . . . 3 Lydia Schumacher b: ABT 1920

. . . 2 Erna Henriette Sophie Papenhagen b: 10 Oct 1888 in Beubukow, Schwerinschen, Mecklenburg, Germany d: 30 Sep 1982 in Dickinson, Stark North Dakota
. . . . . . +William Carl Tegtmeier b: 15 May 1882 in Middleburg Twnshp, OH d: 10 Apr 1955 in Medina Twp., Medina, OH
. . . . . . 3 Loretta Mattie Tegtmeier b: 26 Aug 1911
. . . . +Paul Franklin Berry b: ABT 1908
. . . . 4 David Berry b: ABT 1940
. . . .+Beverly b: ABT 1940
. . . . .5 Wesley Berry b: ABT 1960
. . . . .5 Tammy Berry b: ABT 1962
. . . . .5 Stephanie Berry b: ABT 1965
. . . . +Mr. Estep
. . . . 4 Karen Berry b: ABT 1941
. . . .+Don Boyer b: ABT 1940
. . . . .5 Bryan Boyer b: ABT 1962 in Denver, CO
. . . . .5 Bradley Boyer b: ABT 1963 in Denver, CO
. . . . .5 Lisa Boyer b: ABT 1964 in Denver, CO
. . . . . . 3 Raymond Julius Tegtmeier b: 07 Dec 1912 in Brookpark, OH d: Sep 1982 in Wayne County, Ohio
. . . . +Laura Anna Minichbauer b: 01 Aug 1916 in Cleveland, Cuyahoga County, Ohio d: 10 Oct 1995 in Wayne County, Ohio
. . . . 4 Donna Mae Tegtmeier b: 01 Sep 1944
. . . .+William Schemrich b: ABT 1928
. . . . .5 Ronnie Schemrich b: ABT 1958
. . . . .5 Dale Schemrich b: ABT 1959
. . . . .5 Shawn Schemrich b: ABT 1960
. . . . 4 Sharon Lee Tegtmeier b: 04 Jan 1947
. . . .+Gary Erro b: ABT 1947
. . . . .5 Jody Ann Erro
. . . . .5 Amanda Marie Erro
. . . . 4 Daniel Howard Tegtmeier b: 23 Sep 1957
. . . .+Beth Ann Bougher b: 14 Jan 1959
. . . . .5 Ethan Daniel Tegtmeier b: 26 Jan 1990
. . . . .5 Sarah Christine Tegtmeier b: 16 May 1993
. . . . . . 3 Julia Wihelmina Tegtmeier b: 07 Oct 1914 in Brookpark, Cuyahoga Co., Ohio d: 02 Mar 1934 in Columbus, OH
. . . . . . 3 Alice Henrietta Tegtmeier b: 28 May 1916 in Brookpark, Ohio
. . . . +Edward William Taylor b: 01 Aug 1914 in New York d: 22 Jan 1967 in Jost Van Dyke, US Virgin Islands
. . . . 4 Shirley Ann Taylor b: 11 Oct 1941 in Scranton, PA
. . . .+Eugene Barr b: 13 Nov 1935 in West Virginia
. . . . .5 Jeffrey Barr b: 03 Dec 1963 in Zanesville, Ohio
. . . . +M. Christina Sidwell

. . . . 6 Blake Barr b: 04 Jul 1996
. . . . 6 Blair Barr b: 14 Feb 2001
. . . . 5 Kathy Anne Barr b: 04 Dec 1965 in Zanesville, OH
. . . . +Richard Skillman
. . . . 6 Spencer Skillman b: 04 Oct 1997
. . . . 5 Angela Lynn Barr b: 07 Oct 1969 in Zainesville, Ohio
. . . . +Alan Gresh
. . . . 6 Allison Nicole Gresh b: 27 Jul 2001
. . . . 6 Alec Conner Gresh b: 18 Jun 2004
. . . . 4 Edward William Taylor b: 11 Jan 1944 in Alden, NY
. . . . +Nancy Untezuber b: 03 May 1948
. . . . 5 Craig Edward Taylor b: 07 Sep 1962
. . . . +Debra "Cricket" Jones
. . . . 5 Christine Jean Taylor b: Nov 1974
. . . . +Brian Lee Slone
. . . . 6 Abigail Slone b: 1997
. . . . 6 Victoria Slone b: 2002
. . . . 4 James Robert Taylor b: 22 Mar 1949 in Berea, Ohio
. . . . +Margie Moore b: 01 May 1950 in Newfoundland, Canada
. . . . 5 Shane Edward Taylor b: 01 Aug 1978
. . . . 5 Chasta Taylor b: 21 Mar 1981
. . . . *2nd Wife of James Robert Taylor:
. . . . +Nancy
. . . . 4 Sandra Mina Taylor b: 17 Mar 1950 in Berea, Ohio
. . . . +Peter Graham Bell b: 29 Aug 1937 in Wauseon, Ohio
. . . . 5 Heather Lynne Bell b: 30 Sep 1984 in Sarasota, FL
. . . . 5 Joshua Taylor Bell b: 13 Oct 1986 in Miami, FL
. . . . *2nd Husband of Alice Henrietta Tegtmeier:
. . . . +John Goralsky b: in Coalport, PA d: in Cleveland, OH
. . . . . . 3 Henry Adolph Tegtmeier b: 19 Mar 1918 in Ohio d: 09 Dec 1992 in Fairfield Glade, TN
. . . . +Harriett Barendt b: 09 Jan 1923 in Cleveland, Cuyahoga Co., OH
. . . . 4 Miriam Ann Tegtmeier b: 08 Apr 1946
. . . . +Paul Camper b: ABT 1937
. . . . 5 Nicole Camper
. . . . 5 Nathan Camper
. . . . +Dianne
. . . . 4 Joan Charlotte Tegtmeier b: 07 Aug 1947
. . . . +Tom Truman b: 21 Jul 1946
. . . . 5 Tom Truman b: 14 Sep 1972
. . . . 6 Grace Truman
. . . . 6 Alex Truman
. . . . 6 Abigail Truman

................6 Jonathan Truman
.............5 Jacob Truman b: 13 Sep 1974
................+Maggie
................6 Jacob Truman
................6 Paige Truman
................6 Kaitlyn Truman
.............5 Ashley Truman b: 20 Apr 1976
................+Dan McMaster
.............5 David Truman b: 12 Sep 1978
................+Sara
.... 4 Paul Tegtmeier b: 03 Aug 1948
.............+Sandra Rice b: 19 Jul 1953
.............5 Jamie Tegtmeier b: 25 Apr 1975
................+Richard Hartley
................6 Thaddeus Hartley
.............5 Jeremy Tegtmeier b: 30 Mar 1976
................+Tiffany Sinderyeld
................6 Angela Tegtmeier
...................+Adam Rice
...................7 Jonah Rice
...................7 Beth Rice
...................7 Amelia Grace Rice
................6 Matthew Tegtmeier
...................+Alice
.............5 Jerrod Tegtmeier b: 22 Oct 1984
.... 4 Joel Tegtmeier b: 13 Aug 1959
.............+Tammie b: 30 Jul 1959
.............5 Angela Tegtmeier b: 19 Apr 1979
.............5 Matthew Tegtmeier b: 03 Feb 1981
.............5 Laken Tegtmeier
.............5 Logan Tegtmeier
...... 3 William Edward Tegtmeier b: 06 Mar 1920 in Brookpark, Ohio d: 24 Jul 2000 in Savanah, OH
.... +Lois Genvieve Westlund b: 31 Dec 1922 in Youngstown, Ohio
.... 4 Linda Jean Tegtmeier b: 24 Aug 1947 in Youngstown, OH, North Side Hospital
.............+Larry Gene Fenton b: 02 Mar 1947 in Mansfield, OH
.............5 Shawn Michael Fenton b: 19 Jan 1968 in Columbus, OH
................+Sharon Ann Myers b: 30 Apr 1969 in Dayton, OH
................6 Amanda Michelle Fenton b: 04 Jan 2001 in Dayton, OH
................6 Rachel Elizabeth Fenton b: 21 Mar 2004 in Kettering, OH
.............5 Amy Krista Fenton b: 15 May 1971 in Pittsburgh, PA
................+Paul David Kennedy b: ABT 1970

................6 Jack William Kennedy b: 05 Jan 2003 in Mt. Carmel West Hosp'l, Columbus, OH
.... 4 Terry Tegtmeier b: ABT 1949
.... 4 Timothy Tegtmeier b: 15 Sep 1955
.............+Pam Honaker
.............5 Christine Tegtmeier
.............5 Jonathan Tegtmeier
.... 4 Todd Alan Tegtmeier b: 19 Feb 1962
.............+Wendy Floyd
...... 3 Harold William Tegtmeier b: 02 Mar 1921 in Brookpark, Ohio d: 18 May 2003 in West Salem, Wayne, Ohio
.... +Lucille Clarissa Herman b: 12 Sep 1922 in Hermanville, Creston, Ohio
.... 4 James Herman Tegtmeier b: 14 Feb 1945 in Lodi Hospital, near Wooster, Ohio
.............+Jeanne Marie Gresser b: ABT 1945
.............5 Molly Marie Tegtmeier b: 24 May 1971
................+Brad Stull b: ABT 1971
................6 Katie Marie Stull b: 09 Jun 1999
................6 Riley Ann Stull b: 06 Jun 2003
.............5 Randy James Tegtmeier b: 24 Mar 1975
................+Heather Eubanks
................6 Cody James Tegtmeier b: 10 Jul 2000
................6 Brock Gilbert Tegtmeier b: 17 Jun 2002
.... 4 Donald Phillip Tegtmeier b: 14 Nov 1948 in Lodi Hospital, near Wooster, Ohio
.............+Neva Nestor b: ABT 1948
.............5 Adam Donald Tegtmeier b: 17 Jun 1986
.............5 Heidi Rose Tegtmeier b: 12 Apr 1989
.... 4 Barbara Lucille Tegtmeier b: 15 Dec 1952 in Lodi Hospital, near Wooster, Ohio
.............+James Kramer b: 06 Jun 1950
.............5 William Kramer b: 05 Jan 1974
................+Erin b: ABT 1974
................6 Madeline Kramer b: 16 Jan 1999
................6 Grant Kramer b: 10 Oct 2001
.............5 Matthew James Kramer b: 29 Sep 1982
.... 4 David Harold Tegtmeier b: 15 Sep 1954 in Lodi Hospital, near Wooster, Ohio
.............+Rita Kay Kamp b: 25 Feb 1959 in Ashland, OH
.............5 Luke David Tegtmeier b: 11 May 1983
.............5 Jill Arlene Tegtmeier b: 29 Oct 1985
.............5 Mark David Tegtmeier b: 25 Apr 1990

...... 3 Richard Elmer Tegtmeier b: 03 Jan 1924 in Berea,Cuyahoga Co.OH d: 17 Oct 1995 in Crossville, TN
.... +Sandy Louise Kestner b: 26 Sep 1933 in Ashland, Ashland Co., OH
.... 4 Douglas Richard Tegtmeier b: 06 Dec 1952 in Wooster, Montgomery Co., OH
.............+Suzanne Gulyas b: 09 Jan 1954 in Dayton, OH
.............5 Jeff Tegtmeier b: 22 Dec 1982 in Columbus, Ohio
.............5 Ryan Tegtmeier b: 11 Oct 1984 in Columbus, Ohio
.... 4 Debra Louise Tegtmeier b: 09 Jan 1955 in Wooster, Wayne Co. OH
.............+Terry Miller b: 05 Nov 1952
.............5 Jeremiah Miller b: 20 Jun 1978
.............5 Jonathan Miller b: 24 Aug 1979
................+Rebekah Wright
.... 4 Dean Edward Tegtmeier b: 02 Mar 1957 in Ashland, Ashland Co., OH
.............+Michele Haynes b: 15 Aug 1957 in Toronto, Ohio
.............5 Celeste Tegtmeier b: ABT 1982
.............5 Shawn Tegtmeier b: ABT 1984
................+Michelle
.............5 Sara Tegtmeier b: ABT 1986
... 2 Walter Franklin Papenhagen b: 01 Jun 1892 in Toledo, Lucas, Ohio d: 13 Aug 1944
...... +Elsie Caroline Koester b: 16 May 1893 in Michigan d: 12 May 1982 in Lenawee, Michigan
...... 3 Mildred Wilfred Papenhagen b: ABT 1914 in Michigan
...... 3 Esther Edna Marie Papenhagen b: 07 Sep 1917 in Michigan
.... +Raymond Fredrick Seagert b: 02 May 1913 d: 19 Jul 1981
.... 4 Diana June Seagert b: 12 Jun 1939
.............+Harry BUD Rudolph Pape, Jr. b: 31 Mar 1937
.............5 Nancy Marie Pape b: 24 Jul 1962
................+Dennis Miles Findley b: 16 Apr 1961
................6 Tara Marie Findley b: 29 Sep 1989
................6 Aaron Miles Findley b: 24 Mar 1992
.............5 Dale Rudolph Pape b: 19 Aug 1964
................+Dawn Michele Frazier b: 22 Jan 1968
.............5 Gerald Raymond Pape b: 07 Nov 1967
................+Tammy Lynn (Brock) Loewe b: 07 Jul 1969
................6 Allison Nicole Pape b: 11 Jun 1993
.............5 Yvonne Pearl Pape b: 15 Nov 1975
.... 4 Richard Ray Seagert b: 09 Apr 1943
.............+Donna Eileen Glasgow b: 14 Apr 1944
.............5 Ryan Ray Seagert b: 22 Mar 1972
.............5 Rory Kyle Seagert b: 02 Apr 1974
.............5 Lindsay Lynette Seagert b: 29 Apr 1980

. . . . 4 Linda Marie Seagert b: 04 Jul 1952
. . . .+Richard Doyle Ries b: 01 Apr 1952
. . . . .5 Rachel Erin Ries b: 15 Feb 1976
. . . . .5 Sarah Marie Ries b: 12 Nov 1983
. . . . .5 Emily Diana Ries b: 29 Dec 1987
. . . . . . 3 Erna Ethel Elizabeth Papenhagen b: 02 Dec 1919 in Michigan
. . . . +Arthur William Brenke, Sr. b: 04 Feb 1921
. . . . 4 Arthur Walter Jr. Brenke b: 04 Jul 1944
. . . .+Diana Jean Rittner b: 27 Jan 1945
. . . . .5 Holly Ann Brenke b: 02 Jan 1966
. . . .+Gregory Allen Butts b: 17 May 1965
. . . . .6 Aaron Gregory Butts b: 03 Mar 1992
. . . . .6 Emily Elizabeth Butts b: 05 May 1995
. . . . .5 Christina Marie Brenke b: 23 May 1968 d: 24 May 1968
. . . . .5 Heather Ann Brenke b: 05 Jun 1965
. . . . 4 Sharon Sue Brenke b: 03 Nov 1946
. . . .+Bruce James Wilkes b: 06 Oct 1947
. . . . .5 Gregg James Wilkes b: 06 Sep 1971
. . . . .5 Teresa Sue Wilkes b: 28 Apr 1976
. . . . 4 Brenda Ann Brenke b: 30 Aug 1949
. . . .+Thomas Alan DeBacker b: ABT 1949
. . . . .5 [6] Christopher Alan DeBacker b: 25 Dec 1972
. . . . .5 [7] Amy Michelle DeBacker b: 09 Feb 1977
. . . .*2nd Husband of Brenda Ann Brenke:
. . . .+Michael Jan Andrix b: ABT 1947
. . . . .5 [6] Christopher Alan DeBacker b: 25 Dec 1972
. . . . .5 [7] Amy Michelle DeBacker b: 09 Feb 1977
. . . . . . 3 Clifford W. Papenhagen b: 28 Oct 1923 in Michigan d: 11 Apr 1988 in Peoria, Maricopa, Arizona
. . . . +Arlene Mae Satre b: ABT 1923
. . . . 4 Larry W. Papenhagen b: ABT 1943
. . . . 4 Marsha Papenhagen b: ABT 1944
. . . .+Ledenician
. . . . . . 3 Clyde K. Papenhagen b: 28 Oct 1923 in Michigan
. . . . +Hilda Elizabeth Brenke b: 12 Feb 1925
. . . . 4 Kenneth Roger Papenhagen b: 11 Sep 1946
. . . .+Mary Inez Saxon b: 03 Feb 1946
. . . . .5 Kenneth Roger Papenhagen b: 24 Feb 1968
. . . .+Laura Strite b: 03 Nov 1968
. . . . .6 Boy Papenhagen b: ABT 1994
. . . . .5 Melissa Lynne Papenhagen b: 10 Jul 1969
. . . . 4 Yvonne Jean Papenhagen b: 22 Jul 1950
. . . .+Robert C. Stone b: 16 Aug 1949

. . . . .5 Renee J. Stone b: 26 Oct 1973
. . . . .5 Myra J. Stone b: 17 Dec 1976
. . . . .5 Bryan Charles Stone b: 21 Jan 1978
. . . . . . 3 Donald Papenhagen b: 06 Mar 1908 d: 28 Aug 1987 in Battle Creek, Calhoun, Michigan
. . . . +Marilyn Tagsold
. . . . . . 3 Irma Papenhagen b: 19 Dec 1919 in Riga Twnshp, Lenawee Co., MI d: 01 Apr 2002 in Adrian, MI
. . . . +Arthur W. Brenke, Sr. b: ABT 1919

Descendants of Heinrich Papenhagen

1. HEINRICH[1] PAPENHAGEN was born ABT 1811. He married CHRISTINA NEVERS. She was born ABT 1812.

Notes for HEINRICH PAPENHAGEN:
Bastdorf-Mecklinburg-Schwerin—on the road to Kropline-Doberan-Rostock Westendorf
Villas Brunschaupton—new Kuhlungsborn
—submitted by Michael Hilborn

Children of HEINRICH PAPENHAGEN and CHRISTINA NEVERS are:

2. i. Joachim Christian Johann[2] Papenhagen, b. 01 May 1836, Mechlenburg, Germany; d. 28 Dec 1906, Ottowa Lake, Monroe Co, MI.

ii. MINNIE PAPENHAGEN, b. Mar 1848, Germany; m. FRED JACOBS; b. Oct 1836, Germany.

Notes for MINNIE PAPENHAGEN:
(sister/family needs to be prooved yet as of 6/2004)

also 1900 census/Michigan/Monroe/Whiteford Ed # 83
next door 1900 Michigan/Monroe/Whiteford ED # 83 (check to see if they didn't come over on same ship—the kids are born in Michigan, here some 27 years.)
Fred Jacobs, b Oct 1836 age 63, from Germany; wife Minnie born March 1848, age 51 married 33 years (sister??) George, September 1872 born in Michigan; age 27; John April 1879, age 21, son; Minnie, daughter, May 1883, age 17; George, John and Minnie born in Michigan.

An amazing ship, supporting both steam power and sail with two masts, the Papenhagen family took passage aboard the *Auguste Victoria* , arriving in New York in July 1889.

This ship could had accommodations for 400 passengers in 1st class, 120 in 2nd class and 480 in steerage, with a crew of 245.

The Auguste Victoria

SHIP'S LOG
Joachim Pappenhagen, age 53, merchant
Hilhe, wife, age 40 (this is Wilhelmina) St. Mary's/Ohio Canal
Franz age 16
Herman age 14
Paul age 7
Marie age 6
Joh age 6 (listed as female)
Henri age 5
Rentha age 4 (this is Bertha)
Erna age 9 months, baby

An Effort Toward Translation ...

The / subscribed / administration department government department ministry / certifies / through this / that / the / agrochemical institute / Budner / and / merchant / JOACHIM Christian Johann Papenhagen / from / Neubukow / in the / hiesigen of / Grofsherzogthume, / born / on / Labor Day (1st May) / 1836 / together with / his / wife / : Wilhelmine Marie Johanna, / born / Westendorf / , born on the 13 May 1849, / may pass to the named port with his / these named children: 1. Franz Wilhelm Johann, born on the 24 November 1873 2. Hermann Friedrich Joh. Wilhelm, born on the 15 January 1875, 3. Paul Ludwig Friedrich Christian born on the 15 March 1877; 4. Marie Henriette

Papenhagen, Certificate to Travel

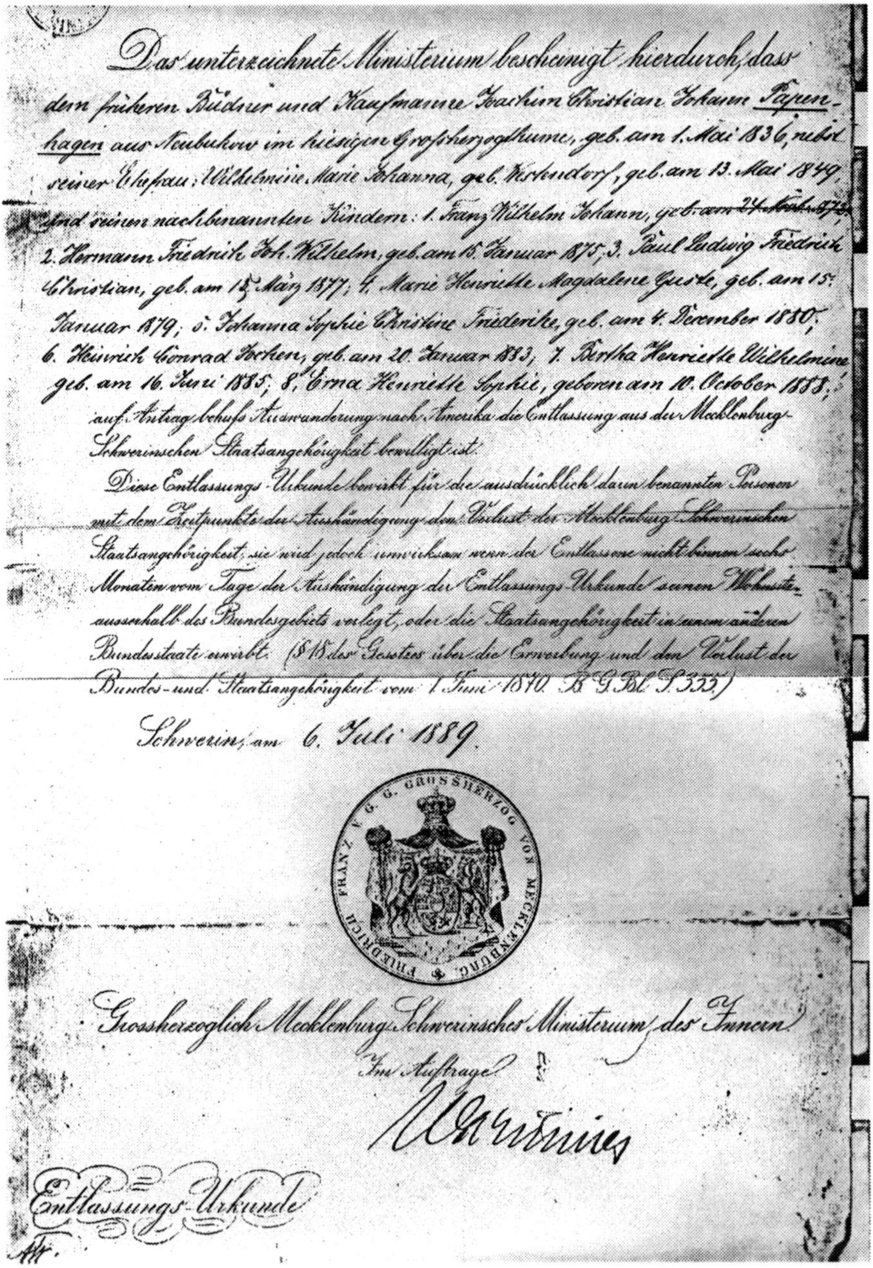

Das unterzeichnete Ministerium bescheinigt hierdurch, dass dem früheren Büdner und Kaufmanne Joachim Christian Johann Papenhagen aus Neubukow im hiesigen Großherzogthume, geb. am 1. Mai 1836, nebst seiner Ehefrau: Wilhelmine Marie Johanna, geb. Wertendorf, geb. am 13. Mai 1849, und seinen nachbenannten Kindern: 1. Franz Wilhelm Johann, geb. am 24. [illegible] 187[illegible], 2. Hermann Friedrich Joh. Wilhelm, geb. am 15. Januar 1875, 3. Paul Ludwig Friedrich Christian, geb. am 15. März 1877; 4. Marie Henriette Magdalene Guste, geb. am 15. Januar 1879; 5. Johanna Sophie Christine Friederike, geb. am 4. December 1880; 6. Heinrich Conrad Jochen, geb. am 20. Januar 1883; 7. Bertha Henriette Wilhelmine geb. am 16. Juni 1885; 8. Erna Henriette Sophie, geboren am 10. October 1888; auf Antrag behufs Auswanderung nach Amerika die Entlassung aus der Mecklenburg-Schwerinschen Staatsangehörigkeit bewilligt ist.

Diese Entlassungs-Urkunde bewirkt für die ausdrücklich darin benannten Personen mit dem Zeitpunkte der Aushändigung den Verlust der Mecklenburg-Schwerinschen Staatsangehörigkeit, sie wird jedoch unwirksam wenn der Entlassene nicht binnen sechs Monaten vom Tage der Aushändigung der Entlassungs-Urkunde seinen Wohnsitz ausserhalb des Bundesgebiets verlegt, oder die Staatsangehörigkeit in einem anderen Bundesstaate erwirbt. (§ 18 des Gesetzes über die Erwerbung und den Verlust der Bundes- und Staatsangehörigkeit vom 1. Juni 1870. B. G. Bl. S. 355.)

Schwerin, am 6. Juli 1889.

Grossherzoglich Mecklenburg-Schwerinsches Ministerium des Innern

Im Auftrage

[illegible]

Entlassungs-Urkunde

Magdalene Guste, born on the 15 January 1879; 5. Johanna Sophie Christine Friedericke, born on the 4 December 1880; Heinrich Conrad Jochen, born on the 20 January 1883; 7. Bertha Henriette Wilhelmine born on the 16 June 1885; 8. Erna Henriette Sophie, born on the 10 October 1888, upon / request / of emigration / towards / America / these / discharged / from / Mecklenburg Schwerinschen Staatsangehougkeit / is granted.

(Second part harder)
That-these-**This**-those / dismissal-notice-removal-resignation certficate-charter-deed-**document**-instrument-record / causes-**effected**-forced-operated / against-for-in **in favor of**-per-pro / **you** / explicit-**expressly**-formally-emphatic / **therein**-in it / **to the named place of delivery**-at of delivery named the point-to the the named port-of the named vessel / **persons** / by-**with** / the-**this**-whom / point in time-**date**-moment-time / **the** / surrender-delivery-**handing over** / The-that one-**this** one-this / **forfeiture**-casualties-damage-deficit-depivation-loss / **the** / **Mecklenburg Schwerinschen Staatsangehvrigkeit** / sic / becomes-**gets**-will / **however**-though-yet / **void**-powerless-ineffective / **if**-unless-wheather / **the** / **dismissed**-unburdened / no-unofficial-un / before-long-**within** hours / **6** / **months** / by-**from**-of / **today**Tage=days / **the** / delivery-surrender-**handing over** / **the** / **dismissal**-notice-removal-resignation / **certificate**-charter-deed-document / causes-**effected**-forced-operated / **to meet one's obligations**, responsibilities / dwelling place-**residence** / exterior-**external** / **Federal territory** / **misplaced** / **or** / **That** / **the** / **this** / **citizenship**-nationality / **in** / **a** an-to a / **anderen** / **federalstate** / erwirbt / (18 / des / act of law / about-above-across-at-by-via-over / die / purchase / and / the-this-this one / damage-forfeiture-loss /

Generation No. 1

1. JOACHIM CHRISTIAN JOHANN[2] PAPENHAGEN *(HEINRICH[1])* was born 01 May 1836 in Mechlenburg, Germany, and died 28 Dec 1906 in Ottowa Lake, Monroe Co, MI. He married WILHELMINA MARIE JOHANNA WESTENDORF ABT 1866 in Germany, daughter of DANIEL WESTENDORF. She was born 13 May 1849 in Germany, and died 05 Feb 1935 in Ottowa Lake, Monroe Co, MI.

Dirk Westendorf in Germany can trace the Westendorf family history back many generations 1300 AD. He said the Westendorfs still own the land that belonged to them in the 1800's.

New York Passenger Lists, 1851–1891 > 1889 > July > Augusta Victoria Destination stated in ship log—New Bucklow (sp?) (Certificate shows Neubukow) (New Brenen, Ohio)—they were headed to New Brenen, Ohio, take the Erie Canal west, then head south on the Canal towards St. Mary's. Something happened, they ended up in Toledo instead … stayed with friends until a house could be obtained. Walter was born in Ohio.

CERTIFICATE OF INTENTION TO BECOME A CITIZEN for Joseph Papenhagen July 24, 1889
(copy courtesy of Michael Hilborn)

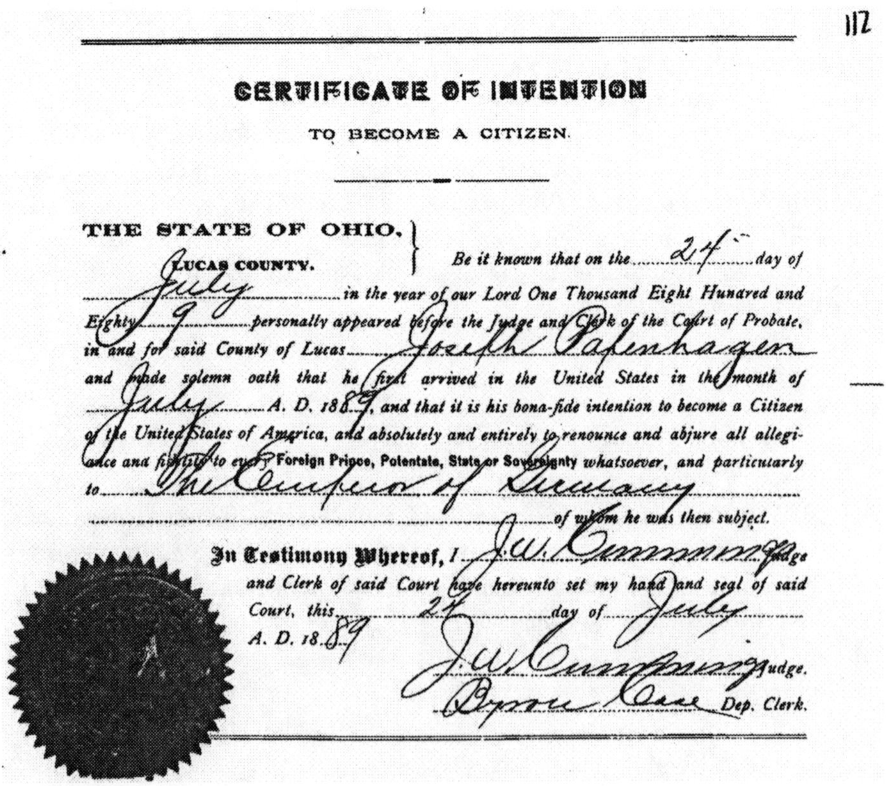
112

CERTIFICATE OF INTENTION

TO BECOME A CITIZEN.

THE STATE OF OHIO, LUCAS COUNTY. } *Be it known that on the* 24 *day of* July *in the year of our Lord One Thousand Eight Hundred and Eighty* 9 *personally appeared before the Judge and Clerk of the Court of Probate, in and for said County of Lucas* Joseph Papenhagen *and made solemn oath that he first arrived in the United States in the month of* July *A. D. 18*89, *and that it is his bona-fide intention to become a Citizen of the United States of America, and absolutely and entirely to renounce and abjure all allegiance and fidelity to every* Foreign Prince, Potentate, State or Sovereignty *whatsoever, and particularly to* The Emperor of Germany *of whom he was then subject.*

In Testimony Whereof, *I* J. W. Cummings *Judge and Clerk of said Court have hereunto set my hand and seal of said Court, this* 24 *day of* July *A. D. 18*89

J. W. Cummings *Judge.*
Byron Case *Dep. Clerk.*

TOLEDO OHIO DIRECTORY 1889–1891
Name: Joseph Papenhagen
Location 2: 441 Wabash
Occupation: laborer
Year: 1890, 1891
City: Toledo
State: OH ***

1900 U.S. Census • Michigan • Monroe • Whiteford • ED# 83
Pappenhagen, Jos, head, born May 1836, age 64, married 30 years, immigrated 1889; farmer, born in Germany, parents born in Germany; Minnie, wife, age 51 May 1850, married 30 years, born in Germany, parents born in Germany, had 9 children, 9 survive; Henry, son, age 17, Jan 1893, day laborer; born in Germany, farmer; Bertha, daughter, June 1886, born in Germany; Annie, daughter born October 1889, age 10, born in Germany; Walter, Son born June 1892 in Ohio; (Note, Jos is 64, not 54, born 1836)

ONE OF THE PAPENHAGENS's was killed by a bear at the zoo near Toledo, but can't remember which one. Does anyone remember this?

—Alice Taylor, 2004

Records from church (Lutheran) at Alt Gaarz date back to 1684. Family came from Germany in summer of 1889, direct to Toledo, Ohio and stayed with friends until a house was found. Citizenship was granted October 25, 1895 by Probate Court, Toledo, Ohio.

—Michael Hilborn

Cemetery records: St. Michaels Lutheran and Zion Lutheran Churches: Tombstones found: Joachim b 1 May 1836 d 2 Jan 1907; William b 1849 d 1935. The cemetery is in Whiteford Township. Monroe Co., Michigan (William-Wilhelmina)

—Joellen Langwell (VNBWJ50B) online

Notes for Wilhelmina Marie Johanna Westendorf:
email: Joellen Langwell (VNWJ50B): Tombstone says William b 1849 d 1935 (I'm sure they messed up reading the headstone on this one. They probably didn't see the "ina" at the end. The cemetery is in Whiteford Twp. Monroe Co.

Wilhelmina Popenhagen
Age in 1910: 61
Estimated Birth Year: 1848
1910 Census: Whiteford Twp, Monroe, Michigan
Popenhagen, Wilhelmina, age 61, head of house, widow, had 10 children, 9 survive, she was born in Germany, emigrated 1889, farmer; Walter, age 17 born in Ohio, farmer; Anna, daughter, age 21.

1920 Census
Wilhelmina, widowed, lived next door to her son,

Paul in 1920:
1920 Census
Paul Popenhagen (sic)
Age: 42 years
Estimated birth year: 1877
Birthplace: Austria; Germany
Race: White

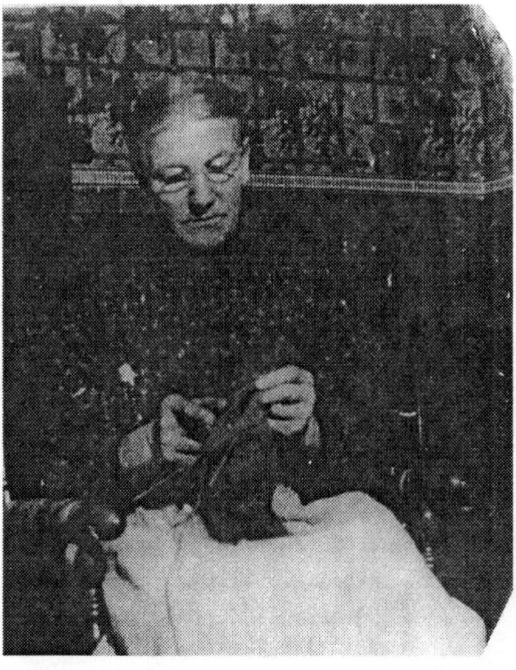
Wilhelmine Westendorf Papenhagen

Home in 1920: Whiteford, Monroe, Michigan
Paul, head, age 42, emigrated 1888; citizen of Germany; Emma wife, age 42, born in Michigan; Ethel 18, Norman 12, Herbert 11, Doris 5

(** Wilhelm Popenhagen, lived next door, age 70, head, widowed.)
(** also next door: Walter Popenhagen, age 27; Elsie age 26; Wilfred, daughter age 5; Esther age 2; Emma, age 1 month.)

More About Joachim Papenhagen and Wilhelmina Westendorf:
Marriage: ABT 1866, Germany

Children of Joachim Papenhagen and Wilhelmina Westendorf are:

2. i. Franz Wilhelm Johann[3] Papenhagen, b. 24 Nov 1872, Germany; d. 04 Oct 1931, Defiance, Ohio.

3. ii. Marie Henriette Magdalene Guste Papenhagen, b. 15 Jan 1879, Germany; d. 20 Oct 1959, Toledo, Lucas, Ohio.

4. iii. Herman Friedrick Johann Wilhelm Papenhagen, b. 15 Jan 1875, Germany; d. 30 Sep 1952, Toledo, Lucas, Ohio.

5. iv. Paul Ludwig Friedrich Christian Papenhagen, b. 15 Mar 1877, Germany; d. 21 Nov 1950, Whiteford, Monroe, Michigan.

6. v. Johanna Sophie Christine Friede Papenhagen, b. 04 Dec 1880, Germany; d. Aft. 1930.

vi. Heinrich Conrad Jochen Papenhagen, b. 20 Jan 1883, Germany; d. 05 Jan 1958, Whiteford Twp., Monroe, Michigan; m. (1) Mattie Oelrich; b. 19 Mar 1881; d. 30 Mar 1941; m. (2) Ida; b. Michigan; m. (3) Bertha.

Notes for Heinrich Conrad Jochen Papenhagen:
1900 U.S. Census • Michigan • Monroe • Whiteford • ED# 83
Pappenhagen, Jos, head, born May 1836, age 64, married 30 years, immigrated 1889; farmer, born in Germany, parents born in Germany; Minnie, wife, age 51 May 1850, married 30 years, born in Germany, parents born in Germany, had 9 children, 9 survive; Henry, son, ** age 17, Jan 1883; born in Germany, farmer; Bertha, daughter, June 1886, born in Germany; Annie, duaghter born October 1889, age 10, born

in Germany; Walter, Son born June 1892 in Ohio; (Note, Jos is 64, not 54, born 1836)

Henry Popenhagen
Age in 1910: 27
Estimated Birth Year: 1882
Home in 1910: WHITEFORD TWP, MONROE, Michigan
Race: White
Gender: Male
Series: T624
Roll: 664
Part: 1
Page: 286B
Year: 1910

1910 U.S. Census • Michigan • Monroe • Monroe City • ED# 110
Henry age 27, born in Germany, farmer; married 1x, 5 years; married to Mattie, first marriage, married, no children listed.

1930 United States Federal Census > Ohio > Wood > Troy > District 47
Henry K, 47 years old, born in Germany, emigrated 1888, field man, sugar factory. wife Mattie E., age 48, born in Michigan, no children listed.

1930: Field Beet manager/banker.

First wife Mattie
Second Wife Ida
Third wife Bertha

Notes for MATTIE OELRICH:
Marriage Record Volume 7–14 M L 7 July 12, 1882–Oct. 13, 1885
Record Location: Porter County, Indiana D. A. P. Submitted by: William Henry Harrison Chapter Daughters of the American Revolution Valparaiso, Indiana
Spouse 1: Geo. Blunk

Spouse 2: Ida Popenhagen (Henry?)
~~Marriage Date: 30 Jul 1883~~ birthdate is 1883
County: Porter
Original Source Page: 219

Joachim "Joseph" & Wilhelmine Papenhagen Family (Joseph is not in the photo.)

Frank Herman Paul Henry Walter

Johanna "Jennie" Marie "Mary" Wilhelmine Bertha Erna (Anna)

7. vii. Bertha Henrietta Wilhelmine Papenhagen, b. 16 Jun 1885, Germany; d. 07 Feb 1966, Lucas Co, Ohio.
8. viii. Erna Henriette Sophie Papenhagen, b. 10 Oct 1888, Beubukow, Schwerinschen, Mecklenburg, Germany; d. 30 Sep 1982, Dickinson, Stark North Dakota.
9. ix. Walter Franklin Papenhagen, b. 01 Jun 1892, Toledo, Lucas, Ohio; d. 13 Aug 1944.

Generation No. 2

2. Franz Wilhelm Johann[3] Papenhagen *(Joachim Christian Johann[2], Heinrich[1])* was born 24 Nov 1872 in Germany, and died 04 Oct 1931 in Defiance, Ohio. He married Winifred Klinger, daughter of Mr. Klinger and Margaret. She was born 26 Sep 1872 in Ohio, and died 02 Mar 1954.

Notes for Franz Wilhelm Johann Papenhagen:
New York Passenger Lists, 1851–1891 > 1889 > July > Augusta Victoria
Franz age 16
children from Mechlenburg.
Destination—New Bucklow (sp?)
(New Brenen, Ohio … maybe … they head for Toledo, Ohio)

1889–1891 TOLEDO OHIO DIRECTORY
Name: Frank Papenhagen
Location 2: boards 441 Wabash
Business Name: Toledo Express
Occupation: printer
Year: 1890, 1891
City: Toledo
State: OH

1900 U.S. Census • Michigan • Monroe • Whiteford • ED# 83
Named Franz Wilhelm Johann Papenhagen, they called him "Frank".

1910 Miracode:
Frank Papenhage, age 37 W GER Defiance, Defiance
Head of Household

Relation	Name	Age	Birth Place
Wife	Winifred	37	Ohio
Son	Frank	10	Ohio
Daughter	Edna	07	Ohio
Mother-in-law	Margaret Klingler	59	PENN

1920 U.S. Census • Ohio • Defiance • Defiance • ED# 5
Frank Papenhagen, age 47, wife Winifred age 47; Frank W. age 20; (spelling awful on this, looks like Ednda (Edna) age 17. ***

1930 Census
Home in 1930: Defiance, Defiance, Ohio
Frank J Papenhausen, age 57, born in Germany, father and mother both born in Germany; Winifred A, wife, born in Ohio, age 57; her father born in Ohio, her mother born in Pennsylvania; no children listed; General Manager for a printing Company. *** (Look back for immigration year)

Historical Newspapers > Lima News (Lima, Ohio) > 1931 > October > 5
FRANK J PAPENHAGEN was shot in the head October 4, 1931
Financial problems, he is in the hospital with his wife, son, Frank W. and daughter Mrs. Robert Emery of Toledo. (He died October 4, 1931)

Notes for Winifred Klinger:
1910 Miracode:
Frank Papenhage, age 37 W GER Defiance, Defiance
Head of Household

Relation	Name	Age	Birth Place
Wife	Winifred	37	Ohio
Son	Frank	10	Ohio
Daughter	Edna	07	Ohio
Mother-in-law	Margaret Klingler	59	PENN

Children of Franz Papenhagen and Winifred Klinger are:

10. i. Frank W.[4] Papenhagen, b. 20 Apr 1899, Ohio; d. Apr 1983, Ft. Meyers, Beach Florida.
11. ii. Edna Papenhagen, b. ABT 1893, Ohio.

3. Marie Henriette Magdalene Guste[3] Papenhagen *(Joachim Christian Johann[2], Heinrich[1])* was born 15 Jan 1879 in Germany, and died 20 Oct 1959 in Toledo, Lucas, Ohio. She married Albert W. Doering ABT 1902 in Toledo Ohio. He was born 12 Jan 1877 in Ohio, and died 27 Jan 1952 in Toledo, Lucas, Ohio.

Notes for Marie Henriette Magdalene Guste Papenhagen:
New York Passenger Lists, 1851–1891 > 1889 > July > Augusta Victoria
Marie age 6
Joh age 6
Henri age 5
Rentha age 4
Erna age 9 months, baby
children from Mechlenburg.
Destination—New Bucklow (sp?) (New Brenen, Ohio)

Notes for Albert W. Doering:
1910 U.S. Census • Ohio • Lucas • Toledo city • ED# 107
Albert W. Doering, age 32, Married 1x, married 8 years; cigarmaker, factory, born in Ohio, parents from Germany; Mary H. age 30, wife, married 8 years, 1 x; had 3 children; 3 survive; born in Germany, parents born in Germany; Helen I age 8; Marie H. age 5; Gertrude S is age 3; children all born in Ohio.

Census 1920 Toledo, Lucas, Ohio
Albert Doering, age 43 born in Ohio, shipping clerk for a hardware company, parents born in Germany; Mary age 41, born in Germany; Helen age 17, bookkeeper, born in Ohio; Marie 15; Gertrude 12; Thelma age 4.

1930 Census Ohio > Lucas > Toledo > District 103
Albert W. Doering, age 52, married 1x, age 23 when first married, shipping clerk; Mary H. age 51, Marie J. age 25, teacher, public school; Gertrude A, age 23, personnel director, department store; Thelma, age 15.

More About Albert Doering and Marie Papenhagen:
Marriage: ABT 1902, Toledo Ohio

Children of MARIE PAPENHAGEN and ALBERT DOERING are:

12. i. Helen I.[4] Doering, b. 02 Nov 1903, Toledo, Ohio.
13. ii. Marie Doering, b. 12 Dec 1904, Toledo, Ohio; d. 08 Jun 1999, Toledo, Ohio.
14. iii. Gertrude Doering, b. 21 Jan 1907, Toledo, Ohio; d. 04 Feb 1997, Whitehall, Trempealeau, Wisconsin.
15. iv. Thelma Doering, b. ABT 1916, Ohio.

4. HERMAN FRIEDRICK JOHANN WILHELM[3] PAPENHAGEN *(JOACHIM CHRISTIAN JOHANN[2], HEINRICH[1])* was born 15 Jan 1875 in Germany, and died 30 Sep 1952 in Toledo, Lucas, Ohio. He married LOUISE H. FREEMAN. She was born 07 Jul 1876 in Ohio, and died 18 Dec 1943.

Notes for HERMAN FRIEDRICK JOHANN WILHELM PAPENHAGEN:
New York Passenger Lists, 1851–1891 > 1889 > July > Augusta Victoria
Herman age 14
children from Mechlenburg.
Destination—New Bucklow (sp?) (New Brenen, Ohio)

TOLEDO OHIO DIRECTORY 1889–1891
Name: Herman Papenhagen
Location 2: boards 441 Wabash
Occupation: machinist hd
Year: 1890, 1891
City: Toledo
State: OH ***

Brother Walter is born in Toledo Ohio in June 1892, but by 1900, Joachim & Wilhelmine, along with the 4 youngest children move to Whiteford Twnship, Monroe, Michigan, next door to the Jacobs (family??) Herman, and Paul remain in Toledo. Frank moves to Defiance, Ohio to set up a printing shop. Mary also stays in Toledo, and marries Doering.

1910 Census
Herman Papenhagen
Age in 1910: 35
Estimated Birth Year: 1874
Home in 1910: 9-WD TOLEDO, LUCAS, Ohio
Race: White

Gender: Male
Series: T624
Roll: 1209
Part: 2
Page: 21B
Year: 1910
Ed #116
Herman, age 35 W GER Lucas, Toledo Head of Household

Relation	Name	Age	Birth Place
Wife	Louise	33	Ohio
Daughter	Marie	10	Ohio
Son	Arnold	09	Ohio

1920 Census • Ohio • Lucas • Toledo • ED# 104
Herman Papenhagen, age 44, bricklayer, single. (Divorced)

Notes for Louise H. Freeman:
1920 Census: Lucas, Toledo, OHIO
Louise age 43, head; Louise daughter, age 20; Arnold, son age 18; Eliz daughter, age 4.

1930 Census: Toledo, Lucas, Ohio
Louise H. Papenhagen, head, age 53, Divorced; Arnold son, age 29; Eloise J. age 14.

More About Herman Papenhagen and Louise Freeman:
Divorce: Bef. 1930, Toledo, Ohio

Children of Herman Papenhagen and Louise Freeman are:

i. Marie[4] Papenhagen, b. Aug 1899, Ohio; m. Jerry; b. ABT 1899.

Notes for Marie Papenhagen:
1910 Census: 9 Ward, Toledo, Lucas, Ohio
Herman, Head age 33, married 1x, born in Germany; Louise, wife age 33 born in Ohio; had 2 children, 2 children survive; Herman and Louise's parents born in Germany; Herman is a brick contractor, works for himself; Marie age 10; Arnold age 9, both born in Ohio. ***

16. ii. ELOISE PAPENHAGEN, b. ABT 1916, Ohio.
17. iii. Ar nol d Papenh agen, b. 11 Mar 1901, Ohio; d. 03 Feb 1982, Perrysburg, Wood, Ohio.

5. PAUL LUDWIG FRIEDRICH CHRISTIAN[3] PAPENHAGEN *(JOACHIM CHRISTIAN JOHANN[2], HEINRICH[1])* was born 15 Mar 1877 in Germany, and died 21 Nov 1950 in Whiteford, Monroe, Michigan. He married (1) MARY PAPENHAGEN. She was born ABT 1889, and died 22 Mar 1964 in Toledo, Lucas, Ohio. He married (2) EMMA ELG 22 Feb 1900 in Whiteford Twnship, Monroe, Michigan. She was born 28 Jun 1877 in Michigan, and died 28 Nov 1943 in Whiteford, Monroe, Michigan.

Notes for PAUL LUDWIG FRIEDRICH CHRISTIAN PAPENHAGEN:
New York Passenger Lists, 1851–1891 > 1889 > July > Augusta Victoria
Paul age 7
children from Mechlenburg.
Destination—New Bucklow (sp?) (New Brenen, Ohio
TOLEDO OHIO DIRECTORY 1889–1891
Name: Paul Papenhagen
Location 2: boards 441 Wabash
Occupation: stirrupmkr
Year: 1890, 1891
City: Toledo
State: OH

1900 Whitfeord Twnship/Monroe County/Michigan page
Popenhagen, Paul, head age 23, March 1877 born in Germany, farmer; married 1 year; Emma, wife born June 1878, born in Michigan, parents born in Germany age 22, no children listed.

1910 • Michigan • Monroe • Monroe City • ED# 110 WHITEFORD TWP
Paul, head, age 33, married 1x, born in Germany, married 10 years, 3 children, all 3 survive; emigrated 1884, farmer, Emma, wife age 32, married 1x, born in Michigan, parents born in Germany, Ethel age 8, Norman age 3, Herbert age 1 1/2.

1920 Census
Paul Popenhagen
Age: 42 years
Estimated birth year: 1877
Birthplace: Austria; Germany
Race: White
Home in 1920: Whiteford, Monroe, Michigan
Paul, head, age 42, emigrated 1888; citizen of Germany; Emma wife, age 42, born in Michigan; Ethel 18, Norman 12, Herbert 11, Doris 5

(** 1920 Wilhelmine Popenhagen, lives next door, age 70, head, widowed.)

(** also next door: 1920 Census Whiteford, Monroe, Michigan Walter Popenhagen (Paul's brother), age 27; Elsie age 26; Wilfred, daughter age 5; Esther age 2; Emma, age 1 month.)

1930 Census: Whiteford, Monroe, Michigan
Paul, head age 52; 22 when he was first married (this is perhaps second marriage) born in Germany, farmer; Emma age 57, age 22 when she was first married, born in Michigan; Norman, age 22; Herbert age 21; and Doris age 15, born in Michigan.

Notes for Mary Papenhagen:
MARY PAPENHAGEN
Gender: Female
Date of Death: March 22, 1964
Volume: 17618
Certificate: 21104
Marital Status: Widowed
Place of Death: Toledo, Lucas County
Race: White
Residence: Toledo, Lucas County
Age: 75

Notes for Emma Elg:
"Emma" or Inez?—perhaps the same person, but alway Emma in the census.

Norman's death certificate: mother's surname is "Elg".

1930 Census (no, but may be family)
Inez V Elg
Age: 27 years
Estimated birth year: 1902
Birthplace: Wisconsin
Relation to Head-of-house: Lodger
Race: White
Home in 1930: Neenah, Winnebago, Wisconsin

More About PAUL PAPENHAGEN and EMMA ELG:
Marriage: 22 Feb 1900, Whiteford Twnship, Monroe, Michigan

Children of PAUL PAPENHAGEN and EMMA ELG are:

18. i. Ethel S.[4] Papenhagen, b. 27 Oct 1901, Michigan; d. 29 Jan 1981, Norvell,Jackson, Michigan.
19. ii. Norman Henry Papenhagen, b. 05 May 1907, Michigan; d. 06 May 1995, Michigan.
20. iii. Doris Papenhagen, b. 23 Jul 1914, Ottawa Lake, Michigan.
21. iv. Herbert Papenhagen, b. 02 Nov 1908, Michigan; d. 05 Jul 1988, Bradenton, Florida.

6. JOHANNA SOPHIE CHRISTINE FRIEDE[3] PAPENHAGEN *(JOACHIM CHRISTIAN JOHANN[2], HEINRICH[1])* was born 04 Dec 1880 in Germany, and died Aft. 1930. She married CHARLES W. HACKER. He was born ABT 1877 in Ohio, and died 1944.

Notes for JOHANNA SOPHIE CHRISTINE FRIEDE PAPENHAGEN:
New York Passenger Lists, 1851–1891 > 1889 > July > Augusta Victoria
Joh age 6
children from Mechlenburg.
Destination—New Bucklow (sp?) (New Brenen, Ohio)

Nicknamed Jennie.

Notes for CHARLES W. HACKER:
Charles W Hacker
Age in 1910: 33
Estimated Birth Year: 1876
Birthplace: Ohio

Home in 1910: 10-WD TOLEDO, LUCAS, Ohio
Race: White Gender: Male
Series: T624 Roll: 1209
Part: 2 Page: 204B

1910 U.S. Census • Ohio • Lucas • Toledo city • ED# 126
Charles W. Hacker, age 33, married 1x, married 8 years, born in Ohio, parents in Germany, machinist, machine making factory; Jennie age 29, 1 child, 1 survive; born in Germany, parents born in Germany; Harold, age 4, son, born in Ohio. Edwin, brother, age 11 born in Ohio.

1930 United States Federal Census > Ohio > Lucas > Toledo > District 119
Charles Hacker, head, 52 years old, born in Ohio, age 24 when he first was married, parents born in Germany, machinist at factory; Jennie, wife age born in Germany, emigrated 1891, 49 years old, age 21 when first married.

Child of JOHANNA PAPENHAGEN and CHARLES HACKER is:

i. HAROLD[4] HACKER, b. ABT 1906, Toledo, Ohio.

Notes for HAROLD HACKER:
1910 U.S. Census • Ohio • Lucas • Toledo city • ED# 126
Charles W. Hacker, age 33, married 1x, married 8 years, born in Ohio, parents in Germany, machinist, machine making factory; Jennie age 29, 1 child, 1 survive; born in Germany, parents born in Germany; Harold ***, age 4, son, born in Ohio. Edwin, brother, age 11 born in Ohio.

1930 United States Federal Census > Ohio > Lucas > Toledo > District 119
Charles Hacker, head, 52 years old, born in Ohio, age 24 when he first was married, parents born in Germany, machinist at factory; Jennie, wife age born in Germany, emigrated 1891, 49 years old, age 21 when first married.

Harold died as a teenager. Is this the boy who was killed by a bear at the Toledo Zoo?

7. BERTHA HENRIETTA WILHELMINE[3] PAPENHAGEN *(JOACHIM CHRISTIAN JOHANN[2], HEINRICH[1])* was born 16 Jun 1885 in Germany, and died 07 Feb 1966 in Lucas Co, Ohio. She married John C. Schumacher 12 Mar 1908. He was born 27 Mar 1880 in Germany, and died 05 Nov 1958 in Lucas Co., Ohio.

Notes for Bertha Henrietta Wilhelmine Papenhagen:
New York Passenger Lists, 1851–1891 > 1889 > July > Augusta Victoria
Rentha age 4—(Bertha??)
children from Mechlenburg.
Destination—New Bucklow (sp?) (New Brenen, Ohio)

1900 U.S. Census • Michigan • Monroe • Whiteford • ED# 83
Pappenhagen, Jos, head, born May 1836, age 64, married 30 years, immigrated 1889; farmer, born in Germany, parents born in Germany; Minnie, wife, age 51 May 1850, married 30 years, born in Germany, parents born in Germany, had 9 children, 9 survive; Henry, son, age 17, Jan 1893; born in Germany, farmer; Bertha, daughter, June 1886, born in Germany; Annie, duaghter born October 1889, age 10, born in Germany; Walter, Son born June 1892 in Ohio; (Note, Jos is 64, not 54, born 1836)

Death certificate:
BERTHA H SCHUMACHER
Gender: Female
Date of Death: February 07, 1966
Volume: 18367
Certificate: 12890
Marital Status: Widowed
Place of Death: Toledo, Lucas County
Race: White
Residence: Out-of-State, Out-of-State
Age: 80

Bertha Schumacher
Age: 43 years
Estimated birth year: 1886
Relation to Head-of-house: Wife
Home in 1930: Woodsfield, Monroe, Ohio

Notes for JOHN C. SCHUMACHER:
1930 United States Federal Census > Michigan > Monroe > Whiteford > District 38
John C. Schumacher, age 50, 28 when he first got married, born in Germany; emigrated 1881, farmer; Bertha age 45 born in Germany, emigrated 1891, age 23 when she first was married; Elmer J age 18, born in Michigan; Frank, 11 born in Michigan; Ray (maybe Roy) age 9, born in Michigan;

More About JOHN SCHUMACHER and BERTHA PAPENHAGEN:
Marriage: 12 Mar 1908

Children of BERTHA PAPENHAGEN and JOHN SCHUMACHER are:
22. i. Elmer[4] Schumacher, b. 10 Jan 1912, Michigan.
23. ii. Frank Schumacher, b. ABT 1909, Michigan.
24. iii. Roy Schumacher, b. 31 Jan 1921, Michigan; d. 12 Sep 1971.
iv. LYDIA SCHUMACHER, b. ABT 1920.

Notes for LYDIA SCHUMACHER:
Died about 6 weeks old.

8. ERNA HENRIETTE SOPHIE[3] PAPENHAGEN *(JOACHIM CHRISTIAN JOHANN[2], HEINRICH[1])* was born 10 Oct 1888 in Beubukow, Schwerinschen, Mecklenburg, Germany, and died 30 Sep 1982 in Dickinson, Stark North Dakota[1,2]. She married WILLIAM CARL TEGTMEIER 24 Nov 1910 in home of her mother by Rev. Albert ZeitnerOttawa Lake, Zion Lutheran, Monroe County, OH, son of JOHANN TEGTMEIER and SOPHIA REINECKE. He was born 15 May 1882 in Middleburg Twnshp, OH, and died 10 Apr 1955 in Medina Twp., Medina, OH.

Notes for ERNA HENRIETTE SOPHIE PAPENHAGEN:
New York Passenger Lists, 1851–1891 > 1889 > July > Augusta Victoria
Erna age 9 months, baby children from Mechlenburg.
Destination—New Bucklow (sp?) (New Brenen, Ohio)

1900 U.S. Census • Michigan • Monroe • Whiteford • ED# 83
Pappenhagen, Jos, head, born May 1836, age 64, married 30 years, immigrated 1889; farmer, born in Germany, parents born in Germany; Minnie, wife, age 51 May 1850, married 30 years, born in Germany, parents born in Germany,

had 9 children, 9 survive; Henry, son, age 17, Jan 1893; born in Germany, farmer; Bertha, daughter, June 1886, born in Germany; Annie, duaghter born October 1889, age 10, born in Germany; Walter, Son born June 1892 in Ohio; (Note, Jos is 64, not 54, born 1836)

1910 Census: Whiteford Twp, Monroe, Michigan
Popenhagen, Wilhelmina, age 61, head of house, widow, had 10 children, 9 survive, born in Germany, emigrated 1889; Walter, age 17 born in Ohio; Anna***, daughter, age 21.

Anna (Erna) nee Papenhagen and William C. Tegtmeier were married November 24, 1920 at Zion Lutheran Church, Ottawa Lake, Monroe County, Michigan. Born in Neubukow, Mecklenburg-Schwerin, Germand October 10, 1888, Anna crossed the ocean with her family, eight months old, losing one shoe on the ship, the Queen Victoria steamer after setting sail July 9.

—Lois Tegtmier Henricks

1930 Census 1930 United States Federal Census > Ohio > Cuyahoga > Chagrin Falls > District 553
Tegtmeier, William, head age 46, farmer, married at age 26, born in Ohio; Anna, wife, age 42, married at age 22, born in Germany; Loretta M age 18, stenographer at a garage; Raymond J age 17; Julia W age age 15; Alice L age 13; Henry A age 12; William Jr. age 10; Harold E. is 9; Richard E. is 6; Lois R. is age 2.

Social Security information
Individual: Tegtmeier, Anna
Issued in: Ohio
Birth date: Oct 10, 1888
Death date: Sep 1982
Residence code: Ohio
ZIP Code of last known residence: 44691

(Please see Tegtmeier, William in the first section of this book for further information to avoid duplication)

Notes for William Carl Tegtmeier:
Baptized May 25, 1882, Berea, Cuyahoga, Ohio

1900 Census: living next to his Uncle Ferd: Cuyahoga—other townships (Middleburgh) ed # 222—page 8
Henry Tegtmeir, head, farmer, single age 24, born October 1875; both parents born in Germany; Christena, sister, single, December 1880, age 19, born in Ohio; WILLIAM ***, brother born May 1882, single, farm laborer; Adolph, brother age 16, Sept 1883, farm laborer.

1910 Census • Ohio • Cuyahoga • Other Townships • ED# 23
Julia, age 59 widow, had 7 children, 6 survive; born in Germany; Henry age 37 works at a factory; WILLIAM age 27**, general farm; Adolph age 26 general farm; children born in Ohio.

(See Tegtmeier/Erna Papenhagen for further info.)

1930 Census 1930 United States Federal Census > Ohio > Cuyahoga > Chagrin Falls > District 553
Tegtmeier, William, head age 46, farmer, married at age 26, born in Ohio; Anna, wife, age 42, married at age 22, born in Germany; Loretta M age 18, stenographer at a garage; Raymond J age 17; Julia W age age 15; Alice L age 13; Henry A age 12; William Jr. age 10; Harold E. is 9; Richard E. is 6; Lois R. age 2.

More about William Tegtmeier and Erna Papenhagen:
Marriage: 24 Nov 1910, home of her mother by Rev. Albert ZeitnerOttawa Lake, Zion Lutheran, Monroe County, OH
Marriage date: home of her mother by Rev. Albert Zeitner

Children of Erna Papenhagen and William Tegtmeier are:

25. i. Lor et t a Mat t ie[4] Tegt meier , b. 26 Aug 1911.

26. ii. Raymond Jul ius Tegt meier , b. 07 Dec 1912, Brookpark, OH; d. Sep 1982, Wayne County, Ohio.

iii. Julia Wihelmina Tegtmeier, b. 07 Oct 1914, Brookpark, Cuyahoga Co., Ohio; d. 02 Mar 1934, Columbus, OH. Died of blood poisoning. (See info under Tegtmeier)

OBITUARY Id#: 0357899
Name: Tegtmeier, Julia W.
Date: Mar 4 1934

Source: Source unknown; Cleveland Necrology File, Reel #079.
Notes: Tegtmeier: Julia W., beloved daughter of William and Anna, at Columbus, O., Friday, March 2, at 8 p. m., aged 19 years. Remains at the funeral home of John C. Murray, Creston, O., where friends may call. Funeral at Canaan Lutheran Church, Creston, O., Monday, March 5, at 2 p. m.

27. iv. ALICE HENRIETTA TEGTMEIER, b. 28 May 1916, Brookpark, Ohio.
28. v. Henry Adolph Tegtmeier, b. 19 Mar 1918, Ohio; d. 09 Dec 1992, Fairfield Glade, TN.
29. vi. William Edward Tegtmeier, b. 06 Mar 1920, Brookpark, Ohio; d. 24 Jul 2000, Savanah, OH.
30. vii. Harold William Tegtmeier, b. 02 Mar 1921, Brookpark, Ohio; d. 18 May 2003, West Salem, Wayne, Ohio.
31. viii. Richard Elmer Tegtmeier, b. 03 Jan 1924, Berea,Cuyahoga Co.OH; d. 17 Oct 1995, Crossville, TN.
32. ix. Lois Ruth Tegtmeier, b. 18 Mar 1928, maybe Brookpark, OH.

9. WALTER FRANKLIN[3] PAPENHAGEN *(JOACHIM CHRISTIAN JOHANN[2], HEINRICH[1])* was born 01 Jun 1892 in Toledo, Lucas, Ohio, and died 13 Aug 1944. He married ELSIE CAROLINE KOESTER, daughter of LOUIS KOESTER and LOUISA SCHMIDT-ESCHENRODER. She was born 16 May 1893 in Michigan, and died 12 May 1982 in Lenawee, Michigan.

Notes for WALTER FRANKLIN PAPENHAGEN:
1900 U.S. Census • Michigan • Monroe • Whiteford • ED# 83
Pappenhagen, Jos, head, born May 1836, age 64, married 30 years, immigrated 1889; farmer, born in Germany, parents born in Germany; Minnie, wife, age 51 May 1850, married 30 years, born in Germany, parents born in Germany, had 9 children, 9 survive; Henry, son, age 17, Jan 1893; born in Germany, farmer; Bertha, daughter, June 1886, born in Germany; Annie, duaghter born October 1889, age 10, born in Germany; Walter, Son born June 1892 in Ohio; (Note, Jos is 64, not 54, born 1836)

1910 Census: Whiteford Twp, Monroe, Michigan
Popenhagen, Wilhelmina, age 61, head of house, widow, had 10 children, 9 survive, born in Germany, emigrated 1889; Walter, age 17 born in Ohio; Anna, daughter, age 21.

1920 920 U.S. Census • Michigan • Monroe • Whiteford • ED# 127
(** Wilhelmina Popenhagen, lives next door, age 70, head, widowed.)
(** also next door: 1920 Census Whiteford, Monroe, Michigan Walter Popenhagen, age 27; Elsie age 26; Wilfred, daughter age 5; Esther age 2; Emma, age 1 month.)

Walter H Popenhagen
Age: 37 years
Estimated birth year: 1892
Birthplace: Ohio
Relation to Head-of-house: Head
Race: White
Home in 1930: Whiteford, Monroe, Michigan
1930 Census: Whiteford, Monroe, Michigan
Walter H Popenhagen, head age 37 born in Ohio; Elsie C. age 36, born in Michigan; Mildred W age 16 born in MI; Esther E, age 12, MI; Erna E age 10; Clifford W age 6; Clyde K age 6.

Notes for Elsie Caroline Koester:
Elsie Papenhagen
Last Residence: 49228 Blissfield, Lenawee, Michigan, United States of America
Born: 16 May 1893
Died: May 1982
State (Year) SSN issued: Michigan (1954)

Elsie C PAPENHAGEN
Birth Date: 16 May 93
Death Date: 12 May 82
Gender: Female
Residence: Adrian, Lenawee, Michigan
Social Security information

Children of WALTER PAPENHAGEN and ELSIE KOESTER are:

i. MILDRED WILFRED[4] PAPENHAGEN, b. ABT 1914, Michigan.

Notes for MILDRED WILFRED PAPENHAGEN:
1930 Census: Whiteford, Monroe, Michigan
Walter H Popenhagen, head age 37 born in Ohio; Elsie C. age 36, born in Michigan; Mildred W age 16 born in MI; Esther E, age 12, MI; Erna E age 10; Clifford W age 6; Clyde K age 6

33. ii. ESTHER EDNA MARIE PAPENHAGEN, b. 07 Sep 1917, Michigan.
34. iii. Erna Ethel Elizabeth Papenhagen, b. 02 Dec 1919, Michigan.
35. iv. Clifford W. Papenhagen, b. 28 Oct 1923, Michigan; d. 11 Apr 1988, Peoria, Maricopa, Arizona.
36. v. Clyde K. Papenhagen, b. 28 Oct 1923, Michigan.
vi. DONALD PAPENHAGEN, b. 06 Mar 1908; d. 28 Aug 1987, Battle Creek, Calhoun, Michigan; m. MARILYN TAGSOLD.

Notes for DONALD PAPENHAGEN:
Death certificate
Donald L POPENHAGEN
Birth Date: 30 06 08
Death Date: 28 August 87
Gender: Male
Residence: Battle Creek, Calhoun, Michigan

vii. IRMA PAPENHAGEN, b. 19 Dec 1919, Riga Twnshp, Lenawee Co., MI; d. 01 Apr 2002, Adrian, MI; m. ARTHUR W. BRENKE, SR.; b. ABT 1919.

Generation No. 3

10. FRANK W.[4] PAPENHAGEN *(FRANZ WILHELM JOHANN[3], JOACHIM CHRISTIAN JOHANN[2], HEINRICH[1])* was born 20 Apr 1899 in Ohio, and died Apr 1983 in Ft. Meyers, Beach Florida. He married MARION D. She was born 16 Jan 1901 in New York, and died Sep 1990.

Notes for Frank W. Papenhagen:
1920 U.S. Census • Ohio • Defiance • Defiance • ED# 5
Frank Papenhagen, age 47, wife Winifred age 47; Frank W. age 20; (spelling awful on this, looks like Ednda (Edna) age 17. ***

1930 United States Federal Census > Ohio > Defiance > Defiance > District 2
Frank W Papenhagenw, head age 30, born in Ohio, father born in Germany, mother born in Ohio. Marion, wife, age 28, born in New York, father born in New York, mother born in Canada. No children listed. He is a printer. ***

Frank W Papenhagen
Age: 30 years
Estimated birth year: 1899
Birthplace: Ohio
Relation to Head-of-house: Head
Race: White
Home in 1930: Defiance, Defiance, Ohio

Notes for Marion D.:
Marion D. Papenhagen
Born: 16 Jan 1901
Died: Sep 1990
State (Year) SSN issued: Ohio (1969)

Children of Frank Papenhagen and Marion D. are:

i. Boy[5] Papenhagen, b. ABT 1921.
ii. Girl Papenhagen, b. ABT 1923.

11. Edna[4] Papenhagen *(Franz Wilhelm Johann[3], Joachim Christian Johann[2], Heinrich[1])* was born ABT 1893 in Ohio. She married Robert W. Emery. He was born ABT 1893 in Ohio.

Notes for Edna Papenhagen:
Historical Newspapers > Lima News (Lima, Ohio) > 1931 > October > 5
FRANK J PAPENHAGEN was shot in the head October 5, 1931
Financial problems, he is in the hospital with his wife, son, Frank W. and daughter Mrs. Robert Emery of Toledo.

Notes for Robert W. Emery:
1930 Census > Ohio > Lucas > Ottawa Hills > District 179
Robert W. Emery, age 27, deparment manager, supermarket store; born in Ohio, both parents born in Ohio; Edna P age 27, born in Ohio; Helen Edwards, 3 1/2 born in Ohio; Carolyn K. 2 4/12 (months) born in Ohio; Joy M. Foer, servant age 27.

Children of Edna Papenhagen and Robert Emery are:

- i. Carolyn K.[5] Emery, b. ABT 1927, Ohio.
- ii. Helen Edwards Emery, b. ABT 1926, Ohio.

12. Helen I.[4] Doering *(Marie Henriette Magdalene Guste[3] Papenhagen, Joachim Christian Johann[2], Heinrich[1])* was born 02 Nov 1903 in Toledo, Ohio. She married Elmer Swartz. He was born ABT 1902.

Notes for Helen I. Doering:
1910 U.S. Census • Ohio • Lucas • Toledo city • ED# 107
Albert W. Doering, age 32, Married 1x, married 8 years; cigarmaker, factory, born in Ohio, parents from Germany; Mary H. age 30, wife, married 8 years, 1 x; had 3 children; 3 survive; born in Germany, parents born in Germany; Helen I age 8; Marie H. age 5; Gertrude S is age 3; children all born in Ohio.

Census 1920 Toledo, Lucas, Ohio
Albert Doering, age 43 born in Ohio, shipping clerk for a hardware company, parents born in Germany; Mary age 41, born in Germany; Helen age 17, book-keeper, born in Ohio; Marie 15; Gertrude 12; Thelma age 4.

HELEN M SWARTZ
Gender: Female
Date of Death: 1969 65, Years
Volume: 19803
Certificate: 069106
Place of Death: Hocking County
Race: White
Residence: 12, 09
Age: Married
Helen Swartz
Last Residence: 43138 Logan, Hocking, Ohio, United States of America
Born: 2 Nov 1903

Died: Sep 1969
State (Year) SSN issued: Ohio (1965)

Helen Swartz
Last Residence: 49120 Niles, Berrien, Michigan, United States of America
Born: 25 Dec 1902
Died: Feb 1987
State (Year) SSN issued: Michigan (Before 1951)

Helen used to have fur coats, and would hang them on the line outdoors to air them out.

—Alice Taylor

CANNOT LOCATE Helen or Elmer in 1930 census. Elmer was an electrician around Toledo. Elmer was the one who installed the electric wiring in the Burbank farm house.

Children of HELEN DOERING and ELMER SWARTZ are:

- i. BOY[5] SWARTZ, b. ABT 1923.
- ii. JOANNE SWARTZ, b. ABT 1924; m. NOPPE.

13. MARIE[4] DOERING *(MARIE HENRIETTE MAGDALENE GUSTE[3] PAPENHAGEN, JOACHIM CHRISTIAN JOHANN[2], HEINRICH[1])* was born 12 Dec 1904 in Toledo, Ohio, and died 08 Jun 1999 in Toledo, Ohio. She married DR. HAROLD ERSIG Aft. 1930. He was born 09 Aug 1893 in St. Mary's, Ohio, and died 04 Jan 1970 in Lucas Co, Ohio.

Notes for MARIE DOERING:
1910 U.S. Census • Ohio • Lucas • Toledo city • ED# 107
Albert W. Doering, age 32, Married 1x, married 8 years; cigarmaker, factory, born in Ohio, parents from Germany; Mary H. age 30, wife, married 8 years, 1 x; had 3 children; 3 survive; born in Germany, parents born in Germany; Helen I age 8; Marie H. age 5; Gertrude S is age 3; children all born in Ohio.

Census 1920 Toledo, Lucas, Ohio
Albert Doering, age 43 born in Ohio, shipping clerk for a hardware company, parents born in Germany; Mary age 41, born in Germany; Helen age 17, bookkeeper, born in Ohio; Marie 15; Gertrude 12; Thelma age 4.

1930 Census Ohio > Lucas > Toledo > District 103
Albert W. Doering, age 52, married 1x, age 23 when first married, shipping clerk; Mary H. age 51, Marie J. age 25, teacher, public school; Gertrude A, age 23, personnel director, department store; Thelma, age 15.

Name: MARIE D(oering) ERSIG
Gender: Female
Date of Death: June 8, 1999
Birth Date: December 12, 1904
Volume: 32013
Certificate: 051078
Autopsy: N
Father's Surname: DOERING
Time of Death: 4:01 AM
Marital Status: widowed
Hispanic Origin: Not Hispanic
Place of Death: hospital/inpatient
Years of Schooling: 16
Certifier: Physician
Branch of Service:
Method of Disposition: Cremation
Mother's Surname: PAPENHAGEN
Race: White
Birth Place: TOLEDO, LUCAS, Ohio
Residence: TOLEDO, LUCAS, Ohio
Age: 94 years

Notes for Dr. Harold Ersig:
OHIO MILITARY MEN 1917–1918
Harold Ersig, 315 Buffalo St., Toledo, O. Recruiting Station Newport, R. I.
07 Jul 1917
St Marys, Ohio.
9 Aug 1893

Source Information:
Ancestry.com. Ohio Military Men, 1917–18. [database on-line] Provo, UT: Ancestry.com, 2000. Original data from: Official Roster of Ohio Soldiers, Sailors and Marines in the World War, 1917–1918, Volumes I-XXIII. Columbus, OH: F. J. Heer Printing Co., 1926.

Harold D Ersig
Gender: Male
Date of Death: 04 January 1970
Volume: 19952
Certificate: 005428
Autopsy: No Autopsy
Marital Status: Married
Place of Death:, Lucas County
Certifier: Physician
Race: White
Residence:, Lucas County
Age: 76 Years

More About HAROLD ERSIG and MARIE DOERING:
Marriage: Aft. 1930

Children of MARIE DOERING and HAROLD ERSIG are:

i. DIANNE[5] ERSIG, b. ABT 1925.
ii. DEAN ERSIG, b. ABT 1926.

14. GERTRUDE[4] DOERING *(MARIE HENRIETTE MAGDALENE GUSTE[3] PAPENHAGEN, JOACHIM CHRISTIAN JOHANN[2], HEINRICH[1])* was born 21 Jan 1907 in Toledo, Ohio, and died 04 Feb 1997 in Whitehall, Trempealeau, Wisconsin. She married FRED MATTKA. He was born 28 Nov 1906 in Wisconsin, and died 05 Feb 1988 in Western Springs, Cook, Illinois.

Notes for GERTRUDE DOERING:
1910 U.S. Census • Ohio • Lucas • Toledo city • ED# 107
Albert W. Doering, age 32, Married 1x, married 8 years; cigarmaker, factory, born in Ohio, parents from Germany; Mary H. age 30, wife, married 8 years, 1 x; had 3 children; 3 survive; born in Germany, parents born in Germany; Helen I age 8; Marie H. age 5; Gertrude S is age 3; children all born in Ohio.

Census 1920 Toledo, Lucas, Ohio
Albert Doering, age 43 born in Ohio, shipping clerk for a hardware company, parents born in Germany; Mary age 41, born in Germany; Helen age 17, bookkeeper, born in Ohio; Marie 15; Gertrude 12; Thelma age 4.

1930 Census Ohio > Lucas > Toledo > District 103
Albert W. Doering, age 52, married 1x, age 23 when first married, shipping clerk; Mary H. age 51, Marie J. age 25, teacher, public school; Gertrude A, age 23, personnel director, department store; Thelma, age 15.

Gertrude D. Mattka
Last Residence: 54773 Whitehall, Trempealeau, Wisconsin, United States of America
Born: 21 Jan 1907
Died: 4 Feb 1997
State (Year) SSN issued: Illinois (1957–1959)

Notes for FRED MATTKA:
Fred Mattka
Age: 24 years
Estimated birth year: 1905
Birthplace: Wisconsin
Relation to Head-of-house: Lodger
Race: White
Home in 1930: Schenectady, Schenectady, New York
(under occupation, he lists "radio test".)

Frederick A. Mattka
Last Residence: 60558 Western Springs, Cook, Illinois, United States of America
Born: 28 Nov 1906
Died: 5 Feb 1988
State (Year) SSN issued: Illinois (Before 1951)

Children of GERTRUDE DOERING and FRED MATTKA are:

i. MEREDITH[5] MATTKA, b. ABT 1940.

ii. BILLY MATTKA, b. 01 Feb 1941; d. 02 Apr 2004.

Notes for BILLY MATTKA:
William A. Mattka
Born: 1 Feb 1941
Died: 2 Apr 2004
State (Year) SSN issued: Illinois (1955–1956)

iii. JERRY MATTKA, b. ABT 1943.

15. THELMA[4] DOERING *(MARIE HENRIETTE MAGDALENE GUSTE[3] PAPENHAGEN, JOACHIM CHRISTIAN JOHANN[2], HEINRICH[1])* was born ABT 1916 in Ohio. She married LEONARD JACOBS.

Notes for THELMA DOERING:
Census 1920 Toledo, Lucas, Ohio
Albert Doering, age 43 born in Ohio, shipping clerk for a hardware company, parents born in Germany; Mary age 41, born in Germany; Helen age 17, bookkeeper, born in Ohio; Marie 15; Gertrude 12; Thelma age 4.

1930 Census Ohio > Lucas > Toledo > District 103
Albert W. Doering, age 52, married 1x, age 23 when first married, shipping clerk; Mary H. age 51, Marie J. age 25, teacher, public school; Gertrude A, age 23, personnel director, department store; Thelma, age 15.

Children of THELMA DOERING and LEONARD JACOBS are:
i. ELAINE[5] JACOBS.
ii. MARY JACOBS.

16. ELOISE[4] PAPENHAGEN *(HERMAN FRIEDRICK JOHANN WILHELM[3], JOACHIM CHRISTIAN JOHANN[2], HEINRICH[1])* was born ABT 1916 in Ohio. She married CHARLES QUINN. He was born 09 Nov 1909, and died 19 Nov 1967.

Notes for ELOISE PAPENHAGEN:
1930 Census
Name: Louise H Papenhagen
Age: 53 years
Estimated birth year: 1876
Birthplace: Ohio
Relation to Head-of-house: Head
Race: White
Home in 1930: Toledo, Lucas, Ohio
Louise H Papenhagen age 53, born in Ohio, son Arnold age 29 born in Ohio; Eloise J age 14, born in Ohio.

Elsie C PAPENHAGEN
Birth Date: 16 May 93
Death Date: 12 May 82
Gender: Female
Residence: Adrian, Lenawee, Michigan

1930 Census: Toledo, Lucas, Ohio
Louise H. Papenhagen, head, age 53, Divorced; Arnold son, age 29; Eloise J. age 14.

Child of ELOISE PAPENHAGEN and CHARLES QUINN is:
i. ADOPTED BOY[5] QUINN, b. ABT 1936.

17. ARNOLD[4] PAPENHAGEN *(HERMAN FRIEDRICK JOHANN WILHELM[3], JOACHIM CHRISTIAN JOHANN[2], HEINRICH[1])* was born 11 Mar 1901 in Ohio[3,3,4], and died 03 Feb 1982 in Perrysburg, Wood, Ohio[5,5]. He married HELEN. She was born ABT 1901.

Notes for ARNOLD PAPENHAGEN:
1880 Census: 9 Ward, Toledo, Lucas, Ohio
Herman, Head age 33, married 1x, born in Germany; Louise, wife age 33 born in Ohio; had 2 children, 2 children survive; Herman and Louise's parents born in Germany; Herman is a brick contractor, works for himself; Marie age 10; Arnold age 9 (b abt 1871), both children born in Ohio. ***

1930 Census: Toledo, Lucas, Ohio
Louise H. Papenhagen, head, age 53, Divorced; Arnold son, age 29; Eloise J. age 14.

Historical Newspapers > Lima News (Lima, Ohio) > 1938 > May > 5
Lieutenant Arnold Papenhagen cut by glass in the fire … Toledo, Ohio

Historical Newspapers > Chronicle Telegram (Elyria, Ohio) > 1956 > February
"Fire Chief, Arnold Papenhagen … Toledo, Ohio"

DEATH NOTICE
Name: Arnold F Papenhagen
Gender: Male

Date of Death: 03 February 1982
Birth Date: 11 March 1901
Volume: 24754
Certificate: 011697
Autopsy: Yes—Used for certification
Marital Status: Widowed (NEED TO FIND WIFE)
Hispanic Origin: German
Place of Death: Sylvania, Lucas County
Certifier: Physician
Race: White
Birth Place: Ohio
Residence: Perrysburg, Wood County
Age: 80 Years

1930 Census: Toledo, Lucas, Ohio
Louise H. Papenhagen, head, age 53, Divorced; Arnold son, age 29; Eloise J. age 14.

Arnold Papenhagen
Last Residence: 43551 Perrysburg, Wood, Ohio, United States of America
Born: 11 Mar 1901
Died: Feb 1982
State (Year) SSN issued: Ohio (Before 1951)

Child of ARNOLD PAPENHAGEN and HELEN is:
i. TED[5] PAPENHAGEN, b. ABT 1921.

18. ETHEL S.[4] PAPENHAGEN *(PAUL LUDWIG FRIEDRICH CHRISTIAN[3], JOACHIM CHRISTIAN JOHANN[2], HEINRICH[1])* was born 27 Oct 1901 in Michigan, and died 29 Jan 1981 in Norvell,Jackson, Michigan. She married WALTER H. KOMSTELLER 22 Feb 1925, son of HENRY COMSTELLER and LOUISA. He was born 07 Dec 1901 in Monroe, Michigan[6,7], and died 29 Oct 1973 in Norvell,Jackson, Michigan[8,9].

Notes for ETHEL S. PAPENHAGEN:
Social Security Death Index
Ethel S KOMSTELLER
Birth Date: 27 October 01
Death Date: 29 January 81

Gender: Female
Residence: Norvell, Jackson, Michigan

Notes for WALTER H. KOMSTELLER:
1910 Census Michigan • Monroe • Monroe City • ED# 110
Comsteller, Henry, Head age 50, born in Germany; Louisa, wife age 48 born in Wisconsin; Louis, son age 20 born in Michigan, Alfred age 16, born in MI, Julius age 10 born in MI, Walter age 8 born in Mi, Carl age 4 born in MI.

Individual: Komsteller, Walter
Issued in: Michigan
Birth date: Dec 7, 1901
Death date: Oct 1973
Residence code: Michigan
ZIP Code of last known residence: 49230
Primary location associated with this ZIP Code: Brooklyn, Michigan

Walter H KOMSTELLER
Birth Date: 07 December 01
Death Date: 29 October 73
Gender: Male
Residence: Norvell, Jackson, Michigan

Only listed Komsteller in the United States Census 1920, married to Helen., no children
Julius Komsteller
Age: 22 years
Estimated birth year: 1897
Birthplace: Ohio
Race: White
Home in 1920: Bedford, Monroe, Michigan

More About WALTER KOMSTELLER and ETHEL PAPENHAGEN:
Marriage: 22 Feb 1925

Children of ETHEL PAPENHAGEN and WALTER KOMSTELLER are:

37. i. Loann Clare[5] Komsteller, b. 10 Dec 1932, Los Angeles, CA.
38. ii. Neal Walter Komsteller, b. 07 Dec 1934, Streator, Illinois.
39. iii. Jane Lee Komsteller, b. 18 Dec 1937, Union City.

19. NORMAN HENRY[4] PAPENHAGEN *(PAUL LUDWIG FRIEDRICH CHRISTIAN[3], JOACHIM CHRISTIAN JOHANN[2], HEINRICH[1])* was born 05 May 1907 in Michigan, and died 06 May 1995 in Michigan. He married DORIS 22 Feb 1931.

Notes for NORMAN HENRY PAPENHAGEN:
Name: Norman Henry Papenhagen
Gender: Male
Date of Death: 06 May 1995
Birth Date: 05 May 1907
Volume: 30253
Certificate: 040205
Autopsy: Yes
Father's Surname: Papenhagen
Time of Death: 11:35 PM
Marital Status: Married
Hispanic Origin: Non Hispanic
Place of Death: Hospital/Inpatient
Years of Schooling: 08
Certifier: Coroner
Referred to Coroner: Yes
Method of Disposition: Burial
Mother's Surname: Elg
Race: White
Birth Place: Michigan
Residence: Michigan
Age: 88

1930 Census: Norman Papenhogen
Age: 22 years
Estimated birth year: 1907
Relation to Head-of-house: Son
Home in 1930: Whiteford, Monroe, Michigan

1930 Census: Whiteford, Monroe, Michigan
Paul, head age 52; born in Germany, farmer; Emma age 57, born in Michigan; Norman, age 22; Herbert age 21; and Doris age 15, born in Michigan

More About NORMAN PAPENHAGEN and DORIS:
Marriage: 22 Feb 1931

Children of NORMAN PAPENHAGEN and DORIS are:

40.	i.	Pauline[5] Papenhagen, b. ABT 1932.
	ii.	GERALD PAPENHAGEN, b. ABT 1934.
41.	iii.	Gail Papenhagen, b. ABT 1935.
42.	iv.	Susan Papenhagen, b. ABT 1937.

20. DORIS[4] PAPENHAGEN *(PAUL LUDWIG FRIEDRICH CHRISTIAN[3], JOACHIM CHRISTIAN JOHANN[2], HEINRICH[1])* was born 23 Jul 1914 in Ottawa Lake, Michigan. She married HOWARD NEVER 22 Feb 1936. He was born 15 Feb 1913 in Lucas, Toledo, Ohio, and died 28 Apr 2000 in Sylvania, Lucas, Ohio.

Notes for DORIS PAPENHAGEN:
1930 Census: Whiteford, Monroe, Michigan
Paul, head age 52; 22 when he was first marriage (this is perhaps second marriage) born in Germany, farmer; Emma age 57, age 22 when she was first married. born in Michigan; Norman, age 22; Herbert age 21; and Doris age 15, born in Michigan.

Notes for HOWARD NEVER:
1930 United States Federal Census > Ohio > Lucas > Toledo > District 72
Albert, head, age 43, widow, born in Ohio, works at an auto factory; Clifford, son age 21 works at auto factory; Howard age 16 and Kenneth age 12.

Courtesy of Michael Hilborn.
Howard G. Never
Last Residence: 43560 Sylvania, Lucas, Ohio, United States of America
Born: 15 Feb 1913
Died: 28 Apr 2000
State (Year) SSN issued: Ohio (Before 1951)

More About HOWARD NEVER and DORIS PAPENHAGEN:
Marriage: 22 Feb 1936

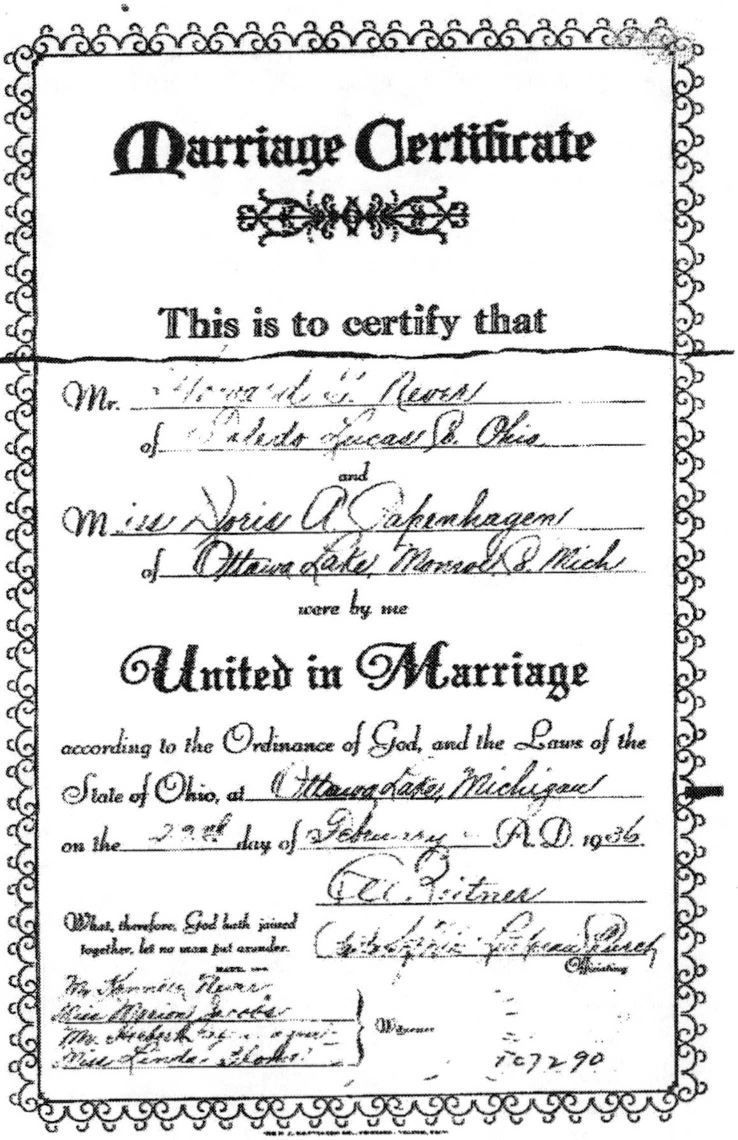

Marriage Certificate

This is to certify that

Mr. [illegible] Never

of [illegible] Lucas Co. Ohio

and

Miss Doris A. Papenhagen

of Ottawa Lake, Monroe Co. Mich

were by me

United in Marriage

according to the Ordinance of God, and the Laws of the State of Ohio, at Ottawa Lake, Michigan

on the 29th day of February A.D. 1936.

[illegible] Reitner

What, therefore, God hath joined together, let no man put asunder.

[illegible] Officiating

Witnesses: [illegible]

Doris A Papenhagen & George Never Marriage Certificate
Courtesy of Les Meier. Circ 1936.

Children of DORIS PAPENHAGEN and HOWARD NEVER are:

43. i. Dathel[5] Never, b. 26 Nov 1938.
44. ii. Marian Bethany Never, b. 14 Jul 1945.
45. iii. Paul Grant Never, b. 18 Nov 1941.
46. iv. Rebecca Sue Never, b. 12 Oct 1948.

21. HERBERT[4] PAPENHAGEN *(PAUL LUDWIG FRIEDRICH CHRISTIAN[3], JOACHIM CHRISTIAN JOHANN[2], HEINRICH[1])* was born 02 Nov 1908 in Michigan[10,10,11,11], and died 05 Jul 1988 in Bradenton, Florida[12,12,13]. He married LINDA BLOME 22 Feb 1937. She was born 20 Jun 1916.

Notes for HERBERT PAPENHAGEN:
1930 Census: Whiteford, Monroe, Michigan
Paul, head age 52; 22 when he was first married (this is perhaps second marriage) born in Germany, farmer; Emma age 57, age 22 when she was first married, born in Michigan; Norman, age 22; Herbert age 21; and Doris age 15, born in Michigan.

Herbert Papenhagen
Last Residence: 34210 Bradenton, Manatee, Florida, United States of America
Born: 2 Nov 1908
Died: 5 Jul 1988

Herbert Papenhagen died on July 5, 1988. Born November 2, 1908, Papenhagen was 79 years old and lived in Bradenton, FL.

Herbert L Papenhagen
Gender: Male
Date of Death: 05 July 1988
Birth Date: 02 November 1908
Volume: 27368
Certificate: 053975
Autopsy: Yes—Used for certification
Social Security
Marital Status: Married
Hispanic Origin: German
Place of Death: Toledo, Lucas County
Certifier: Physician
Race: White

Birth Place: Michigan
Residence: Out-of-State, Out-of-State
Age: 79 Years

More About HERBERT PAPENHAGEN and LINDA BLOME:
Marriage: 22 Feb 1937

Children of HERBERT PAPENHAGEN and LINDA BLOME are:

47. i. David Herbert[5] Papenhagen, b. 12 Sep 1939.
48. ii. Diann Papenhagen, b. ABT 1940.
49. iii. Brian Papenhagen, b. ABT 1942.

22. ELMER[4] SCHUMACHER *(BERTHA HENRIETTA WILHELMINE[3] PAPENHAGEN, JOACHIM CHRISTIAN JOHANN[2], HEINRICH[1])* was born 10 Jan 1912 in Michigan. He married EUNICE. She was born 09 Mar 1913, and died 05 Sep 1985.

Notes for ELMER SCHUMACHER:
1930 United States Federal Census > Michigan > Monroe > Whiteford > District 38
John C. Schumacher, age 50, 28 when he first got married, born in Germany; emigrated 1881; Bertha age 45 born in Germany, emigrated 1891, age 23 when she first was married; Elmer J age 18, born in Michigan; Frank, 11 born in Michigan; Ray (maybe Roy) age 9, born in Michigan;

Notes for EUNICE:
POSSIBLE—yet to be proved.
Eunice M Schumacher
Gender: 2
Date of Death: 05 September 1985
Birth Date: 09 March 1913
Volume: 26180
Certificate: 069294
Autopsy: 9
Marital Status: Married
Hispanic Origin: German
Place of Death: Sylvania, Lucas County
Certifier: Physician
Race: White
Birth Place: Ohio

Residence: Sylvania, Lucas County
Age: 72 Years

Children of ELMER SCHUMACHER and EUNICE are:

i. BARBARA[5] SCHUMACHER, b. 09 Nov 1934.
50. ii. James R. Schumacher, b. 05 Sep 1945.

23. FRANK[4] SCHUMACHER *(BERTHA HENRIETTA WILHELMINE[3] PAPENHAGEN, JOACHIM CHRISTIAN JOHANN[2], HEINRICH[1])* was born ABT 1909 in Michigan. He married ALGIE. She was born ABT 1909.

Notes for FRANK SCHUMACHER:
1930 United States Federal Census > Michigan > Monroe > Whiteford > District 38
John C. Schumacher, age 50, 28 when he first got married, born in Germany; emigrated 1881, farmer; Bertha age 45 born in Germany, emigrated 1891, age 23 when she first was married; Elmer J age 18, born in Michigan; Frank, 11 born in Michigan; Ray (maybe Roy) age 9, born in Michigan

----
POSSIBLE OTHER FAMILY MEMBERS:
1930 Census: 1930 United States Federal Census > Ohio > Monroe > Woodsfield > District 4
Frank E. Schumacher, age 44 born in Ohio, clerk in a furniture store, Bertha, wife age 43, born in Ohio; James age 6, son, born in Ohio. married about 12 years.

1930 United States Federal Census > Ohio > Monroe > Woodsfield > District 4 (next store) George, age 23, born in Ohio, head; Minnie, wife age 23 born in Ohio.

Margurite Schumacher, age 71, (same page) head, widow. no one else in family.

Children of FRANK SCHUMACHER and ALGIE are:

i. LARRY[5] SCHUMACHER.
ii. TOM SCHUMACHER.
iii. CINDY SCHUMACHER.
iv. JOAN SCHUMACHER.
v. JOHN JR. SCHUMACHER.

24. Roy[4] Schumacher *(Bertha Henrietta Wilhelmine[3] Papenhagen, Joachim Christian Johann[2], Heinrich[1])* was born 31 Jan 1921 in Michigan, and died 12 Sep 1971. He married Donna.

Notes for Roy Schumacher:
1930 United States Federal Census > Michigan > Monroe > Whiteford > District 38
John C. Schumacher, age 50, 28 when he first got married, born in Germany; emigrated 1881, farmer; Bertha age 45 born in Germany, emigrated 1891, age 23 when she first was married; Elmer J age 18, born in Michigan; Frank, 11 born in Michigan; Ray (maybe Roy) age 9, born in Michigan;

Children of Roy Schumacher and Donna are:
i. Richard[5] Schumacher.
ii. Robert Schumacher.
iii. Susan Schumacher.
iv. Ronald Schumacher.

25. Loretta Mattie[4] Tegtmeier *(Erna Henriette Sophie[3] Papenhagen, Joachim Christian Johann[2], Heinrich[1])* was born 26 Aug 1911. She married Paul Franklin Berry 15 Jun 1935. He was born ABT 1908.

(Please see Tegtmeier Family for further information.)

Children of Loretta Tegtmeier and Paul Berry are:
51. i. David[5] Berry, b. ABT 1940.
52. ii. Karen Berry, b. ABT 1941.

26. Raymond Julius[4] Tegtmeier *(Erna Henriette Sophie[3] Papenhagen, Joachim Christian Johann[2], Heinrich[1])* was born 07 Dec 1912 in Brookpark, OH[14,14,15], and died Sep 1982 in Wayne County, Ohio[16,16,17]. He married Laura Anna Minichbauer. She was born 01 Aug 1916 in Cleveland, Cuyahoga County, Ohio[18,18,19], and died 10 Oct 1995 in Wayne County, Ohio[20,20,21].

(Please see Tegtmeier Family for further information.)

Children of Raymond Tegtmeier and Laura Minichbauer are:

53.	i.	Donna Mae[5] Tegtmeier, b. 01 Sep 1944.
54.	ii.	Sharon Lee Tegtmeier, b. 04 Jan 1947.
55.	iii.	Daniel Howard Tegtmeier, b. 23 Sep 1957.

27. Alice Henrietta[4] Tegtmeier *(Erna Henriette Sophie[3] Papenhagen, Joachim Christian Johann[2], Heinrich[1])* was born 28 May 1916 in Brookpark, Ohio. She married (1) Edward William Taylor 02 Jul 1940 in Buffalo, NY, son of George Taylor and Mayme Trautman. He was born 01 Aug 1914 in New York, and died 22 Jan 1967 in Jost Van Dyke, US Virgin Islands. She married (2) John Goralsky ABT 1973. He was born in Coalport, PA, and died in Cleveland, OH.

(Please see Tegtmeier Family for further information.)

Children of Alice Tegtmeier and Edward Taylor are:

56.	i.	Shirley Ann[5] Taylor, b. 11 Oct 1941, Scranton, PA.
57.	ii.	Edward William Taylor, b. 11 Jan 1944, Alden, NY.
58.	iii.	James Robert Taylor, b. 22 Mar 1949, Berea, Ohio.
59.	iv.	Sandra Mina Taylor, b. 17 Mar 1950, Berea, Ohio.

28. Henry Adolph[4] Tegtmeier *(Erna Henriette Sophie[3] Papenhagen, Joachim Christian Johann[2], Heinrich[1])* was born 19 Mar 1918 in Ohio[22,22,23], and died 09 Dec 1992 in Fairfield Glade, TN[24,24,25]. He married Harriett Barendt 28 May 1945. She was born 09 Jan 1923 in Cleveland, Cuyahoga Co., OH.

(Please see Tegtmeier Family for further information.)

Children of Henry Tegtmeier and Harriett Barendt are:

	i.	Miriam Ann[5] Tegtmeier, b. 08 Apr 1946; m. Paul Camper; b. ABT 1937.
60.	ii.	Joan Charlotte Tegtmeier, b. 07 Aug 1947.
61.	iii.	Paul Tegtmeier, b. 03 Aug 1948.
62.	iv.	Joel Tegtmeier, b. 13 Aug 1959.

29. William Edward[4] Tegtmeier *(Erna Henriette Sophie[3] Papenhagen, Joachim Christian Johann[2], Heinrich[1])* was born 06 Mar 1920 in Brookpark, Ohio, and died 24 Jul 2000 in Savanah, OH. He married Lois Genvieve

WESTLUND 15 Jun 1946, daughter of EMIL WESTLUND and SIGRID. She was born 31 Dec 1922 in Youngstown, Ohio.

(Please see Tegtmeier Family for further information.)

Children of WILLIAM TEGTMEIER and LOIS WESTLUND are:

63. i. Linda Jean[5] Tegtmeier, b. 24 Aug 1947, Youngstown, OH, North Side Hospital.

ii. TERRY TEGTMEIER, b. ABT 1949.

64. iii. Timothy Tegtmeier, b. 15 Sep 1955.

iv. TODD ALAN TEGTMEIER, b. 19 Feb 1962; m. WENDY FLOYD, 19 Dec 1993.

More About TODD TEGTMEIER and WENDY FLOYD:
Marriage: 19 Dec 1993

30. HAROLD WILLIAM[4] TEGTMEIER *(ERNA HENRIETTE SOPHIE[3] PAPENHAGEN, JOACHIM CHRISTIAN JOHANN[2], HEINRICH[1])* was born 02 Mar 1921 in Brookpark, Ohio, and died 18 May 2003 in West Salem, Wayne, Ohio. He married LUCILLE CLARISSA HERMAN 02 Mar 1943 in Jackson Presbyterian Church, Creston, Ohio. She was born 12 Sep 1922 in Hermanville, Creston, Ohio.

(Please see Tegtmeier Family for further information.)

Children of HAROLD TEGTMEIER and LUCILLE HERMAN are:

65. i. James Herman[5] Tegtmeier, b. 14 Feb 1945, Lodi Hospital, near Wooster, Ohio.

66. ii. Donald Phillip Tegtmeier, b. 14 Nov 1948, Lodi Hospital, near Wooster, Ohio.

67. iii. Barbara Lucille Tegtmeier, b. 15 Dec 1952, Lodi Hospital, near Wooster, Ohio.

68. iv. David Harold Tegtmeier, b. 15 Sep 1954, Lodi Hospital, near Wooster, Ohio.

31. RICHARD ELMER[4] TEGTMEIER *(ERNA HENRIETTE SOPHIE[3] PAPENHAGEN, JOACHIM CHRISTIAN JOHANN[2], HEINRICH[1])* was born 03 Jan 1924 in Berea,Cuyahoga Co.OH, and died 17 Oct 1995 in Crossville, TN[26,26,27]. He married SANDY LOUISE KESTNER 29 Sep 1951 in Ashland, Ashland Co. OH, daughter of FREDERICK KESTNER and ADELAIDE FAIR. She was born 26 Sep 1933 in Ashland, Ashland Co., OH.

(Please see Tegtmeier Family for further information.)

Children of RICHARD TEGTMEIER and SANDY KESTNER are:

69. i. Douglas Richard[5] Tegtmeier, b. 06 Dec 1952, Wooster, Montgomery Co., OH.
70. ii. Debra Louise Tegtmeier, b. 09 Jan 1955, Wooster, Wayne Co. OH.
71. iii. Dean Edward Tegtmeier, b. 02 Mar 1957, Ashland, Ashland Co., OH.

32. LOIS RUTH[4] TEGTMEIER *(ERNA HENRIETTE SOPHIE[3] PAPENHAGEN, JOACHIM CHRISTIAN JOHANN[2], HEINRICH[1])* was born 18 Mar 1928 in maybe Brookpark, OH. She married PETER CORNELIUS HINRICHS 03 Jun 1950 in W. Canaan, Wayne Co., Ohio at Canaan Lutheran Church, son of PETER HINRICHS and EMMA GROTH. He was born 23 Oct 1925 in Arlington, Kingsbury, SD, and died 31 Jul 1994 in Dickinson, Stark Co. ND.

(Please see Tegtmeier Family for further information.)

More About PETER HINRICHS and LOIS TEGTMEIER:
Marriage: 03 Jun 1950, W. Canaan, Wayne Co., Ohio at Canaan Lutheran Church

Children of LOIS TEGTMEIER and PETER HINRICHS are:

72. i. Mark Peter[5] Hinricks, b. 30 Oct 1951, Redfield, SD.
73. ii. Steven Heye Hinricks, b. 23 Jan 1954, Redfield, Spink Co, SD.

33. ESTHER EDNA MARIE[4] PAPENHAGEN *(WALTER FRANKLIN[3], JOACHIM CHRISTIAN JOHANN[2], HEINRICH[1])* was born 07 Sep 1917 in Michigan. She married RAYMOND FREDRICK SEAGERT 17 Mar 1938. He was born 02 May 1913, and died 19 Jul 1981.

Notes for ESTHER EDNA MARIE PAPENHAGEN:
1930 Census: Whiteford, Monroe, Michigan
Walter H Popenhagen, head age 37 born in Ohio; Elsie C. age 36, born in Michigan; Mildred W age 16 born in MI; Esther E, age 12, MI; Erna E age 10; Clifford W age 6; Clyde K age 6

More About RAYMOND SEAGERT and ESTHER PAPENHAGEN:
Marriage: 17 Mar 1938

Children of ESTHER PAPENHAGEN and RAYMOND SEAGERT are:
74. i. Diana June[5] Seagert, b. 12 Jun 1939.
75. ii. Richard Ray Seagert, b. 09 Apr 1943.
76. iii. Linda Marie Seagert, b. 04 Jul 1952.

34. ERNA ETHEL ELIZABETH[4] PAPENHAGEN *(WALTER FRANKLIN[3], JOACHIM CHRISTIAN JOHANN[2], HEINRICH[1])* was born 02 Dec 1919 in Michigan. She married ARTHUR WILLIAM BRENKE, SR. 19 Nov 1941 in Lenawee, Michigan. He was born 04 Feb 1921.

Notes for ERNA ETHEL ELIZABETH PAPENHAGEN:
1930 Census: Whiteford, Monroe, Michigan
Walter H Popenhagen, head age 37 born in Ohio; Elsie C. age 36, born in Michigan; Mildred W age 16 born in MI; Esther E, age 12, MI; Erna E age 10; Clifford W age 6; Clyde K age 6

More About ARTHUR BRENKE and ERNA PAPENHAGEN:
Marriage: 19 Nov 1941, Lenawee, Michigan

Children of ERNA PAPENHAGEN and ARTHUR BRENKE are:
77. i. Arthur Walter Jr.[5] Brenke, b. 04 Jul 1944.
78. ii. Sharon Sue Brenke, b. 03 Nov 1946.
79. iii. Brenda Ann Brenke, b. 30 Aug 1949.

35. CLIFFORD W.[4] PAPENHAGEN *(WALTER FRANKLIN[3], JOACHIM CHRISTIAN JOHANN[2], HEINRICH[1])* was born 28 Oct 1923 in Michigan, and died 11 Apr 1988 in Peoria, Maricopa, Arizona. He married ARLENE MAE SATRE 14 Jul 1945. She was born ABT 1923.

Notes for CLIFFORD W. PAPENHAGEN:
1930 Census: Whiteford, Monroe, Michigan
Walter H Popenhagen, head age 37 born in Ohio; Elsie C. age 36, born in Michigan; Mildred W age 16 born in MI; Esther E, age 12, MI; Erna E age 10; Clifford W age 6; Clyde K age 6

Clifford W. Papenhagen
Last Residence: 85345 Peoria, Maricopa, Arizona, United States of America
Born: 28 Oct 1923
Died: 11 Apr 1988
State (Year) SSN issued: Michigan (Before 1951)

More About CLIFFORD PAPENHAGEN and ARLENE SATRE:
Marriage: 14 Jul 1945

Children of CLIFFORD PAPENHAGEN and ARLENE SATRE are:
i. LARRY W.[5] PAPENHAGEN, b. ABT 1943.
ii. MARSHA PAPENHAGEN, b. ABT 1944; m. LEDENICIAN.

36. CLYDE K.[4] PAPENHAGEN *(WALTER FRANKLIN[3], JOACHIM CHRISTIAN JOHANN[2], HEINRICH[1])* was born 28 Oct 1923 in Michigan. He married HILDA ELIZABETH BRENKE 19 Apr 1944. She was born 12 Feb 1925.

Notes for CLYDE K. PAPENHAGEN:
1930 Census: Whiteford, Monroe, Michigan
Walter H Popenhagen, head age 37 born in Ohio; Elsie C. age 36, born in Michigan; Mildred W age 16 born in MI; Esther E, age 12, MI; Erna E age 10; Clifford W age 6; Clyde K age 6

More About CLYDE PAPENHAGEN and HILDA BRENKE:
Marriage: 19 Apr 1944

Children of CLYDE PAPENHAGEN and HILDA BRENKE are:
80. i. Kenneth Roger[5] Papenhagen, b. 11 Sep 1946.
81. ii. Yvonne Jean Papenhagen, b. 22 Jul 1950.

Generation No. 4

37. Loann Clare[5] Komsteller *(Ethel S.[4] Papenhagen, Paul Ludwig Friedrich Christian[3], Joachim Christian Johann[2], Heinrich[1])* was born 10 Dec 1932 in Los Angeles, CA. She married Gene B. Fairweather 04 Oct 1953. He was born 08 Jun 1932.

More About Gene Fairweather and Loann Komsteller:
Marriage: 04 Oct 1953

Children of Loann Komsteller and Gene Fairweather are:

82.	i.	Michael B.[6] Fairweather, b. 23 Nov 1954.
83.	ii.	Linda Lee Fairweather, b. 01 Jun 1956.
	iii.	Jean Marie Fairweather, b. 11 Oct 1960; m. David West.

38. Neal Walter[5] Komsteller *(Ethel S.[4] Papenhagen, Paul Ludwig Friedrich Christian[3], Joachim Christian Johann[2], Heinrich[1])* was born 07 Dec 1934 in Streator, Illinois. He married Donna Hayes 12 Feb 1955. She was born 11 Jan 1933.

More About Neal Komsteller and Donna Hayes:
Marriage: 12 Feb 1955

Children of Neal Komsteller and Donna Hayes are:

84.	i.	Kimberly Ann[6] Komsteller, b. 12 Dec 1955.
85.	ii.	Jill Marie Komsteller, b. 23 Jul 1959.
86.	iii.	Jeff Neal Komsteller, b. 05 Jun 1961.

39. Jane Lee[5] Komsteller *(Ethel S.[4] Papenhagen, Paul Ludwig Friedrich Christian[3], Joachim Christian Johann[2], Heinrich[1])* was born 18 Dec 1937 in Union City. She married Donald D. Strange 30 Oct 1959. He was born 12 Jun 1936.

More About Donald Strange and Jane Komsteller:
Marriage: 30 Oct 1959

Children of JANE KOMSTELLER and DONALD STRANGE are:

i. MELINDA LEE[6] STRANGE, b. 28 Jan 1961; d. 28 Oct 1961.

87. ii. Bradley John Strange, b. 18 Feb 1962.

88. iii. Brenda Lee Strange, b. 12 Apr 1964.

iv. LORI ANN STRANGE, b. 07 Jan 1969; m. TIMOTHY LYELL, 11 May 1991; b. 23 Jul 1968.

More About TIMOTHY LYELL and LORI STRANGE:
Marriage: 11 May 1991

40. PAULINE[5] PAPENHAGEN *(NORMAN HENRY[4], PAUL LUDWIG FRIEDRICH CHRISTIAN[3], JOACHIM CHRISTIAN JOHANN[2], HEINRICH[1])* was born ABT 1932. She married ROGER WESSENDORF.

Children of PAULINE PAPENHAGEN and ROGER WESSENDORF are:

i. BARBARA[6] WESSENDORF, b. ABT 1950.

ii. ROBERT WESSENDORF, b. ABT 1952.

iii. BRUCE WESSENDORF, b. ABT 1955.

41. GAIL[5] PAPENHAGEN *(NORMAN HENRY[4], PAUL LUDWIG FRIEDRICH CHRISTIAN[3], JOACHIM CHRISTIAN JOHANN[2], HEINRICH[1])* was born ABT 1935. He married RITA. She was born ABT 1935.

Children of GAIL PAPENHAGEN and RITA are:

i. DARLENE[6] PAPENHAGEN, b. ABT 1955.

ii. KELLY PAPENHAGEN, b. ABT 1957.

42. SUSAN[5] PAPENHAGEN *(NORMAN HENRY[4], PAUL LUDWIG FRIEDRICH CHRISTIAN[3], JOACHIM CHRISTIAN JOHANN[2], HEINRICH[1])* was born ABT 1937. She married TERRI ALDRICH. He was born ABT 1937.

Children of SUSAN PAPENHAGEN and TERRI ALDRICH are:

i. DANIEL[6] ALDRICH, b. ABT 1957.

ii. TARA ALDRICH, b. ABT 1960.

43. DATHEL[5] NEVER *(DORIS[4] PAPENHAGEN, PAUL LUDWIG FRIEDRICH CHRISTIAN[3], JOACHIM CHRISTIAN JOHANN[2], HEINRICH[1])* was born 26 Nov 1938. She married ROBERT HILBORN 06 Oct 1962. He was born 18 Oct 1941.

Notes for DATHEL NEVER:
RN, Winter Park, Florida

More About ROBERT HILBORN and DATHEL NEVER:
Marriage: 06 Oct 1962

Children of DATHEL NEVER and ROBERT HILBORN are:
89. i. Mark Robert[6] Hilborn, b. 01 Sep 1963.
90. ii. Scott Alan Hilborn, b. 20 Nov 1965.
91. iii. Michael David Hilborn, b. 16 Nov 1966.

44. MARIAN BETHANY[5] NEVER *(DORIS[4] PAPENHAGEN, PAUL LUDWIG FRIEDRICH CHRISTIAN[3], JOACHIM CHRISTIAN JOHANN[2], HEINRICH[1])* was born 14 Jul 1945. She married (1) BILL DECATOR. She married (2) JOSEPH DONOFRIO. He was born ABT 1945.

Notes for MARIAN BETHANY NEVER:
D-H Machinery, Owner, Toledo OH

Children of MARIAN NEVER and BILL DECATOR are:
92. i. John H.[6] Decator, b. 05 Oct.
93. ii. Jonelle Decator, b. 11 Oct.

45. PAUL GRANT[5] NEVER *(DORIS[4] PAPENHAGEN, PAUL LUDWIG FRIEDRICH CHRISTIAN[3], JOACHIM CHRISTIAN JOHANN[2], HEINRICH[1])* was born 18 Nov 1941. He married JOYCE PHILAUM 03 Aug. She was born 17 Dec 1942.

Notes for PAUL GRANT NEVER:
Ottawa Lake, Michigan, Farmer

More About PAUL NEVER and JOYCE PHILAUM:
Marriage: 03 Aug

Children of PAUL NEVER and JOYCE PHILAUM are:
i. KEITH[6] NEVER, b. June 14, ABT 1962.
ii. TERRI NEVER, b. May 3, ABT 1963.

May 3, no year for birthdate.

Doris Papenhagen Never & Children
Back row: Marian, Rebecca
Front row: Dathel, Doris & Paul

Doris Never sitting with ten of her eleven grandchildren: Back Row: Gina Hooker (Carlson), Lisa Delong (Carlson), Jonelle Montes (DeCator), Terri Never, Laurie Pieper (Never),

94. iii. LAURIE NEVER, b. ABT 1964.

46. REBECCA SUE[5] NEVER *(DORIS[4] PAPENHAGEN, PAUL LUDWIG FRIEDRICH CHRISTIAN[3], JOACHIM CHRISTIAN JOHANN[2], HEINRICH[1])* was born 12 Oct 1948. She married GEORGE CARLSON ABT 1969. He was born 30 Oct 1948.

Notes for REBECCA SUE NEVER:
Office, Louisville.

More About GEORGE CARLSON and REBECCA NEVER:
Divorced: ABT 2003
Marriage: ABT 1969

Children of REBECCA NEVER and GEORGE CARLSON are:

i. TODD[6] CARLSON, b. ABT 1970.

Notes for TODD CARLSON:
Deceased

95. ii. LISA CARLSON, b. 26 Feb 1969.

iii. GINA CARLSON, b. 15 Apr 1972; m. A. JACK HOOKER, 13 Apr 1995.

More About A. HOOKER and GINA CARLSON:
Marriage: 13 Apr 1995

iv. MICHAEL CARLSON, b. 20 Mar 1974.

47. DAVID HERBERT[5] PAPENHAGEN *(HERBERT[4], PAUL LUDWIG FRIEDRICH CHRISTIAN[3], JOACHIM CHRISTIAN JOHANN[2], HEINRICH[1])* was born 12 Sep 1939. He married SHIRLEY GOETZ. She was born ABT 1940.

Children of DAVID PAPENHAGEN and SHIRLEY GOETZ are:

i. DAWN[6] PAPENHAGEN, b. 29 Oct 1963; m. JOEL MAKZIS; b. ABT 1963.

ii. CHRISTIE PAPENHAGEN, b. 21 Jan 1967; m. GARY CHILDERS; b. ABT 1967.

iii. DAVID PAUL PAPENHAGEN, b. 22 Jun 1968.

48. DIANN[5] PAPENHAGEN *(HERBERT[4], PAUL LUDWIG FRIEDRICH CHRISTIAN[3], JOACHIM CHRISTIAN JOHANN[2], HEINRICH[1])* was born ABT 1940. She married JAMES PAVELKA. He was born ABT 1940.

Children of DIANN PAPENHAGEN and JAMES PAVELKA are:

i. PAULA[6] PAVELKA, b. ABT 1960.
ii. STEVEN PAVELKA, b. ABT 1962.
iii. ERIC PAVELKA, b. ABT 1964.

49. BRIAN[5] PAPENHAGEN *(HERBERT[4], PAUL LUDWIG FRIEDRICH CHRISTIAN[3], JOACHIM CHRISTIAN JOHANN[2], HEINRICH[1])* was born ABT 1942. He married VICKIE. She was born ABT 1943.

Children of BRIAN PAPENHAGEN and VICKIE are:

i. TRACEY[6] PAPENHAGEN, b. ABT 1963.
ii. JODEE PAPENHAGEN, b. ABT 1965.
iii. COREY PAPENHAGEN, b. ABT 1966.

50. JAMES R.[5] SCHUMACHER *(ELMER[4], BERTHA HENRIETTA WILHELMINE[3] PAPENHAGEN, JOACHIM CHRISTIAN JOHANN[2], HEINRICH[1])* was born 05 Sep 1945. He married KARALENE 14 Sep 1966.

More About JAMES SCHUMACHER and KARALENE:
Marriage: 14 Sep 1966

Children of JAMES SCHUMACHER and KARALENE are:

i. LAURIE[6] SCHUMACHER.
ii. KENNETH SCHUMACHER.

51. DAVID[5] PAUL BERRY *(LORETTA MATTIE[4] TEGTMEIER, ERNA HENRIETTE SOPHIE[3] PAPENHAGEN, JOACHIM CHRISTIAN JOHANN[2], HEINRICH[1])* was born October 31, 1936. He married BEVERLY ANNE COOPER. She was born August 3, 1939.

(Please see Tegtmeier Family for further information.)

Children of DAVID PAUL BERRY and BEVERLY are:

i. WESLEY[6] DAVID BERRY, b. October 15, 1958.
ii. TAMALA ANNE BERRY, b. Nov 8 1961.
iii. STEPHANIE RENEE BERRY, b. March 7 1969; m. VONDON TIMOTHY ESTEP.

(Please see Tegtmeier Family for further information.)

52. KAREN[5] BERRY *(LORETTA MATTIE[4] TEGTMEIER, ERNA HENRIETTE SOPHIE[3] PAPENHAGEN, JOACHIM CHRISTIAN JOHANN[2], HEINRICH[1])* was born March 22 1942. She married DON BOYER. He was born ABT 1940.

(Please see Tegtmeier Family for further information.)

Children of KAREN BERRY and DON BOYER are:

- i. BRYAN[6] BOYER, b. ABT 1962, Denver, CO.
- ii. BRADLEY BOYER, b. ABT 1963, Denver, CO.
- iii. LISA BOYER, b. ABT 1964, Denver, CO.

53. DONNA MAE[5] TEGTMEIER *(RAYMOND JULIUS[4], ERNA HENRIETTE SOPHIE[3] PAPENHAGEN, JOACHIM CHRISTIAN JOHANN[2], HEINRICH[1])* was born 01 Sep 1944. She married WILLIAM SCHEMRICH 07 Dec 1962. He was born ABT 1928.

(Please see Tegtmeier Family for further information.)

Children of DONNA TEGTMEIER and WILLIAM SCHEMRICH are:

- i. RONNIE[6] SCHEMRICH, b. ABT 1958.
- ii. DALE SCHEMRICH, b. ABT 1959.
- iii. SHAWN SCHEMRICH, b. ABT 1960.

54. SHARON LEE[5] TEGTMEIER *(RAYMOND JULIUS[4], ERNA HENRIETTE SOPHIE[3] PAPENHAGEN, JOACHIM CHRISTIAN JOHANN[2], HEINRICH[1])* was born 04 Jan 1947. She married GARY ERRO 16 May 1967. He was born ABT 1947.

(Please see Tegtmeier Family for further information.)

Children of SHARON TEGTMEIER and GARY ERRO are:

- i. JODY ANN[6] ERRO.
- ii. AMANDA MARIE ERRO.

55. DANIEL HOWARD[5] TEGTMEIER *(RAYMOND JULIUS[4], ERNA HENRIETTE SOPHIE[3] PAPENHAGEN, JOACHIM CHRISTIAN JOHANN[2], HEINRICH[1])* was born 23 Sep 1957. He married BETH ANN BOUGHER 05 May 1978. She was born 14 Jan 1959.

(Please see Tegtmeier Family for further information.)

Children of DANIEL TEGTMEIER and BETH BOUGHER are:

i. ETHAN DANIEL[6] TEGTMEIER, b. 26 Jan 1990.
ii. SARAH CHRISTINE TEGTMEIER, b. 16 May 1993.

56. SHIRLEY ANN[5] TAYLOR *(ALICE HENRIETTA[4] TEGTMEIER, ERNA HENRIETTE SOPHIE[3] PAPENHAGEN, JOACHIM CHRISTIAN JOHANN[2], HEINRICH[1])* was born 11 Oct 1941 in Scranton, PA. She married EUGENE BARR 01 Jun 1963 in Berea, Ohio, son of GEORGE BARR and RENA DAVIS. He was born 13 Nov 1935 in West Virginia.

(Please see Tegtmeier Family for further information.)

Children of SHIRLEY TAYLOR and EUGENE BARR are:

96. i. Jeffrey[6] Barr, b. 03 Dec 1963, Zanesville, Ohio.
97. ii. Kathy Anne Barr, b. 04 Dec 1965, Zanesville, OH.
98. iii. Angela Lynn Barr, b. 07 Oct 1969, Zainesville, Ohio.

57. EDWARD WILLIAM[5] TAYLOR *(ALICE HENRIETTA[4] TEGTMEIER, ERNA HENRIETTE SOPHIE[3] PAPENHAGEN, JOACHIM CHRISTIAN JOHANN[2], HEINRICH[1])* was born 11 Jan 1944 in Alden, NY. He married NANCY UNTEZUBER. She was born 03 May 1948.

(Please see Tegtmeier Family for further information.)

Children of EDWARD TAYLOR and NANCY UNTEZUBER are:

i. CRAIG EDWARD[6] TAYLOR, b. 07 Sep 1962; m. DEBRA "CRICKET" JONES, 23 Apr 1999, Christ the King Lutheran, Twinsburg, OH.
99. ii. Christine Jean Taylor, b. Nov 1974.

58. JAMES ROBERT[5] TAYLOR *(ALICE HENRIETTA[4] TEGTMEIER, ERNA HENRIETTE SOPHIE[3] PAPENHAGEN, JOACHIM CHRISTIAN JOHANN[2], HEINRICH[1])* was born 22 Mar 1949 in Berea, Ohio. He married (1) MARGIE MOORE 28 Aug 1971 in Newfoundland, Canada. She was born 01 May 1950 in Newfoundland, Canada. He married (2) NANCY ABT 1998.

(Please see Tegtmeier Family for further information.)

Children of JAMES TAYLOR and MARGIE MOORE are:

i. SHANE EDWARD[6] TAYLOR, b. 01 Aug 1978.
ii. CHASTA TAYLOR, b. 21 Mar 1981.

59. SANDRA MINA[5] TAYLOR *(ALICE HENRIETTA[4] TEGTMEIER, ERNA HENRIETTE SOPHIE[3] PAPENHAGEN, JOACHIM CHRISTIAN JOHANN[2], HEINRICH[1])* was born 17 Mar 1950 in Berea, Ohio. She married PETER GRAHAM BELL 03 Jun 1984 in Pine Shores Presb. Church, Sarasota, Fl, son of HAL BELL and JANE KLUEPFEL. He was born 29 Aug 1937 in Wauseon, Ohio.

(Please see Tegtmeier Family for further information.)

Children of SANDRA TAYLOR and PETER BELL are:

i. HEATHER LYNNE[6] BELL, b. 30 Sep 1984, Sarasota, FL.
ii. JOSHUA TAYLOR BELL, b. 13 Oct 1986, Miami, FL.

60. JOAN CHARLOTTE[5] TEGTMEIER *(HENRY ADOLPH[4], ERNA HENRIETTE SOPHIE[3] PAPENHAGEN, JOACHIM CHRISTIAN JOHANN[2], HEINRICH[1])* was born 07 Aug 1947. She married TOM TRUMAN 13 Jun 1970. He was born 21 Jul 1946.

(Please see Tegtmeier Family for further information.)

Children of JOAN TEGTMEIER and TOM TRUMAN are:

i. TOM[6] TRUMAN, b. 14 Sep 1972.
ii. JACOB TRUMAN, b. 13 Sep 1974.
iii. ASHLEY TRUMAN, b. 20 Apr 1976.
iv. DAVID TRUMAN, b. 12 Sep 1978.

61. PAUL[5] TEGTMEIER *(HENRY ADOLPH[4], ERNA HENRIETTE SOPHIE[3] PAPENHAGEN, JOACHIM CHRISTIAN JOHANN[2], HEINRICH[1])* was born 03 Aug 1948. He married SANDRA RICE 04 Nov 1972. She was born 19 Jul 1953.

(Please see Tegtmeier Family for further information.)

Children of PAUL TEGTMEIER and SANDRA RICE are:

i. JAMIE[6] TEGTMEIER, b. 25 Apr 1975.
ii. JEREMY TEGTMEIER, b. 30 Mar 1976.
iii. JERROD TEGTMEIER, b. 22 Oct 1984.

62. Joel[5] Tegtmeier *(Henry Adolph[4], Erna Henriette Sophie[3] Papenhagen, Joachim Christian Johann[2], Heinrich[1])* was born 13 Aug 1959. He married Tammie 20 Oct 1978. She was born 30 Jul 1959.

(Please see Tegtmeier Family for further information.)

Children of Joel Tegtmeier and Tammie are:

i. Angela[6] Tegtmeier, b. 19 Apr 1979.
ii. Matthew Tegtmeier, b. 03 Feb 1981.

63. Linda Jean[5] Tegtmeier *(William Edward[4], Erna Henriette Sophie[3] Papenhagen, Joachim Christian Johann[2], Heinrich[1])* was born 24 Aug 1947 in Youngstown, OH, North Side Hospital. She married Larry Gene Fenton 19 Dec 1992 in Germantown, OH, son of Waldo Fenton and Sara Bell. He was born 02 Mar 1947 in Mansfield, OH.

(Please see Tegtmeier Family for further information.)

Children of Linda Tegtmeier and Larry Fenton are:

100. i. Shawn Michael[6] Fenton, b. 19 Jan 1968, Columbus, OH.
101. ii. Amy Krista Fenton, b. 15 May 1971, Pittsburgh, PA.

64. Timothy[5] Tegtmeier *(William Edward[4], Erna Henriette Sophie[3] Papenhagen, Joachim Christian Johann[2], Heinrich[1])* was born 15 Sep 1955. He married Pam Honaker 15 Jun 1977.

(Please see Tegtmeier Family for further information.)

Children of Timothy Tegtmeier and Pam Honaker are:

i. Christine[6] Tegtmeier.
ii. Jonathan Tegtmeier.

65. James Herman[5] Tegtmeier *(Harold William[4], Erna Henriette Sophie[3] Papenhagen, Joachim Christian Johann[2], Heinrich[1])* was born 14 Feb 1945 in Lodi Hospital, near Wooster, Ohio. He married Jeanne Marie Gresser 20 Jun 1965. She was born ABT 1945.

(Please see Tegtmeier Family for further information.)

Children of James Tegtmeier and Jeanne Gresser are:

102. i. Molly Marie[6] Tegtmeier, b. 24 May 1971.

ii. Randy James Tegtmeier, b. 24 Mar 1975.

66. Donald Phillip[5] Tegtmeier *(Harold William[4], Erna Henriette Sophie[3] Papenhagen, Joachim Christian Johann[2], Heinrich[1])* was born 14 Nov 1948 in Lodi Hospital, near Wooster, Ohio. He married Neva Nestor 20 Oct 1984. She was born ABT 1948.

(Please see Tegtmeier Family for further information.)

Children of Donald Tegtmeier and Neva Nestor are:

i. Adam Donald[6] Tegtmeier, b. 17 Jun 1986.

ii. Heidi Rose Tegtmeier, b. 12 Apr 1989.

67. Barbara Lucille[5] Tegtmeier *(Harold William[4], Erna Henriette Sophie[3] Papenhagen, Joachim Christian Johann[2], Heinrich[1])* was born 15 Dec 1952 in Lodi Hospital, near Wooster, Ohio. She married James Kramer 08 Jun 1979. He was born 06 Jun 1950.

(Please see Tegtmeier Family for further information.)

Children of Barbara Tegtmeier and James Kramer are:

103. i. William[6] Kramer, b. 05 Jan 1974.

ii. Matthew James Kramer, b. 29 Sep 1982.

68. David Harold[5] Tegtmeier *(Harold William[4], Erna Henriette Sophie[3] Papenhagen, Joachim Christian Johann[2], Heinrich[1])* was born 15 Sep 1954 in Lodi Hospital, near Wooster, Ohio. He married RITA KAY KAMP 24 Jun 1979, daughter of Norman Kamp and Arlene Rastetter. She was born 25 Feb 1959 in Ashland, OH.

(Please see Tegtmeier Family for further information.)

Children of David Tegtmeier and Rita Kamp are:

i. Luke David[6] Tegtmeier, b. 11 May 1983.

ii. Jill Arlene Tegtmeier, b. 29 Oct 1985.

iii. Mark David Tegtmeier, b. 25 Apr 1990.

69. DOUGLAS RICHARD[5] TEGTMEIER *(RICHARD ELMER[4], ERNA HENRIETTE SOPHIE[3] PAPENHAGEN, JOACHIM CHRISTIAN JOHANN[2], HEINRICH[1])* was born 06 Dec 1952 in Wooster, Montgomery Co., OH. He married SUZANNE GULYAS 14 Aug 1976 in Centerville, Montgomery Co., OH. She was born 09 Jan 1954 in Dayton, OH.

(Please see Tegtmeier Family for further information.)

Children of DOUGLAS TEGTMEIER and SUZANNE GULYAS are:

i. JEFF[6] TEGTMEIER, b. 22 Dec 1982, Columbus, Ohio.
ii. RYAN TEGTMEIER, b. 11 Oct 1984, Columbus, Ohio.

70. DEBRA LOUISE[5] TEGTMEIER *(RICHARD ELMER[4], ERNA HENRIETTE SOPHIE[3] PAPENHAGEN, JOACHIM CHRISTIAN JOHANN[2], HEINRICH[1])* was born 09 Jan 1955 in Wooster, Wayne Co. OH. She married TERRY MILLER 06 Jul 1974 in Wooster, Wayne Co., OH. He was born 05 Nov 1952.

(Please see Tegtmeier Family for further information.)

Children of DEBRA TEGTMEIER and TERRY MILLER are:

i. JEREMIAH[6] MILLER, b. 20 Jun 1978.
ii. JONATHAN MILLER, b. 24 Aug 1979; m. REBEKAH WRIGHT, 10 Aug 2002, Wooster, Wayne Co. Ohio.

More About JONATHAN MILLER and REBEKAH WRIGHT:
Marriage: 10 Aug 2002, Wooster, Wayne Co. Ohio

71. DEAN EDWARD[5] TEGTMEIER *(RICHARD ELMER[4], ERNA HENRIETTE SOPHIE[3] PAPENHAGEN, JOACHIM CHRISTIAN JOHANN[2], HEINRICH[1])* was born 02 Mar 1957 in Ashland, Ashland Co., OH. He married MICHELE HAYNES 21 Jun 1980 in Toronto, Canada. She was born 15 Aug 1957 in Toronto, Ohio.

(Please see Tegtmeier Family for further information.)

Children of DEAN TEGTMEIER and MICHELE HAYNES are:

i. CELESTE[6] TEGTMEIER, b. ABT 1982.
ii. SHAWN TEGTMEIER, b. ABT 1984; m. MICHELLE.
iii. SARA TEGTMEIER, b. ABT 1986.

72. Mark Peter^5 Hinricks *(Lois Ruth^4 Tegtmeier, Erna Henriette Sophie^3 Papenhagen, Joachim Christian Johann^2, Heinrich^1)* was born 30 Oct 1951 in Redfield, SD. He married Sandra Kae Landgrebe 26 Dec 1976, daughter of Mortimer Landgrebe and Arlene Weeks. She was born 16 Apr 1952 in Bismarck, ND.

(Please see Tegtmeier Family for further information.)

Children of Mark Hinricks and Sandra Landgrebe are:

i. Lucas Alexander^6 Hinricks, b. 19 Mar 1982, Dickinson, Stark, ND.

ii. Rachel Elizabeth Hinricks, b. 16 Oct 1987, Dickinson, Stark, ND.

73. Steven Heye^5 Hinricks *(Lois Ruth^4 Tegtmeier, Erna Henriette Sophie^3 Papenhagen, Joachim Christian Johann^2, Heinrich^1)* was born 23 Jan 1954 in Redfield, Spink Co, SD. He married Deborah Martin 02 May 1981 in Dickinson, Stark, ND, daughter of Norman Martin and Winnifred Dwyer. She was born 10 Aug 1949 in Bismarck, Burleigh, ND.

(Please see Tegtmeier Family for further information.)

Children of Steven Hinricks and Deborah Martin are:

i. Benjamin Heye^6 Hinricks, b. 29 Nov 1983, Sacramento, CA.

ii. Andrew Peter Hinricks, b. 30 Mar 1988.

74. Diana June^5 Seagert *(Esther Edna Marie^4 Papenhagen, Walter Franklin^3, Joachim Christian Johann^2, Heinrich^1)* was born 12 Jun 1939. She married Harry Bud Rudolph Pape, Jr. 24 Jun 1961. He was born 31 Mar 1937.

More About Harry Pape and Diana Seagert:
Marriage: 24 Jun 1961

Children of Diana Seagert and Harry Pape are:

104. i. Nancy Marie^6 Pape, b. 24 Jul 1962.

ii. Dale Rudolph Pape, b. 19 Aug 1964; m. Dawn Michele Frazier, 14 Oct 1989; b. 22 Jan 1968.

More About DALE PAPE and DAWN FRAZIER:
Marriage: 14 Oct 1989

105. iii. GERALD RAYMOND PAPE, b. 07 Nov 1967.
iv. YVONNE PEARL PAPE, b. 15 Nov 1975.

75. RICHARD RAY^5 SEAGERT *(ESTHER EDNA MARIE^4 PAPENHAGEN, WALTER FRANKLIN^3, JOACHIM CHRISTIAN JOHANN^2, HEINRICH^1)* was born 09 Apr 1943. He married DONNA EILEEN GLASGOW 15 Jun 1968. She was born 14 Apr 1944.

More About RICHARD SEAGERT and DONNA GLASGOW:
Marriage: 15 Jun 1968

Children of RICHARD SEAGERT and DONNA GLASGOW are:
i. RYAN RAY^6 SEAGERT, b. 22 Mar 1972.
ii. RORY KYLE SEAGERT, b. 02 Apr 1974.
iii. LINDSAY LYNETTE SEAGERT, b. 29 Apr 1980.

76. LINDA MARIE^5 SEAGERT *(ESTHER EDNA MARIE^4 PAPENHAGEN, WALTER FRANKLIN^3, JOACHIM CHRISTIAN JOHANN^2, HEINRICH^1)* was born 04 Jul 1952. She married RICHARD DOYLE RIES 13 Apr 1973. He was born 01 Apr 1952.

More About RICHARD RIES and LINDA SEAGERT:
Marriage: 13 Apr 1973

Children of LINDA SEAGERT and RICHARD RIES are:
i. RACHEL ERIN^6 RIES, b. 15 Feb 1976.
ii. SARAH MARIE RIES, b. 12 Nov 1983.
iii. EMILY DIANA RIES, b. 29 Dec 1987.

77. ARTHUR WALTER JR.^{5} BRENKE *(ERNA ETHEL ELIZABETH^4 PAPENHAGEN, WALTER FRANKLIN^3, JOACHIM CHRISTIAN JOHANN^2, HEINRICH^1)* was born 04 Jul 1944. He married DIANA JEAN RITTNER 29 Jan 1965. She was born 27 Jan 1945.

More About ARTHUR BRENKE and DIANA RITTNER:
Marriage: 29 Jan 1965

Children of Arthur Brenke and Diana Rittner are:

106. i. Holly Ann[6] Brenke, b. 02 Jan 1966.

ii. Christina Marie Brenke, b. 23 May 1968; d. 24 May 1968.

iii. Heather Ann Brenke, b. 05 Jun 1965.

78. Sharon Sue[5] Brenke *(Erna Ethel Elizabeth[4] Papenhagen, Walter Franklin[3], Joachim Christian Johann[2], Heinrich[1])* was born 03 Nov 1946. She married Bruce James Wilkes 28 Jul 1967. He was born 06 Oct 1947.

More About Bruce Wilkes and Sharon Brenke:
Marriage: 28 Jul 1967

Children of Sharon Brenke and Bruce Wilkes are:

i. Gregg James[6] Wilkes, b. 06 Sep 1971.

ii. Teresa Sue Wilkes, b. 28 Apr 1976.

79. Brenda Ann[5] Brenke *(Erna Ethel Elizabeth[4] Papenhagen, Walter Franklin[3], Joachim Christian Johann[2], Heinrich[1])* was born 30 Aug 1949. She married (1) Thomas Alan Debacker. He was born ABT 1949. She married (2) Michael Jan Andrix. He was born ABT 1947.

Children of Brenda Brenke and Thomas Debacker are:

i. Christopher Alan[6] Debacker, b. 25 Dec 1972.

ii. Amy Michelle Debacker, b. 09 Feb 1977.

80. Kenneth Roger[5] Papenhagen *(Clyde K.[4], Walter Franklin[3], Joachim Christian Johann[2], Heinrich[1])* was born 11 Sep 1946. He married Mary Inez Saxon 22 Apr 1964. She was born 03 Feb 1946.

More About Kenneth Papenhagen and Mary Saxon:
Marriage: 22 Apr 1964

Children of Kenneth Papenhagen and Mary Saxon are:

107. i. Kenneth Roger[6] Papenhagen, b. 24 Feb 1968.

ii. Melissa Lynne Papenhagen, b. 10 Jul 1969.

81. Yvonne Jean[5] Papenhagen *(Clyde K.[4], Walter Franklin[3], Joachim Christian Johann[2], Heinrich[1])* was born 22 Jul 1950. She married Robert C. Stone 03 Jan 1970. He was born 16 Aug 1949.

More About Robert Stone and Yvonne Papenhagen:
Marriage: 03 Jan 1970

Children of Yvonne Papenhagen and Robert Stone are:
- i. Renee J.[6] Stone, b. 26 Oct 1973.
- ii. Myra J. Stone, b. 17 Dec 1976.
- iii. Bryan Charles Stone, b. 21 Jan 1978.

Generation No. 5

82. Michael B.[6] Fairweather *(Loann Clare[5] Komsteller, Ethel S.[4] Papenhagen, Paul Ludwig Friedrich Christian[3], Joachim Christian Johann[2], Heinrich[1])* was born 23 Nov 1954. He married Patty Macorie 07 Feb 1981. She was born 02 Mar 1956.

More About Michael Fairweather and Patty Macorie:
Marriage: 07 Feb 1981

Children of Michael Fairweather and Patty Macorie are:
- i. Renee M.[7] Fairweather, b. 28 Aug 1979.
- ii. Rachel Fairweather, b. ABT 1980.
- iii. Randi M. Fairweather, b. 08 Apr 1988.
- iv. Rikki L. Fairweather, b. 15 May 1989.

83. Linda Lee[6] Fairweather *(Loann Clare[5] Komsteller, Ethel S.[4] Papenhagen, Paul Ludwig Friedrich Christian[3], Joachim Christian Johann[2], Heinrich[1])* was born 01 Jun 1956. She married (1) David Arnold. He was born ABT 1956. She married (2) Don Sharp. He was born ABT 1956.

Children of Linda Fairweather and David Arnold are:
- i. Michele Lee[7] Arnold, b. 23 Oct 1978.
- ii. Bradley John Arnold, b. 27 Mar 1984.

84. KIMBERLY ANN[6] KOMSTELLER *(NEAL WALTER[5], ETHEL S.[4] PAPENHAGEN, PAUL LUDWIG FRIEDRICH CHRISTIAN[3], JOACHIM CHRISTIAN JOHANN[2], HEINRICH[1])* was born 12 Dec 1955. She married ROBERT SCHULTZ 01 Jun 1973. He was born 28 Jul 1951.

More About ROBERT SCHULTZ and KIMBERLY KOMSTELLER:
Marriage: 01 Jun 1973

Children of KIMBERLY KOMSTELLER and ROBERT SCHULTZ are:

i. MEGAN LEE[7] SCHULTZ, b. 28 Jan 1975.
ii. MISTY LYNN SCHULTZ, b. 14 Sep 1977.
iii. COREY ROBERT SCHULTZ, b. 16 Dec 1981.
iv. CASEY SCHULTZ, b. 14 May 1985.

85. JILL MARIE[6] KOMSTELLER *(NEAL WALTER[5], ETHEL S.[4] PAPENHAGEN, PAUL LUDWIG FRIEDRICH CHRISTIAN[3], JOACHIM CHRISTIAN JOHANN[2], HEINRICH[1])* was born 23 Jul 1959. She married MARVIN QUICK 04 Aug 1977. He was born 19 Mar 1955.

More About MARVIN QUICK and JILL KOMSTELLER:
Marriage: 04 Aug 1977

Children of JILL KOMSTELLER and MARVIN QUICK are:

i. LEE MARVIN[7] QUICK, b. 11 Jul 1978.
ii. AMBER MARIE QUICK, b. 18 May 1982.
iii. ASHLEY LYNN QUICK, b. 02 Oct 1985.

86. JEFF NEAL[6] KOMSTELLER *(NEAL WALTER[5], ETHEL S.[4] PAPENHAGEN, PAUL LUDWIG FRIEDRICH CHRISTIAN[3], JOACHIM CHRISTIAN JOHANN[2], HEINRICH[1])* was born 05 Jun 1961. He married DEBBIE HALL HEIDER 02 Dec 1985. She was born 02 Jan 1956.

More About JEFF KOMSTELLER and DEBBIE HEIDER:
Marriage: 02 Dec 1985

Child of JEFF KOMSTELLER and DEBBIE HEIDER is:

i. MICHAEL[7] KOMSTELLER, b. 16 May 1987.

87. BRADLEY JOHN[6] STRANGE *(JANE LEE[5] KOMSTELLER, ETHEL S.[4] PAPENHAGEN, PAUL LUDWIG FRIEDRICH CHRISTIAN[3], JOACHIM CHRISTIAN JOHANN[2], HEINRICH[1])* was born 18 Feb 1962. He married TERRI CARLTON 18 Nov 1989. She was born 01 May 1964.

More About BRADLEY STRANGE and TERRI CARLTON:
Marriage: 18 Nov 1989

Child of BRADLEY STRANGE and TERRI CARLTON is:

i. LYNDI ELIZABETH[7] STRANGE, b. 03 Mar 1994.

88. BRENDA LEE[6] STRANGE *(JANE LEE[5] KOMSTELLER, ETHEL S.[4] PAPENHAGEN, PAUL LUDWIG FRIEDRICH CHRISTIAN[3], JOACHIM CHRISTIAN JOHANN[2], HEINRICH[1])* was born 12 Apr 1964. She married JEFF B. POTTER 06 Aug 1983. He was born 18 Aug 1960.

More About JEFF POTTER and BRENDA STRANGE:
Marriage: 06 Aug 1983

Children of BRENDA STRANGE and JEFF POTTER are:

i. JEFF DANE[7] POTTER, b. 05 Sep 1984.
ii. KATIE LEE POTTER, b. 01 Jul 1991.

89. MARK ROBERT[6] HILBORN *(DATHEL[5] NEVER, DORIS[4] PAPENHAGEN, PAUL LUDWIG FRIEDRICH CHRISTIAN[3], JOACHIM CHRISTIAN JOHANN[2], HEINRICH[1])* was born 01 Sep 1963. He married SANDRA 26 Apr 1988. She was born ABT 1963.

Notes for MARK ROBERT HILBORN:
In 2004 living in Huntsville, Alabama.

More About MARK HILBORN and SANDRA:
Marriage: 26 Apr 1988

Children of MARK HILBORN and SANDRA are:

i. TIMOTHY MARK[7] HILBORN, b. 11 Apr 1989, Minnesota.
ii. JENNA MICHELLE HILBORN, b. 28 Nov 1990, Minnesota.

90. Scott Alan^{6} Hilborn *(Dathel^{5} Never, Doris^{4} Papenhagen, Paul Ludwig Friedrich Christian^{3}, Joachim Christian Johann^{2}, Heinrich^{1})* was born 20 Nov 1965. He married Shannon 23 Mar 1991. She was born ABT 1965.

Notes for Scott Alan Hilborn:
2004, living in Orlando, Florida

More About Scott Hilborn and Shannon:
Marriage: 23 Mar 1991

Children of Scott Hilborn and Shannon are:

i. Kristen Eileen^{7} Hilborn, b. 27 Feb 1993, Brandon, Fl.

ii. Trevor David Hilborn, b. 17 Jun 1996, Orlando, Fl.

iii. Sheriana Genevieve Hilborn, b. 15 May 1998, Orlando, Fl.

91. Michael David^{6} Hilborn *(Dathel^{5} Never, Doris^{4} Papenhagen, Paul Ludwig Friedrich Christian^{3}, Joachim Christian Johann^{2}, Heinrich^{1})* was born 16 Nov 1966. He married (1) Terri Sue Crunk 27 Dec 1986. She was born 07 Aug 1967 in Woodburn, IN. He married (2) Tracey Anne Clark 05 Aug 1995. She was born 29 Aug 1968 in Fort Wayne, IN.

About Michael Hilborn and Terri Crunk:
Divorce: Nov 1989
Marriage: 27 Dec 1986

More About Michael Hilborn and Tracey Clark:
Divorce: 01 Feb 2001
Marriage: 05 Aug 1995

Child of Michael Hilborn and Tracey Clark is:

i. Aubrey Rachelle^{7} Hilborn, b. 10 Sep 1998, Ft. Wayne, IN.

92. John H.^{6} Decator *(Marian Bethany^{5} Never, Doris^{4} Papenhagen, Paul Ludwig Friedrich Christian^{3}, Joachim Christian Johann^{2}, Heinrich^{1})* was born 05 Oct. He married Tamera 03 Sep 1994. She was born ABT 1965.

More About JOHN DECATOR and TAMERA:
Marriage: 03 Sep 1994

Children of JOHN DECATOR and TAMERA are:
- i. MADISON[7] DECATOR, b. 05 Jan 1994.
- ii. MARINA DECATOR, b. 19 Apr 1995.

93. JONELLE[6] DECATOR *(MARIAN BETHANY[5] NEVER, DORIS[4] PAPENHAGEN, PAUL LUDWIG FRIEDRICH CHRISTIAN[3], JOACHIM CHRISTIAN JOHANN[2], HEINRICH[1])* was born 11 Oct. She married BILLY MONTES 05 Jun 1993. He was born ABT 1965.

More About BILLY MONTES and JONELLE DECATOR:
Marriage: 05 Jun 1993

Children of JONELLE DECATOR and BILLY MONTES are:
- i. ALEC[7] MONTES, b. 09 Jul 1994.
- ii. GABRIEL MONTES, b. 27 Dec 1995.

94. LAURIE[6] NEVER *(PAUL GRANT[5], DORIS[4] PAPENHAGEN, PAUL LUDWIG FRIEDRICH CHRISTIAN[3], JOACHIM CHRISTIAN JOHANN[2], HEINRICH[1])* was born November 19, abt 1964. She married GREG PIEPER 28 Sep 1991. He was born 09 Feb 1960.

Notes for LAURIE NEVER:
birthdate November 19th

More About GREG PIEPER and LAURIE NEVER:
Marriage: 28 Sep 1991

Child of LAURIE NEVER and GREG PIEPER is:
- i. ALEX[7] PIEPER, b. 23 Mar 1992.

95. LISA[6] CARLSON *(REBECCA SUE[5] NEVER, DORIS[4] PAPENHAGEN, PAUL LUDWIG FRIEDRICH CHRISTIAN[3], JOACHIM CHRISTIAN JOHANN[2], HEINRICH[1])* was born 26 Feb 1969. She married TONY DELONG 11 Aug 1989. He was born 13 Nov 1966.

More About TONY DELONG and LISA CARLSON:
Marriage: 11 Aug 1989

Children of LISA CARLSON and TONY DELONG are:

i. CASEY[7] DELONG, b. 16 Jan 1989.

ii. SAMANTHA DELONG, b. 16 Jan 1989.

96. JEFFREY[6] BARR *(SHIRLEY ANN[5] TAYLOR, ALICE HENRIETTA[4] TEGTMEIER, ERNA HENRIETTE SOPHIE[3] PAPENHAGEN, JOACHIM CHRISTIAN JOHANN[2], HEINRICH[1])* was born 03 Dec 1963 in Zanesville, Ohio. He married M. CHRISTINA SIDWELL 20 Feb 1993 in Columbus, Ohio.

(Please see Tegtmeier Family for further information.)

Children of JEFFREY BARR and M. SIDWELL are:

i. BLAKE[7] BARR, b. 04 Jul 1996.

ii. BLAIR BARR, b. 14 Feb 2001.

97. KATHY ANNE[6] BARR *(SHIRLEY ANN[5] TAYLOR, ALICE HENRIETTA[4] TEGTMEIER, ERNA HENRIETTE SOPHIE[3] PAPENHAGEN, JOACHIM CHRISTIAN JOHANN[2], HEINRICH[1])* was born 04 Dec 1965 in Zanesville, OH. She married RICHARD SKILLMAN 03 Jan 1998 in Grace Lutheran, Thornville, OH, son of LEROY SKILLMAN and BETTY.

(Please see Tegtmeier Family for further information.)

Child of KATHY BARR and RICHARD SKILLMAN is:

i. SPENCER[7] SKILLMAN, b. 04 Oct 1997.

98. ANGELA LYNN[6] BARR *(SHIRLEY ANN[5] TAYLOR, ALICE HENRIETTA[4] TEGTMEIER, ERNA HENRIETTE SOPHIE[3] PAPENHAGEN, JOACHIM CHRISTIAN JOHANN[2], HEINRICH[1])* was born 07 Oct 1969 in Zainesville, Ohio. She married ALAN GRESH.

(Please see Tegtmeier Family for further information.)

Children of ANGELA BARR and ALAN GRESH are:

i. ALLISON NICOLE[7] GRESH, b. 27 Jul 2001.

ii. ALEC CONNER GRESH, b. 18 Jun 2004.

99. CHRISTINE JEAN[6] TAYLOR *(EDWARD WILLIAM[5], ALICE HENRIETTA[4] TEGTMEIER, ERNA HENRIETTE SOPHIE[3] PAPENHAGEN, JOACHIM CHRISTIAN JOHANN[2], HEINRICH[1])* was born Nov 1974. She married BRIAN LEE SLONE 18 Jul 1998 in Christ the King Lutheran, Twinsburg, OH.

(Please see Tegtmeier Family for further information.)

Children of CHRISTINE TAYLOR and BRIAN SLONE are:

i. ABIGAIL[7] SLONE, b. 1997.
ii. VICTORIA SLONE, b. 2002.

100. SHAWN MICHAEL[6] FENTON *(LINDA JEAN[5] TEGTMEIER, WILLIAM EDWARD[4], ERNA HENRIETTE SOPHIE[3] PAPENHAGEN, JOACHIM CHRISTIAN JOHANN[2], HEINRICH[1])* was born 19 Jan 1968 in Columbus, OH. He married SHARON ANN MYERS 19 Dec 1992 in Germantown, OH, daughter of ROBERT MYERS and CAROL ASKINS. She was born 30 Apr 1969 in Dayton, OH.

(Please see Tegtmeier Family for further information.)

Children of SHAWN FENTON and SHARON MYERS are:

i. AMANDA MICHELLE[7] FENTON, b. 04 Jan 2001, Dayton, OH.
ii. RACHEL ELIZABETH FENTON, b. 21 Mar 2004, Kettering, OH.

101. AMY KRISTA[6] FENTON *(LINDA JEAN[5] TEGTMEIER, WILLIAM EDWARD[4], ERNA HENRIETTE SOPHIE[3] PAPENHAGEN, JOACHIM CHRISTIAN JOHANN[2], HEINRICH[1])* was born 15 May 1971 in Pittsburgh, PA. She married PAUL DAVID KENNEDY 10 Sep 1994 in Columbus, OH, son of JOHN KENNEDY and EILEEN JOHNSON. He was born ABT 1970.

(Please see Tegtmeier Family for further information.)

Child of AMY FENTON and PAUL KENNEDY is:

i. JACK WILLIAM[7] KENNEDY, b. 05 Jan 2003, Mt. Carmel West Hosp'l, Columbus, OH.

102. MOLLY MARIE[6] TEGTMEIER *(JAMES HERMAN[5], HAROLD WILLIAM[4], ERNA HENRIETTE SOPHIE[3] PAPENHAGEN, JOACHIM CHRISTIAN JOHANN[2], HEINRICH[1])* was born 24 May 1971. She married BRAD STULL. He was born ABT 1971.

(Please see Tegtmeier Family for further information.)

Children of MOLLY TEGTMEIER and BRAD STULL are:

i. KATIE MARIE[7] STULL, b. 09 Jun 1999.
ii. RILEY ANN STULL, b. 06 Jun 2003.

103. WILLIAM[6] KRAMER *(BARBARA LUCILLE[5] TEGTMEIER, HAROLD WILLIAM[4], ERNA HENRIETTE SOPHIE[3] PAPENHAGEN, JOACHIM CHRISTIAN JOHANN[2], HEINRICH[1])* was born 05 Jan 1974. He married ERIN 20 Jun 1997. She was born ABT 1974.

(Please see Tegtmeier Family for further information.)

Children of WILLIAM KRAMER and ERIN are:

i. MADELINE[7] KRAMER, b. 16 Jan 1999.
ii. GRANT KRAMER, b. 10 Oct 2001.

104. NANCY MARIE[6] PAPE *(DIANA JUNE[5] SEAGERT, ESTHER EDNA MARIE[4] PAPENHAGEN, WALTER FRANKLIN[3], JOACHIM CHRISTIAN JOHANN[2], HEINRICH[1])* was born 24 Jul 1962. She married DENNIS MILES FINDLEY 26 Mar 1983. He was born 16 Apr 1961.

More About DENNIS FINDLEY and NANCY PAPE:
Marriage: 26 Mar 1983

Children of NANCY PAPE and DENNIS FINDLEY are:

i. TARA MARIE[7] FINDLEY, b. 29 Sep 1989.
ii. AARON MILES FINDLEY, b. 24 Mar 1992.

105. GERALD RAYMOND[6] PAPE *(DIANA JUNE[5] SEAGERT, ESTHER EDNA MARIE[4] PAPENHAGEN, WALTER FRANKLIN[3], JOACHIM CHRISTIAN JOHANN[2], HEINRICH[1])* was born 07 Nov 1967. He married TAMMY LYNN (BROCK) LOEWE 22 Jul 1989. She was born 07 Jul 1969.

More About GERALD PAPE and TAMMY LOEWE:
Marriage: 22 Jul 1989

Child of GERALD PAPE and TAMMY LOEWE is:

i. ALLISON NICOLE^{7} PAPE, b. 11 Jun 1993.

106. HOLLY ANN^{6} BRENKE *(ARTHUR WALTER JR.^{5}, ERNA ETHEL ELIZABETH^{4} PAPENHAGEN, WALTER FRANKLIN^{3}, JOACHIM CHRISTIAN JOHANN^{2}, HEINRICH^{1})* was born 02 Jan 1966. She married GREGORY ALLEN BUTTS 25 Apr 1987. He was born 17 May 1965.

More About GREGORY BUTTS and HOLLY BRENKE:
Marriage: 25 Apr 1987

Children of HOLLY BRENKE and GREGORY BUTTS are:

i. AARON GREGORY^{7} BUTTS, b. 03 Mar 1992.

ii. EMILY ELIZABETH BUTTS, b. 05 May 1995.

107. KENNETH ROGER^{6} PAPENHAGEN *(KENNETH ROGER^{5}, CLYDE K.^{4}, WALTER FRANKLIN^{3}, JOACHIM CHRISTIAN JOHANN^{2}, HEINRICH^{1})* was born 24 Feb 1968. He married LAURA STRITE. She was born 03 Nov 1968.

Child of KENNETH PAPENHAGEN and LAURA STRITE is:

i. BOY^{7} PAPENHAGEN, b. ABT 1994.

Cousins and Their Locations

Name	Spouse	Birth date	Birth location	Death date	Death location
Adams, Andrew	Schultz, Connie Ann				
Ahleman, Almeta Bertha Christine	Meier, John Bernard	26 Jan 1901	Riga Twp, Riga, MI	15 Nov 1979	
Ahleman, Arthur G.	Dedering, Olive A.	12 Feb 1896	Riga Twp., Riga, MI	11 Apr 1988	Riga Twp., Riga, MI
Ahleman, Damaris Anne	Bromley, Ronald	10 Jun 1944	Lowrey Air Force Base, CO		
Ahleman, David John		16 Oct 1969	Toledo, OH		
Ahleman, Donald Ernest	Stevens, Marilyn Lou	04 Mar 1934	Liberty Center, Henry Co., OH		
Ahleman, Elsie Emma Hulda	Marks, Elwin C.	20 Apr 1903	Riga Twp., Riga MI	15 May 1994	
Ahleman, Florence Elsie	Henning, Richard F.	30 Nov 1930	Henry Co., Liberty Center, OH		
Ahleman, Frederick Wm.		19 Jul 1894	Riga Twp, Ottawa Lake, MI	01 Dec 1905	Riga Twp, Ottawa Lake, MI
Ahleman, Heinrich Ernst A.	Tegtmeier, Hulda Louise Maria	25 May 1869	Riga Twp, Ottawa Lake, Michigan	21 Dec 1948	Riga, MI
Ahleman, Larry Ernest		22 Mar 1943	Lincoln, NE		
Ahleman, Paul Ernest	Huff, Lola E.	06 Apr 1917	Riga Twn, Riga, MI		
Ahleman, Shelly Joanne	Parsell, Rodney Richard	05 Aug 1967	Toledo, OH		
Ahleman, Walter Adolph	Strayer, Ethel M.	16 Jan 1907	Riga Twn, Riga, MI	17 Feb 1959	Napolean, Henry Co.,
Ahrens, Jerry	Papenhagen, Marie	ABT 1899			
Alas, Candace Clare Fairweather Scully		23 Nov 1985			
Alas, Doug	Fairweather, Jean Marie				
Alas, Emilio Mauricio Fairweather Alas		06 Nov 1991			
Alas, James Alexander		08 Oct 1993			
Aldrich, Daniel		ABT 1957			

Aldrich, Tara		ABT 1960			
Aldrich, Terri	Papenhagen, Susan	ABT 1937			
Algie	Schumacher, Frank	ABT 1909			
Alice	Tegtmeier, Matthew				
Allen, Alice	Smith, Leland J.	ABT 1910	Ohio		
Andrix, Michael Jan	Brenke, Brenda Ann	ABT 1947			
Angie	Papenhagen, Norman Henry	13 Jan			
Arnold, Bradley John		27 Mar 1984			
Arnold, David	Fairweather, Linda Lee	ABT 1956			
Arnold, Michele Lee		23 Oct 1978			
Arters, Jane	Teckmyer, William L.	14 Aug 1915		Feb 1986	Cleveland, Cuyahoga, Ohio
Ashdown, Terry	Marks, Todd Bernard	16 Mar 1958	Pierre, S. Dakota		
Backman, Judith Katherine	Marks, Stanley Arthur	11 Oct 1946	Fresno, CA		
Bailey, Andrew Paul		08 Sep 1989			
Bailey, Justine Nicole		16 Dec 1986			
Bailey, Paul J.	Berry, Tamala Anne				
Bailey, Priscilla Joy	Sigler, Christopher Allen	20 Dec 1984	Medina, Ohio		
Bailey, Timothy Adam		12 Dec 1980			
Balliet, Dennis	Schultz, Cynthia Sue				
Ballou, Robert Allen	Berry, Tamala Anne	26 Jan 1969			
Barendt, Harriett	Tegtmeier, Henry Adolph	09 Jan 1923	Cleveland, Cuyahoga Co., OH		
Barr, Angela Lynn	Gresh, Alan	07 Oct 1969	Zainesville, Ohio		
Barr, Blair		14 Feb 2001			
Barr, Blake		04 Jul 1996			
Barr, Eugene	Taylor, Shirley Ann	13 Nov 1935	West Virginia		
Barr, Jeffrey	Sidwell, M. Christina	03 Dec 1963	Zanesville, Ohio		
Barr, Kathy Anne	Skillman, Richard	04 Dec 1965	Zanesville, OH		
Bartel, xxx	Tegtmeier, Nina				
Bartels, Maria Fridericka Johane	Tegtmeier, Karl Ferdinand	Apr 1859	Germany	04 Oct 1942	Cleveland, Cuyahoga Co., O
Bauer, Alma Marie	Tegtmeier, Gustav Adolph	ABT 1893	Ohio	Bef. 1966	
Bauer, Douglas Charles	Meier, Laureen Marie	23 Mar 1956	Denver, CO		
Bauer, Scott Ryan		10 Aug 1987	San Francisco, CA		
Bauer, William Taylor		08 Sep 1990	San Francisco, CA		

Beaubien, Audrey Kay		18 Aug 1985			
Beaubien, Christopher J.		31 Aug 1982	Adrian, MI		
Beaubien, Leonard J.	Marks, Nancy Kay	29 Nov 1958	Adrian, MI		
Behner, Elmer	Tegtmeier, Erma Maria	ABT 1904			
Behner, Glenn		18 Aug 1937	Berea, Cuyahoga Co. OH	29 Jan 1999	Brookpark, Cuyahoga Co. OH
Behny, Kory Lea	Stamper, Joshua Noel Thomas	01 Mar 1973	Wheat Ridge, CO		
Bell, Heather Lynne		30 Sep 1984	Sarasota, FL		
Bell, Joshua Taylor		13 Oct 1986	Miami, FL		
Bell, Peter Graham	Taylor, Sandra Mina	29 Aug 1937	Wauseon, Ohio		
Bergstedt, Alyssa Kathleen		07 Nov 1991	Wauseon, OH		
Bergstedt, Jennifer Elizabeth		09 Jun 1984	Wauseon, OH		
Bergstedt, Jessica Elyse		19 Apr 1985	Wauseon, OH		
Bergstedt, Joey Donald	Henning, Debra Kay	12 Jul 1959	Napoleon, OH		
Berry, David Paul	Cooper, Beverly Ann	01 Oct 1936	Lodi, Ohio		
Berry, Karen Diane	Boyer, Don	22 Mar 1942	West Salem, Ohio		
Berry, Paul Franklin	Tegtmeier, Loretta Mattie	26 Apr 1910		07 May 1998	
Berry, Stephanie Renee	Estep, Vondon Timothy	07 Mar 1969			
Berry, Tamala Anne	Ballou, Robert Allen	08 Nov 1961			
Berry, Wesley David	Frazier, Susan Annette	15 Oct 1958	Ashland, Ohio		
Bertha	Papenhagen, Heinrich Conrad Jochen				
Biller, xxx	Tegtmeier, Rose				
Blome, Linda	Papenhagen, Herbert	20 Jun 1916			
Bougher, Beth Ann	Tegtmeier, Daniel Howard	14 Jan 1959			
Boyer, Bradley		ABT 1963	Denver, CO		
Boyer, Bryan		ABT 1962	Denver, CO		
Boyer, Don	Berry, Karen Diane	ABT 1940			
Boyer, Lisa		ABT 1964	Denver, CO		
Brandes, Augusta Christine	Tegtmeier, Henry William Carl	18 Jan 1879	Ohio	02 Apr 1967	Strongsville, Ohio
Bree, Maria Dorothea	Tegtmeier, Johann Friedrich	29 Sep 1823	Iden, Osterburg, Prussia	29 May 1903	Middleburg Twp. Cuyahoga Co. OH
Brenke, Arthur W., Sr.	Papenhagen, Irma	ABT 1919			
Brenke, Arthur Walter Jr.	Rittner, Diana Jean	04 Jul 1944			
Brenke, Arthur William, Sr.	Papenhagen, Erna Ethel Elizabeth	04 Feb 1921			
Brenke, Brenda Ann	DeBacker, Thomas Alan	30 Aug 1949			

Brenke, Christina Marie		23 May 1968		24 May 1968	
Brenke, Heather Ann		05 Jun 1965			
Brenke, Hilda Elizabeth	Papenhagen, Clyde K.	12 Feb 1925			
Brenke, Holly Ann	Butts, Gregory Allen	02 Jan 1966			
Brenke, Sharon Sue	Wilkes, Bruce James	03 Nov 1946			
Bromley, Maria Ann		08 Jun 1973	Boise, ID		
Bromley, Robert Paul		07 Oct 1971	Boise, ID		
Bromley, Ronald	Ahleman, Damaris Anne	06 Jan 1940	CA		
Butts, Aaron Gregory		03 Mar 1992			
Butts, Emily Elizabeth		05 May 1995			
Butts, Gregory Allen	Brenke, Holly Ann	17 May 1965			
Byers, xxx	Puls, Arlene	ABT 1915			
Camper, Nathan	Dianne				
Camper, Nicole					
Camper, Paul	Tegtmeier, Miriam Ann	ABT 1937			
Carlson, George	Never, Rebecca Sue	30 Oct 1948			
Carlson, Gina	Hooker, A. Jack	15 Apr 1972			
Carlson, Lisa	Delong, Tony	26 Feb 1969			
Carlson, Michael		20 Mar 1974			
Carlson, Todd		ABT 1970			
Carlton, Terri	Strange, Bradley John	01 May 1964			
Carol	Smith, Glen A.				
Caruthers, Dana Lynne	Marks, Gregg Herbert	17 Jun 1962	Denver, CO		
Childers, Gary	Papenhagen, Christie	ABT 1967			
Clark, Tracey Anne	Hilborn, Michael David	29 Aug 1968	Fort Wayne, IN		
Coey, Alfred	Henning, Lori Jean	27 Sep 1956	Wauseon, OH		
Coey, Jacob Lee		12 May 1990	Wauseon, OH		
Coey, Jason Tyler		26 Mar 1980	Wauseon, OH		
Cooper, Beverly Ann	Berry, David Paul	03 Aug 1939			
Crunk, Terri Sue	Hilborn, Michael David	07 Aug 1967	Woodburn, IN		
D., Marion	Papenhagen, Frank W.	16 Jan 1901	New York	Sep 1990	
Davidson, Francis P.	Tegtmeier, Ruth	09 Jul 1908	Cuyahoga Co., OH	05 Mar 1996	Richfield, Summit, Ohio
Davidson, Nancy	Jones, xxx	ABT 1935			

Davidson, Richard		ABT 1936			
Davidson, Susan	Hahn, xxx	ABT 1938			
DeBacker, Amy Michelle		09 Feb 1977			
DeBacker, Christopher Alan		25 Dec 1972			
DeBacker, Thomas Alan	Brenke, Brenda Ann	ABT 1949			
DeBoer, Sherry	Wessendorf, Robert				
Decator, Bill	Never, Marian Bethany				
Decator, Brendan W.		07 Jun 2005			
Decator, John H.	Tamera	05 Oct			
Decator, Jonelle	Montes, Billy	11 Oct			
Decator, Madison		05 Jan 1994			
Decator, Marina		19 Apr 1995			
Dedering, Olive A.	Ahleman, Arthur G.	20 Oct 1903	Port Huron, MI	08 Jan 1958	
DeFrancisco, Janice	Wessendorf, Robert	30 Jun 1954			
Delong, Casey		16 Jan 1989			
Delong, Samantha		16 Jan 1989			
Delong, Tony	Carlson, Lisa	13 Nov 1966			
Dianne	Camper, Nathan				
Dingman, Gary Allyn	Meier, Cynthia Ann	10 Jun 1957	Longmont, CO		
Dingman, Justin Cody		18 Jun 1997	Denver, CO		
Doering, Albert W.	Papenhagen, Marie Henriette Magdalene Guste	12 Jan 1877	Ohio	27 Jan 1952	Toledo, Lucas, Ohio
Doering, Gertrude	Mattka, Fred	21 Jan 1907	Toledo, Ohio	04 Feb 1997	Whitehall, Trempealeau, Wisconsin
Doering, Helen I.	Swartz, Elmer	02 Nov 1903	Toledo, Ohio		
Doering, Marie	Ersig, Harold	12 Dec 1904	Toledo, Ohio	08 Jun 1999	Toledo, Ohio
Doering, Thelma	Jacobs, Leonard	ABT 1916	Ohio		
Donna	Schumacher, Roy				
Donofrio, Joseph	Never, Marian Bethany	ABT 1945			
Droege, Magdelena M.	Tegtmeier, Friedrich Wilhelm	Apr 1857	Ohio	04 Aug 1936	Cleveland, Cuyahoga Co., O
Dyke, Gloria J.	Schultz, James William				
Edna	Papenhagen, Norman Henry			Sep 2004	
Elg, Emma	Papenhagen, Paul Ludwig Friedrich Christian	28 Jun 1877	Michigan	18 Nov 1943	Whiteford, Monroe, Michigan
Emery, Carolyn K.		ABT 1927	Ohio		
Emery, Helen Edwards		ABT 1926	Ohio		

Emery, Mildred Irene	Marks, William Carl Elwin	03 Jan 1933	Adrian, MI		
Emery, Robert W.	Papenhagen, Edna	ABT 1893	Ohio		
Erin	Kramer, William	ABT 1974			
Erro, Amanda Marie					
Erro, Gary	Tegtmeier, Sharon Lee	ABT 1947			
Erro, Jody Ann					
Ersig, Dean		ABT 1926			
Ersig, Dianne		ABT 1925			
Ersig, Harold	Doering, Marie	09 Aug 1893	St. Mary's, Ohio	04 Jan 1970	Lucas Co, Ohio
Estep, Tristan Samuel		13 Dec 2000			
Estep, Vondon Timothy	Berry, Stephanie Renee	13 Jun 1960			
Estep, Vondon Timothy II		16 Mar 1993			
Eubanks, Heather	Tegtmeier, Randy James				
Euler, Abel W.		12 Sep 1976	Bowling Green, OH		
Euler, Allyn Kent	Meier, Beverly Ann	08 Oct 1945	Bowling Green, OH		
Euler, Jason Allyn		02 Apr 1981	Bowling Green, OH		
Eunice	Schumacher, Elmer	09 Mar 1913		05 Sep 1985	
Fairbank, Louis G.	Tegtmeier, Elsie		Akron, Ohio		
Fairbank, Robert Lewis		07 Jan 1912	Cleveland, Cuyahoga Co., OH	18 Sep 1998	Ohio
Fairweather, Eugene B.	Komsteller, Loann Clare	08 Jun 1932			
Fairweather, Jean Marie	West, David	11 Oct 1960			
Fairweather, Linda Lee	Arnold, David	01 Jun 1956			
Fairweather, Michael B.	MaCrorie, Patty	23 Nov 1954			
Fairweather, Rachel		24 Dec 1982			
Fairweather, Randi M.		08 Apr 1988			
Fairweather, Renee M.		28 Aug 1979			
Fairweather, Rikki L.		15 May 1989			
Fenton, Amanda Michelle		04 Jan 2001	Dayton, OH		
Fenton, Amy Krista	Kennedy, Paul David	15 May 1971	Pittsburgh, PA		
Fenton, Larry Gene	Tegtmeier, Linda Jean	02 Mar 1947	Mansfield, OH		
Fenton, Rachel Elizabeth		21 Mar 2004	Kettering, OH		
Fenton, Shawn Michael	Myers, Sharon Ann	19 Jan 1968	Columbus, OH		
Findley, Aaron Miles		24 Mar 1992			

Findley, Dennis Miles	Pape, Nancy Marie	16 Apr 1961			
Findley, Tara Marie		29 Sep 1989			
Fink, Marvin	Papenhagen, Pauline				
Fishbaugh, Allison Jane		17 Jul 2003	Toledo, Ohio		
Fishbaugh, Jack Michael		17 Jul 2000	Maumee, Ohio		
Fishbaugh, Kasey Jane		23 Nov 1998	Columbus, Ohio		
Fishbaugh, Michael Raymond	Simmons, Sarah Jane	12 Feb 1971	Toledo, OH		
Floyd, Wendy	Tegtmeier, Todd Alan				
Fowler, Inez	Papenhagen, Paul Ludwig Friedrich Christian	04 Apr 1889		20 Mar 1945	
Frazier, Dawn Michele	Pape, Dale Rudolph	22 Jan 1968			
Frazier, Susan Annette	Berry, Wesley David	02 Jul 1958			
Freeman, Louise H.	Papenhagen, Herman Friedrick Johann Wilhelm	07 Jul 1876	Ohio	18 Dec 1943	
Garrelts, Nate	Wilcox, Beth Marie				
Geyser, Erin Christine	Thompson, Andrew Scott	24 Apr 1980	Fairfield, CA		
Gibson, Janice	Marks, Herbert Bernard	12 May 1936	Toledo, OH		
Glasgow, Donna Eileen	Seagert, Richard Ray	14 Apr 1944			
Goetz, Shirley	Papenhagen, David Herbert	ABT 1940			
Goralsky, John	Tegtmeier, Alice Henrietta		Coalport, PA		Cleveland, OH
Gresh, Alan	Barr, Angela Lynn				
Gresh, Alec Conner		18 Jun 2004			
Gresh, Allison Nicole		27 Jul 2001			
Gresser, Jeanne Marie	Tegtmeier, James Herman	ABT 1945			
Gulyas, Suzanne	Tegtmeier, Douglas Richard	09 Jan 1954	Dayton, OH		
Hacker, Charles W.	Papenhagen, Johanna Sophie Christine Friede	ABT 1877	Ohio	1944	
Hacker, Harold		ABT 1906	Toledo, Ohio		
Hahn, xxx	Davidson, Susan				
Hansen, Clara	Scrivens, Edwin A.	ABT 1900	Ohio		
Hartley, Richard	Tegtmeier, Jamie				
Hartley, Thaddeus					
Hayes, Donna Jean	Komsteller, Neal Walter	11 Jan 1933		11 Jan 1996	
Haynes, Michele	Tegtmeier, Dean Edward	15 Aug 1957	Toronto, Ohio		
Heider, Debbie Hall	Komsteller, Jeff Neal	02 Jan 1956			
Helen	Papenhagen, Arnold	ABT 1901			

Henning, Chari Lynn		29 Nov 1953	Henry Co., OH	06 Jul 1959	
Henning, Debra Kay	Bergstedt, Joey Donald	16 Oct 1956	Napoleon, OH		
Henning, Lori Jean	Coey, Alfred	07 Oct 1959	Wauseon, OH		
Henning, Richard F.	Ahleman, Florence Elsie	30 Oct 1929	Napoleon, OH		
Herman, Lucille Clarissa	Tegtmeier, Harold William	12 Sep 1922	Hermanville, Creston, Ohio		
Hickok, xxx	Tegtmeier, Celia				
Hilborn, Aubrey Rachelle		10 Sep 1998	Ft. Wayne, IN		
Hilborn, Jenna Michelle		28 Nov 1990	Minnesota		
Hilborn, Kristen Eileen		27 Feb 1993	Brandon, Fl		
Hilborn, Mark Robert	Sandra	01 Sep 1963			
Hilborn, Michael David	Crunk, Terri Sue	16 Nov 1966			
Hilborn, Robert	Never, Dathel	18 Oct 1941			
Hilborn, Scott Alan	Shannon	20 Nov 1965			
Hilborn, Sheriana Genevieve		15 May 1998	Orlando, Fl		
Hilborn, Timothy Mark		11 Apr 1989	Minnesota		
Hilborn, Trevor David		17 Jun 1996	Orlando, Fl		
Hille, Dale Herman	Meier, Doris Hulda	14 Aug 1924	Wood Do., Bowling Green, OH		
Hille, Dennis Kay		08 Apr 1953	Bowling Green, OH		
Hille, Karen Rae	Roman, William Kristopher	21 Apr 1951	Perrysburg, OH		
Hille, Karlyn Sue	Stamper, Terry Lee	19 Jul 1955	Bowling Green, OH		
Hines, Dolores Ann	Schultz, William L.	02 Dec 1934			
Hinrichs, Peter Cornelius	Tegtmeier, Lois Ruth	23 Oct 1925	Arlington, Kingsbury, SD	31 Jul 1994	Dickinson, Stark Co. ND
Hinricks, Andrew Peter		30 Mar 1988			
Hinricks, Benjamin Heye		29 Nov 1983	Sacramento, CA		
Hinricks, Lucas Alexander		19 Mar 1982	Dickinson, Stark, ND		
Hinricks, Mark Peter	Landgrebe, Sandra Kae	30 Oct 1951	Redfield, SD		
Hinricks, Rachel Elizabeth		16 Oct 1987	Dickinson, Stark, ND		
Hinricks, Steven Heye	Martin, Deborah	23 Jan 1954	Redfield, Spink Co, SD		
Honaker, Pam	Tegtmeier, Timothy				
Hooker, A. Jack	Carlson, Gina				
Huff, Lola E.	Ahleman, Paul Ernest	10 Aug 1908	Toledo, OH	17 Apr 1954	Henry Co., OH
Hughes, Rhonda	Schultz, David Alan				
Hunt, Karen Jane	Shoner, Daniel George	11 Feb 1962	Adrian,MI		

Hunt, Wesley Alger	Marks, Leola May	04 Oct 1928	Franklyn Twp., MI		
Ida	Papenhagen, Heinrich Conrad Jochen		Michigan		
Jacobs, Elaine					
Jacobs, Leonard	Doering, Thelma				
Jacobs, Mary					
Jacobs, Mary	Papenhagen, Paul Ludwig Friedrich Christian	ABT 1889		22 Mar 1964	Toledo, Lucas, Ohio
Jennifer	Quick, Lee Marvin				
Jones, Debra “Cricket”	Taylor, Craig Edward				
Jones, Elizabeth		Bef. 1967	Ohio		
Jones, xxx	Davidson, Nancy				
Jozwiak, Mary	Scrivens, Clayton	ABT 1885	Ohio		Berea, Ohio
Jr., William L., Teckmyer		29 Dec 1943	Cleveland, Cuyahoga Co., Ohio	21 Dec 1998	
Kamp, Rita Kay	Tegtmeier, David Harold	25 Feb 1959	Ashland, OH		
Karalene	Schumacher, James R.				
Keck, xxx	Puls, Carol Jean				
Kennedy, Jack William		05 Jan 2003	Mt. Carmel West Hosp'l, Columbus, OH		
Kennedy, Paul David	Fenton, Amy Krista	02 Oct 1970			
Kestner, Sandy Louise	Tegtmeier, Richard Elmer	26 Sep 1933	Ashland, Ashland Co., OH		
Kirsch, Brian Scott		04 Mar 1994	Beaufort, NC		
Kirsch, Steven Scott	Simmons, Katherine Kramer	28 Jan 1970	South Bend, IN		
Klebold, Mary Lou	Meier, Lester Bernard	04 Jun 1932	Columbus, OH		
Klinger, Winifred	Papenhagen, Franz Wilhelm Johann	26 Sep 1872	Ohio	02 Mar 1954	
Koester, Elsie Caroline	Papenhagen, Walter Franklin	16 May 1893	Michigan	12 May 1982	Lenawee, Michigan
Kolasinaki, Sally Helen	Meier, Richard Allen	02 Dec 1958	Toledo, OH		
Komsteller, Jane Lee	Strange, Donald D.	18 Dec 1937	Union City		
Komsteller, Jeff Neal	Heider, Debbie Hall	05 Jun 1961			
Komsteller, Jill Marie	Quick, Marvin	23 Jul 1959			
Komsteller, Kimberly Ann	Schultz, Robert	12 Dec 1955			
Komsteller, Loann Clare	Fairweather, Eugene B.	10 Dec 1932	Los Angeles, CA		
Komsteller, Michael		16 May 1987			
Komsteller, Neal Walter	Hayes, Donna Jean	07 Dec 1934	Streator, Illinois		
Komsteller, Walter H.	Papenhagen, Ethel S.	07 Dec 1901	Monroe, Michigan	29 Oct 1973	Norvell,Jackson, Michigan
Konzen, Claretta R.	Scrivens, William A.	ABT 1907	Ohio	24 Oct 1960	Cleveland, Cuyahoga Co., Ohio

Koppin, Adelaide	Ahleman, Arthur G.	19 Jul 1901			
Kovalik, Rose	Tegtmeier, Karl Ferdinand			19 Jun 1947	Cleveland, Cuyahoga, Ohio
Kramer, Grant		10 Oct 2001			
Kramer, James	Tegtmeier, Barbara Lucille	06 Jun 1950			
Kramer, Madeline		16 Jan 1999			
Kramer, Matthew James		29 Sep 1982			
Kramer, William	Erin	05 Jan 1974			
Landgrebe, Sandra Kae	Hinricks, Mark Peter	16 Apr 1952	Bismarck, ND		
Laser, Bentley John	Marks, Wendy Lee	01 Dec 1958	Wauseon, OH		
Laser, Bently John II		29 Mar 1991	Toledo, OH		
Laser, Holly Jeanne		19 Nov 1992	Grayling, MI		
Laser, Shelby Lee		16 Oct 1996	Toledo, OH		
Ledenician	Papenhagen, Marsha				
Lenthe, LENA	Tegtmeier, Karl Ferdinand	ABT 1883	Ohio	Bef. 1926	Cuyahoga Co, Ohio
Leogrande, Jim	Papenhagen, Pauline				
Loewe, Tammy Lynn (Brock)	Pape, Gerald Raymond	07 Jul 1969			
Lowe, Marion	Teckmyer, Fred C.	25 May 1888	Ohio	May 1982	Seffner, Hillsborough, Florida
Lucy	Quick, Lee Marvin				
Lyell, Brandon Baird		01 Jul 1996			
Lyell, Brittany Lee		23 Jul 1998			
Lyell, Timothy	Strange, Lori Ann	23 Jul 1968			
MaCrorie, Patty	Fairweather, Michael B.	02 Mar 1956			
Maggie	Truman, Jacob				
Makzis, Joel	Papenhagen, Dawn	ABT 1963			
Malone, xxx	Puls, Myrtle				
Marks, Elwin C.	Ahleman, Elsie Emma Hulda	20 Aug 1898	Blissfield, MI	01 Nov 1997	Clayton, MI
Marks, Gregg Herbert	Caruthers, Dana Lynne	18 Jan 1960	Mt. Clemens, MI		
Marks, Herbert Bernard	Gibson, Janice	31 Mar 1936	Deerfield, MI		
Marks, Jaycee Marie		03 Dec 1991	Elgin, IL		
Marks, Judy Lyn	Schneiderbuer, Craig	04 Jun 1960	Adrian, MI		
Marks, Leola May	Hunt, Wesley Alger	12 Oct 1925	Henry Co., OH		
Marks, Nancy Kay	Beaubien, Leonard J.	12 Dec 1957	Adrian, MI		
Marks, Scott Edward	Shupick, Marie Colleen	18 May 1964	Lansing, MI		

Marks, Stanley Arthur	Backman, Judith Katherine	23 Jan 1940	Deerfield, MI		
Marks, Todd Bernard	Ashdown, Terry	29 Nov 1957	Hudson, MI		
Marks, Travis Stanley		05 Sep 1981	Fresno, CA		
Marks, Trevor Scott E.		14 Jan 1994	Elgin, IL		
Marks, Troy William		31 Dec 1989	Fresno, CA		
Marks, Wendy Lee	Laser, Bentley John	25 Jul 1964	Adrian, MI		
Marks, William Carl Elwin	Emery, Mildred Irene	01 Mar 1930	Monroe Co., MI		
Martin, Deborah	Hinricks, Steven Heye	10 Aug 1949	Bismarck, Burleigh, ND		
Matheson, Robert	Wessendorf, Brandie Lynn				
Mattka, Billy		01 Feb 1941		02 Apr 2004	
Mattka, Fred	Doering, Gertrude	28 Nov 1906	Wisconsin	05 Feb 1988	Western Springs, Cook, Illinois
Mattka, Jerry		ABT 1943			
Mattka, Meredith		ABT 1940			
McClenahan, Ernie	Berry, Tamala Anne				
McMaster, Dan	Truman, Ashley				
Meier, Beverly Ann	Euler, Allyn Kent	16 Aug 1954	Perrysburg, OH		
Meier, Cynthia Ann	Thompson, Robert Eugene	06 Apr 1956	Toledo, OH		
Meier, David John		24 Aug 1971	Toledo, OH		
Meier, Doris Hulda	Hille, Dale Herman	22 Oct 1925	Curtice, OH		
Meier, Eileen Kay	Stamper, Barton Thomas	19 Oct 1952	Bowling Green, OH		
Meier, Elizabeth Jane		20 Aug 1987	Toledo, OH		
Meier, James Andrew		17 Jan 1982	Toledo, OH		
Meier, John Arthur	Metzker, Doris Jane	25 Dec 1922	Curtice, OH		
Meier, John Bernard	Ahleman, Almeta Bertha Christine	02 Jun 1887	Toledo, OH	01 Jun 1969	
Meier, Laureen Marie	Bauer, Douglas Charles	31 May 1958	Bowling Green, OH		
Meier, Lester Bernard	Klebold, Mary Lou	07 Jan 1931	Curtice, OH		
Meier, Linda Christine	Simmons, Jack Richard	25 Apr 1951	Toledo, OH		
Meier, Lucene Elsie	Pyers, Victor Junior	15 Nov 1924	Curtice, OH		
Meier, Mark Arthur		24 Aug 1971	Toledo, OH		
Meier, Paul Jacob		17 May 1984	Toledo, OH		
Meier, Richard Allen	Kolasinaki, Sally Helen	06 Mar 1949	Toledo, OH	18 Jun 2000	
Meier, Ronald Arthur	Williams, Janice Marie	21 Feb 1946	Toledo, OH		
Meier, William Joseph		20 Oct 1985	Toledo, OH		

Metzker, Doris Jane	Meier, John Arthur	17 Jun 1923	Toledo, OH	09 Jan 2003	Bellville, OH
Michelle	Tegtmeier, Shawn				
Miller, Brian	Fairweather, Jean Marie				
Miller, Jeremiah		20 Jun 1978			
Miller, Jonathan Paul	Wright, Rebekah	24 Aug 1979			
Miller, Paul	Carlson, Gina				
Miller, Terry G.	Tegtmeier, Debra Louise	05 Nov 1952			
Minichbauer, Laura Anna	Tegtmeier, Raymond Julius	01 Aug 1916	Cleveland, Cuyahoga County, Ohio	10 Oct 1995	Wayne County, Ohio
Montes, Alec		09 Jul 1994			
Montes, Billy	Decator, Jonelle	ABT 1965			
Montes, Gabriel		27 Dec 1995			
Moore, Margie	Taylor, James Robert	01 May 1950	Newfoundland, Canada		
Murphy, Jana	Wessendorf, Robert				
Mutz, Lena		ABT 1872			
Mutz, Philip J.	Tegtmeier, Augusta Maria Elizabeth	ABT 1848	Germany		Cuyahoga Co, Ohio
Mutz, Robert		ABT 1879			
Myers, Sharon Ann	Fenton, Shawn Michael	30 Apr 1969	Dayton, OH		
Nancy	Taylor, James Robert				
Nestor, Neva	Tegtmeier, Donald Phillip	ABT 1948			
Never, Dathel	Hilborn, Robert	26 Nov 1938			
Never, Howard	Papenhagen, Doris	15 Feb 1913	Lucas, Toledo, Ohio	28 Apr 2000	Sylvania, Lucas, Ohio
Never, Keith		14 Jun 1965			
Never, Laurie	Pieper, Greg	19 Nov 1968			
Never, Marian Bethany	Decator, Bill	14 Jul 1945			
Never, Paul Grant	Philaum, Joyce	18 Nov 1941			
Never, Rebecca Sue	Carlson, George	12 Oct 1948			
Never, Terri		03 May 1967			
Noppe	Swartz, Joanne				
Oelrich, Mattie	Papenhagen, Heinrich Conrad Jochen	19 Mar 1881		30 Mar 1941	
Pape, Allison Nicole		11 Jun 1993			
Pape, Dale Rudolph	Frazier, Dawn Michele	19 Aug 1964			
Pape, Gerald Raymond	Loewe, Tammy Lynn (Brock)	07 Nov 1967			
Pape, Harry BUD Rudolph, Jr.	Seagert, Diana June	31 Mar 1937			

Pape, Nancy Marie	Findley, Dennis Miles	24 Jul 1962			
Pape, Yvonne Pearl		15 Nov 1975			
Papenhagen, Arnold	Helen	11 Mar 1901	Ohio	03 Feb 1982	Perrysburg, Wood, Ohio
Papenhagen, Bertha Henrietta Wilhelmine	Schumacher, John C.	16 Jun 1885	Germany	07 Feb 1966	Lucas Co, Ohio
Papenhagen, Boy		ABT 1921			
Papenhagen, Boy		ABT 1994			
Papenhagen, Brian	Vickie	ABT 1942			
Papenhagen, Christie	Childers, Gary	21 Jan 1967			
Papenhagen, Clifford W.	Satre, Arlene Mae	28 Oct 1923	Michigan	11 Apr 1988	Peoria, Maricopa, Arizona
Papenhagen, Clyde K.	Brenke, Hilda Elizabeth	28 Oct 1923	Michigan		
Papenhagen, Corey		ABT 1966			
Papenhagen, Darlene		ABT 1955			
Papenhagen, David Herbert	Goetz, Shirley	12 Sep 1939			
Papenhagen, David Paul		22 Jun 1968			
Papenhagen, Dawn	Makzis, Joel	29 Oct 1963			
Papenhagen, Diann	Pavelka, James	ABT 1940			
Papenhagen, Donald	Tagsold, Marilyn	06 Mar 1908		28 Aug 1987	Battle Creek, Calhoun, Michigan
Papenhagen, Doris	Never, Howard	23 Jul 1914	Ottawa Lake, Michigan		
Papenhagen, Edna	Emery, Robert W.	ABT 1893	Ohio		
Papenhagen, Eloise	Quinn, Charles	ABT 1916	Ohio		
Papenhagen, Erna Ethel Elizabeth	Brenke, Arthur William, Sr.	02 Dec 1919	Michigan		
Papenhagen, Erna Henriette Sophie	Tegtmeier, William Carl	10 Oct 1888	Beubukow, Schwerinschen, Mecklenburg, Germany		30 Sep 1982 Dickinson, Stark North Dakota
Papenhagen, Esther Edna Marie	Seagert, Raymond Fredrick	07 Sep 1917	Michigan		
Papenhagen, Ethel S.	Komsteller, Walter H.	27 Oct 1901	Michigan	29 Jan 1981	Norvell,Jackson, Michigan
Papenhagen, Frank W.	D., Marion	20 Apr 1899	Ohio	Apr 1983	Ft. Meyers, Beach Florida
Papenhagen, Franz Wilhelm Johann	Klinger, Winifred	24 Nov 1872	Germany	04 Oct 1931	Defiance, Ohio
Papenhagen, Gail	Rita	ABT 1935			
Papenhagen, Gerald		27 Nov 1936		14 Dec 1951	
Papenhagen, Girl		ABT 1923			
Papenhagen, Heinrich Conrad Jochen	Oelrich, Mattie	20 Jan 1883	Germany	05 Jan 1958	Whiteford Twp., Monroe, Michigan
Papenhagen, Herbert	Blome, Linda	02 Nov 1908	Michigan	05 Jul 1988	Bradenton, Florida
Papenhagen, Herman Friedrick Johann Wilhelm	Freeman, Louise H.	15 Jan 1875	Germany	30 Sep 1952	Toledo, Lucas, Ohio
Papenhagen, Irma	Brenke, Arthur W., Sr.	19 Dec 1919	Riga Twnshp, Lenawee Co., MI	01 Apr 2002	Adrian, MI

Papenhagen, Joachim Christian Johann	Westendorf, Wilhelmina Marie Johanna	01 May 1836	Mechlenburg, Germany	28 Dec 1906	Ottowa Lake, Monroe Co, MI
Papenhagen, Jodee		ABT 1965			
Papenhagen, Johanna Sophie Christine Friede	Hacker, Charles W.	04 Dec 1880	Germany	Aft. 1930	
Papenhagen, Kelly		ABT 1957			
Papenhagen, Kenneth Roger	Saxon, Mary Inez	11 Sep 1946			
Papenhagen, Kenneth Roger	Strite, Laura	24 Feb 1968			
Papenhagen, Larry W.		ABT 1943			
Papenhagen, Marie	Ahrens, Jerry	Aug 1899	Ohio		
Papenhagen, Marie Henriette Magdalene Guste	Doering, Albert W.	15 Jan 1879	Germany	20 Oct 1959	Toledo, Lucas, Ohio
Papenhagen, Marsha	Ledenician	ABT 1944			
Papenhagen, Melissa Lynne		10 Jul 1969			
Papenhagen, Mildred Wilfred		ABT 1914	Michigan		
Papenhagen, Norman Henry	Viers, Doris Laverne	05 May 1907	Michigan	06 May 1995	Michigan
Papenhagen, Paul Ludwig Friedrich Christian	Elg, Emma	15 Mar 1877	Germany	21 Nov 1950	Whiteford, Monroe, Michigan
Papenhagen, Pauline	Wessendorf, Roger	01 Sep 1933			
Papenhagen, Susan	Aldrich, Terri	ABT 1937			
Papenhagen, Ted		ABT 1921			
Papenhagen, Tracey		ABT 1963			
Papenhagen, Walter Franklin	Koester, Elsie Caroline	01 Jun 1892	Toledo, Lucas, Ohio	13 Aug 1944	
Papenhagen, Yvonne Jean	Stone, Robert C.	22 Jul 1950			
Parker, Anna	Puls, William H.	ABT 1885		09 Sep 1963	Cuyahoga Co, Ohio
Parsell, Lucas Prescott		15 Jul 1994	Napoleon, OH		
Parsell, Rodney Richard	Ahleman, Shelly Joanne	24 Apr 1968	Unionville, MI		
Pavelka, Eric		ABT 1964			
Pavelka, James	Papenhagen, Diann	ABT 1940			
Pavelka, Paula		ABT 1960			
Pavelka, Steven		ABT 1962			
Pernoja, xxx	Tegtmeier, Norma				
Peterson, Dale					
Pfizenmayer, Ariene				27 Mar 1942	Cleveland, Cuyahoga Co., Ohio
Pfizenmayer, Henry	Tegtmeier, Madeline	ABT 1873		28 Nov 1949	Lakewood, Cuyahoga, Ohio
Pfizenmayer, Lucille		ABT 1909	Ohio	04 Sep 1916	Lakewood, Cuyahoga, Ohio
Pfizenmayer, Thomas David					

Pfizenmayer, Victor C.					
Pfizenmayer, Victor C.					
Philaum, Joyce	Never, Paul Grant	17 Dec 1942			
Phillips, xxx	Puls, Thelma				
Pieper, Alex		23 Mar 1992			
Pieper, Greg	Never, Laurie	09 Feb 1960			
Pincombe, Ethel L.	Puls, Leonard	ABT 1896	Ohio	03 Mar 1956	Berea, Cuyahoga Co.,Ohio
Porter, Vesper Ivy	Stamper, Benjamin Jacob	12 Jan 1977	Nuremburg, Germany		
Potter, Jeff B.	Strange, Brenda Lee	18 Aug 1960			
Potter, Jeff Dane		05 Sep 1984			
Potter, Katie Lee		01 Jul 1991			
Prechtel, xxx	Scrivens, Mary Lou	ABT 1930			
Proud, Vern	Komsteller, Jill Marie				
Puls, Adeline					
Puls, Arlene	Byers, xxx	ABT 1917			
Puls, Carol Jean	Keck, xxx	ABT 1915			
Puls, Elsie	Rohde, xxx	Dec 1888	Cuyahoga Co, Ohio		
Puls, Elva	Rhode, xxx	ABT 1890			
Puls, Emile					
Puls, LaVerne	Woddups, xxx	ABT 1902			
Puls, Leah	Svat, xxx	ABT 1900			
Puls, Leonard	Pincombe, Ethel L.	Jun 1895	Cuyahoga Co, Ohio	04 Oct 1957	Berea, Cuyahoga Co.,Ohio
Puls, Loretta					
Puls, Myrtle	Malone, xxx	ABT 1919			
Puls, Thelma	Phillips, xxx	ABT 1904			
Puls, William		ABT 1906			
Puls, William H.	Parker, Anna	Jan 1884	Cuyahoga Co, Ohio	18 Apr 1943	Berea, Cuyahoga Co.,Ohio
Puls, William W.	Tegtmeier, Adeline Louise	Nov 1856	Cuyahoga Co., OH	19 Jun 1926	Cuyahoga Co, Ohio
Pyers, Dean Hale		07 Aug 1962	Toledo, OH		
Pyers, Victor Junior	Meier, Lucene Elsie	15 Dec 1919	Lime City, OH	17 Jun 1993	Fort Meigs Cemetery, Perrysburg, OH
Quick, Amber Marie	Smith, Shawn	18 May 1982			
Quick, Ashley Lynn		02 Oct 1985			
Quick, Breann		2004			

Quick, Donavan Lee		Jan 2003			
Quick, Girl		Feb 2005			
Quick, Lee Marvin	Jennifer	11 Jul 1978			
Quick, Marvin	Komsteller, Jill Marie	19 Mar 1955			
Quinn, Adopted Boy		ABT 1936			
Quinn, Charles	Papenhagen, Eloise	09 Nov 1909		19 Nov 1967	
Reinecke, Sophia Louise Juliana	Tegtmeier, Johann Heinrich	19 Jan 1848	Prussia	11 May 1933	Washington Twp, Henry, OH
Renee	Decator, John H.				
Rhode, xxx	Puls, Elva		Brookpark, Cuyahoga, Ohio		
Rice, Adam	Tegtmeier, Angela				
Rice, Amelia Grace					
Rice, Beth					
Rice, Jonah					
Rice, Sandra	Tegtmeier, Paul	19 Jul 1953			
Rich, Celia E.		ABT 1917	Ohio		
Rich, Louis	Tegtmeier, Celia F.	16 Mar 1885	Ohio	30 Jul 1943	Lakewood, Ohio
Rich, Louis Jr.		03 Jan 1920	Ohio	12 Dec 2001	Moore, NC
Rich, Shirley M		ABT 1926	Ohio		
Ries, Emily Diana		29 Dec 1987			
Ries, Rachel Erin		15 Feb 1976			
Ries, Richard Doyle	Seagert, Linda Marie	01 Apr 1952			
Ries, Sarah Marie		12 Nov 1983			
Rita	Papenhagen, Gail	ABT 1935			
Rittner, Diana Jean	Brenke, Arthur Walter Jr.	27 Jan 1945			
Rohde, xxx	Puls, Elsie				
Roley, Paul R.	Tegtmeier, Jennifer L.	12 Nov 1976			
Roman, Meghan Grier		26 Oct 1982	Columbus, OH		
Roman, Sarah Elizabeth		09 Jul 1978	Columbus, OH		
Roman, William Kristopher	Hille, Karen Rae	15 Oct 1949	Canton, OH		
Sandra	Hilborn, Mark Robert	ABT 1963			
Sara	Truman, David				
Satre, Arlene Mae	Papenhagen, Clifford W.	ABT 1923			
Saxon, Mary Inez	Papenhagen, Kenneth Roger	03 Feb 1946			

Schemrich, Dale		ABT 1959			
Schemrich, Ronnie		ABT 1958			
Schemrich, Shawn		ABT 1960			
Schemrich, William	Tegtmeier, Donna Mae	ABT 1928			
Schneiderbuer, Craig	Marks, Judy Lyn	17 Jun 1955	Toledo, OH		
Schneiderbuer, Emily Lyn		09 Jan 1991	Toledo, OH		
Schneiderbuer, Eric Stephen		29 Jul 1988	Toledo, OH		
Schultz, Casey		14 May 1985			
Schultz, Connie Ann	Adams, Andrew	21 Jul 1954			
Schultz, Corey Robert		16 Dec 1981			
Schultz, Cynthia Sue	Balliet, Dennis	07 Jan 1958			
Schultz, David Alan	Hughes, Rhonda	07 Apr 1956			
Schultz, James William	Dyke, Gloria J.	05 May 1953			
Schultz, Lloyd William	Scrivens, Florence Julia	18 Oct 1899	Ohio	30 Jul 1979	Ohio
Schultz, Megan Lee		28 Jan 1975		1975	
Schultz, Misty Lynn	Smith, Allan B.	14 Sep 1977			
Schultz, Robert	Komsteller, Kimberly Ann	28 Jul 1951			
Schultz, Timothy Ben		18 Mar 1960			
Schultz, William L.	Hines, Dolores Ann	02 Aug 1931	Berea, Cuyahoga, OH		
Schumacher, Barbara		09 Nov 1934			
Schumacher, Cindy					
Schumacher, Elmer	Eunice	10 Jan 1912	Michigan		
Schumacher, Frank	Algie	ABT 1909	Michigan		
Schumacher, James R.	Karalene	05 Sep 1945			
Schumacher, Joan					
Schumacher, John C.	Papenhagen, Bertha Henrietta Wilhelmine	27 Mar 1880	Germany	05 Nov 1958	Lucas Co., Ohio
Schumacher, John Jr.					
Schumacher, Kenneth					
Schumacher, Larry					
Schumacher, Laurie					
Schumacher, Lydia		ABT 1920			
Schumacher, Richard					
Schumacher, Robert					

Schumacher, Ronald					
Schumacher, Roy	Donna	31 Jan 1921	Michigan	12 Sep 1971	
Schumacher, Susan					
Schumacher, Tom					
Scrivens, Clayton	Jozwiak, Mary	30 Oct 1904	Ohio	26 Aug 1977	Berea, Ohio
Scrivens, Edwin A.	Hansen, Clara	24 Jan 1899	Ohio	Jul 1976	Cleveland, OH
Scrivens, Florence Julia	Schultz, Lloyd William	21 Jan 1903	Berea, Cuyahoga Co. OH	04 May 1993	Ohio
Scrivens, Jay D.		ABT 1933			
Scrivens, Mary Lou	Prechtel, xxx	Aft. 1930			
Scrivens, Peter A.		ABT 1934			
Scrivens, William A.	Konzen, Claretta R.	30 Apr 1901	Cuyahoga Co., OH	06 Jul 1997	Cleveland, OH
Scrivens, William R.	Tegtmeier, Lucie Adeline Julianna	ABT 1870	Ohio	07 Apr 1927	Middleburg Twp. Cuyahoga OH
Seagert, Diana June	Pape, Harry BUD Rudolph, Jr.	12 Jun 1939			
Seagert, Linda Marie	Ries, Richard Doyle	04 Jul 1952			
Seagert, Lindsay Lynette		29 Apr 1980			
Seagert, Raymond Fredrick	Papenhagen, Esther Edna Marie	02 May 1913		19 Jul 1981	
Seagert, Richard Ray	Glasgow, Donna Eileen	09 Apr 1943			
Seagert, Rory Kyle		02 Apr 1974			
Seagert, Ryan Ray		22 Mar 1972			
Shannon	Hilborn, Scott Alan	ABT 1965			
Sharp, Don	Fairweather, Linda Lee	ABT 1956			
Sharp, Kristi Lea	Thompson, Ian Robert	12 Sep 1980	Tuscon, AZ		
Shoner, Daniel George	Hunt, Karen Jane	21 Feb 1959	Ypsilanti, MI		
Shoner, Jenna Marie		26 Jan 1994	Saline, MI		
Shoner, Michael W.		05 May 1992		17 Sep 1992	Saline Mi.
Shoner, Rachel Nicole		21 Dec 1995	Ann Arbor, MI	30 Sep 1996	
Shupick, Marie Colleen	Marks, Scott Edward	15 Oct 1965	Eagle Butte, S. Dakota		
Sidwell, M. Christina	Barr, Jeffrey				
Sigler, Christopher Allen	Bailey, Priscilla Joy	08 Jun 1972			
Simmons, Abigail Christine		06 Nov 1986	Toledo, OH		
Simmons, Jack Richard	Meier, Linda Christine	05 Feb 1949	Toledo, OH		
Simmons, Katherine Kramer	Kirsch, Steven Scott	15 Jun 1970	Bowling Green, OH		
Simmons, Megan Meier		22 Jun 1983	Toledo, OH		

Simmons, Sarah Jane	Fishbaugh, Michael Raymond	12 Aug 1973	Toledo, OH		
Simons, Mary Araujo	Komsteller, Neal Walter	20 Apr 1939			
Sinderyeld, Tiffany	Tegtmeier, Jeremy				
Skillman, Richard	Barr, Kathy Anne				
Skillman, Spencer		04 Oct 1997			
Slone, Abigail		1997			
Slone, Brian Lee	Taylor, Christine Jean				
Slone, Victoria		2002			
Smith, Allan B.	Schultz, Misty Lynn				
Smith, Bertha		ABT 1913			
Smith, Caria					
Smith, Cindy					
Smith, Glen A.	Carol	ABT 1938	Cleveland, Cuyahoga Co., OH		
Smith, Gregory					
Smith, Haley Ann		03 Jul 2003			
Smith, Julius Carl	Tegtmeier, Christina Dorothea Emilie	ABT 1879	Ohio	12 Dec 1949	Longview, Texas
Smith, Leland J.	Allen, Alice	ABT 1910	Ohio	1972	Brookpark, Ohio
Smith, Samantha Kay		11 Feb 2001			
Smith, Shawn	Quick, Amber Marie				
Snapp, Pauline	Ahleman, Paul Ernest	30 Sep 1929	Maryland		
Staley, Daniel	Berry, Tamala Anne				
Stamper, Aaron Christopher		25 Jun 1981	Stamford, CT		
Stamper, Alban Jack Comfort		03 Feb 2003	West Orange, NJ		
Stamper, Ansa Rachel		11 Jun 1996	N. Hampton, MA		
Stamper, Arden Lille Evangeline		03 Oct 2005	West Orange, NJ		
Stamper, Barton Thomas	Meier, Eileen Kay	21 Aug 1949	Denver, CO		
Stamper, Benjamin Jacob	Porter, Vesper Ivy	11 Apr 1975	Denver, CO		
Stamper, Hilja Kay		11 Apr 1999	Hartford, CT		
Stamper, Joshua Noel Thomas	Behny, Kory Lea	27 Sep 1972	Denver, CO		
Stamper, Terry Lee	Hille, Karlyn Sue	09 Mar 1956	Grayson, KY		
Stevens, Marilyn Lou	Ahleman, Donald Ernest	03 Jul 1934	Holgate, OH		
Stone, Bryan Charles		21 Jan 1978			
Stone, Myra J.		17 Dec 1976			

Stone, Renee J.		26 Oct 1973			
Stone, Robert C.	Papenhagen, Yvonne Jean	16 Aug 1949			
Strange, Bradley John	Carlton, Terri	18 Feb 1962			
Strange, Brenda Lee	Potter, Jeff B.	12 Apr 1964			
Strange, Donald D.	Komsteller, Jane Lee	12 Jun 1936			
Strange, Lori Ann	Lyell, Timothy	07 Jan 1969			
Strange, Lyndi Elizabeth		03 Mar 1994			
Strange, Melinda Lee		28 Jan 1961		28 Oct 1961	
Strayer, Ethel M.	Ahleman, Walter Adolph	10 Sep 1906	Grand Rapids, OH	17 Apr 1996	
Strite, Laura	Papenhagen, Kenneth Roger II	03 Nov 1968			
Stull, Brad	Tegtmeier, Molly Marie	ABT 1971			
Stull, Katie Marie		09 Jun 1999			
Stull, Riley Ann		06 Jun 2003			
Svat, xxx	Puls, Leah	ABT 1900			
Swartz, Boy		ABT 1923			
Swartz, Elmer	Doering, Helen I.	ABT 1902			
Swartz, Joanne	Noppe	ABT 1924			
Tagsold, Marilyn	Papenhagen, Donald				
Tamera	Decator, John H.	ABT 1965			
Tammie	Tegtmeier, Joel	30 Jul 1959			
Taylor, Chasta		21 Mar 1981			
Taylor, Christine Jean	Slone, Brian Lee	Nov 1974			
Taylor, Craig Edward	Jones, Debra "Cricket"	07 Sep 1962			
Taylor, Edward William	Tegtmeier, Alice Henrietta	01 Aug 1914	New York	22 Jan 1967	Jost Van Dyke, US Virgin Islands
Taylor, Edward William	Untezuber, Nancy	11 Jan 1944	Alden, NY		
Taylor, James Robert	Moore, Margie	22 Mar 1949	Berea, Ohio		
Taylor, Sandra Mina	Bell, Peter Graham	17 Mar 1950	Berea, Ohio		
Taylor, Shane Edward		01 Aug 1978			
Taylor, Shirley Ann	Barr, Eugene	11 Oct 1941	Scranton, PA		
Teckmyer, Fred C.	Lowe, Marion	May 1881	Ohio	19 Mar 1961	Eustis, Florida
Teckmyer, Fred C., Jr.		20 Feb 1914	Ohio	21 Oct 2000	Naples, Collier, Florida
Teckmyer, Isabel M.		ABT 1918	Ohio		
Teckmyer, William L.	Arters, Jane	17 Jun 1912	Ohio	Feb 1978	Cleveland, Cuyahoga, Ohio

Tegtmeier, Adam Donald		17 Jun 1986			
Tegtmeier, Adelbert E.		Jun 1913	Ohio	17 Dec 1991	Ohio
Tegtmeier, Adeline Elizabeth Emma (died in inf)		08 Apr 1876	Berea, Cuyahoga Co. OH	18 Sep 1876	Berea, Cuyahoga Co. OH
Tegtmeier, Adeline Louise	Puls, William W.	22 Aug 1862	Middleburg Twp. Cuyahoga, Oh	21 Feb 1903	
Tegtmeier, Alice Henrietta	Taylor, Edward William	28 May 1916	Brookpark, Ohio		
Tegtmeier, Angela	Rice, Adam				
Tegtmeier, Angela		19 Apr 1979			
Tegtmeier, Augusta Maria Elizabeth	Mutz, Philip J.	05 Dec 1852	Iden, Osterburg, Prussia	02 Oct 1894	Cleveland, Cuyahoga Co. OH
Tegtmeier, Barbara Lucille	Kramer, James	15 Dec 1952	Lodi Hospital, near Wooster, Ohio		
Tegtmeier, Brenda G.	Tegtmeier, Terry	08 Mar 1949			
Tegtmeier, Brock Gilbert		17 Jun 2002			
Tegtmeier, Celeste		ABT 1982			
Tegtmeier, Celia	Hickok, xxx	ABT 1912			
Tegtmeier, Celia F.	Rich, Louis	Apr 1889	Ohio	31 Aug 1960	Lakewood, Ohio
Tegtmeier, Christina Dorothea Emilie	Smith, Julius Carl	01 Dec 1880	Berea, Cuyahoga Co. OH	17 Nov 1963	Middleburg Hts. Cuyahoga Co. OH
Tegtmeier, Christine					
Tegtmeier, Cody James		10 Jul 2000			
Tegtmeier, Daniel Howard	Bougher, Beth Ann	23 Sep 1957			
Tegtmeier, David Harold	Kamp, Rita Kay	15 Sep 1954	Lodi Hospital, near Wooster, Ohio		
Tegtmeier, Dean Edward	Haynes, Michele	02 Mar 1957	Ashland, Ashland Co., OH		
Tegtmeier, Debra Louise	Miller, Terry G.	09 Jan 1955	Wooster, Wayne Co. OH		
Tegtmeier, Donald Phillip	Nestor, Neva	14 Nov 1948	Lodi Hospital, near Wooster, Ohio		
Tegtmeier, Donna Mae	Schemrich, William	01 Sep 1944			
Tegtmeier, Douglas Richard	Gulyas, Suzanne	06 Dec 1952	Wooster, Montgomery Co., OH		
Tegtmeier, Elsie	Fairbank, Louis G.	Jan 1887	Ohio		
Tegtmeier, Erma Maria	Behner, Elmer	25 Mar 1904	Berea, Cuyahoga Co. OH	16 Feb 1977	Medina Co. Ohio
Tegtmeier, Ernest Arthur		17 Nov 1886	Middleburg Twp. Cuyahoga Co. OH	18 Feb 1893	Middleburg Twp. Cuyahoga Co. OH
Tegtmeier, Ethan Daniel		26 Jan 1990			
Tegtmeier, Frieda Magdelena		09 Jan 1885	Middleburg Twp. Cuyahoga Co. OH	09 Jul 1946	Berea, Cuyahoga Co.,Ohio
Tegtmeier, Friedrich Wilhelm	Droege, Magdelena M.	28 Sep 1845	Iden, Osterburg, Prussia	16 Jan 1909	Cleveland, Cuyahoga Co. OH
Tegtmeier, Friedrich Wilhelm		14 May 1890	Berea, Cuyahoga Co. OH	Dec 1967	Brookpark, Cuyahoga Co. OH
Tegtmeier, Gustav Adolph	Bauer, Alma Marie	06 Sep 1883	Middleburg Twp, Cuyahoga Co. OH	24 Nov 1937	Erie, Erie Co. PA
Tegtmeier, Harold William	Herman, Lucille Clarissa	02 Mar 1921	Brookpark, Ohio	18 May 2003	West Salem, Wayne, Ohio

Tegtmeier, Heidi Rose		12 Apr 1989			
Tegtmeier, Henry Adolph	Barendt, Harriett	19 Mar 1918	Ohio	09 Dec 1992	Fairfield Glade, TN
Tegtmeier, Henry William Carl	Brandes, Augusta Christine	04 Nov 1874	Middleburg Twp., Cuyahoga, OH	08 Jun 1963	Millersburg, Holmes, OH
Tegtmeier, Howard J.		ABT 1913	Ohio		
Tegtmeier, Howard Jr.		ABT 1934			
Tegtmeier, Hulda Louise Maria	Ahleman, Heinrich Ernst A.	21 May 1873	Independence, OH	25 Feb 1968	Adrian, Lenawee, MI
Tegtmeier, Ida Louise (died in inf)		21 Jan 1872	Berea, Cuyahoga Co. OH	21 Jul 1872	Berea, Cuyahoga Co. OH
Tegtmeier, James Herman	Gresser, Jeanne Marie	14 Feb 1945	Lodi Hospital, near Wooster, Ohio		
Tegtmeier, Jamie	Hartley, Richard	25 Apr 1975			
Tegtmeier, Jeff		22 Dec 1982	Columbus, Ohio		
Tegtmeier, Jennifer L.	Roley, Paul R.	12 Dec 1976			
Tegtmeier, Jeremy	Sinderyeld, Tiffany	30 Mar 1976			
Tegtmeier, Jerrod		22 Oct 1984			
Tegtmeier, Jill Arlene		29 Oct 1985			
Tegtmeier, Joan Charlotte	Truman, Tom	07 Aug 1947			
Tegtmeier, Joel	Tammie	13 Aug 1959			
Tegtmeier, Johann Friedrich	Bree, Maria Dorothea	31 Aug 1821	Iden, Osterburg, Prussia	27 Aug 1903	Middleburg Twp, Cuyahoga OH
Tegtmeier, Johann Heinrich	Reinecke, Sophia Louise Juliana	08 Jan 1844	Iden, Osterburg, Prussia	24 Jan 1897	Middleburg Twp, Cuyahoga, OH
Tegtmeier, Jonathan					
Tegtmeier, Julia Wihelmina		07 Oct 1914	Brookpark, Cuyahoga Co., Ohio	02 Mar 1934	Columbus, OH
Tegtmeier, Karl Ferdinand	Bartels, Maria Fridericka Johane	05 Feb 1848	Iden, Osterburg, Prussia	03 Jul 1907	Middleburg Twp, Cuyahoga OH
Tegtmeier, Karl Ferdinand	Lenthe, LENA	30 Aug 1883	Berea, Cuyahoga Co. OH	09 Apr 1956	Cuyahoga Co., OH
Tegtmeier, Laken					
Tegtmeier, Linda Jean	Fenton, Larry Gene	24 Aug 1947	Youngstown, OH, North Side Hospital		
Tegtmeier, Logan					
Tegtmeier, Lois Ruth	Hinrichs, Peter Cornelius	18 Mar 1928	maybe Brookpark, OH		
Tegtmeier, Loretta Mattie	Berry, Paul Franklin	26 Aug 1911			
Tegtmeier, Lucie Adeline Julianna	Scrivens, William R.	06 Aug 1877	Berea, Cuyahoga Co. OH	09 Oct 1921	Middleburg Twp, Cuyahoga OH
Tegtmeier, Luke David		11 May 1983			
Tegtmeier, Madeline	Pfizenmayer, Henry	May 1879	Ohio	13 Sep 1950	Cuyahoga Co, Ohio
Tegtmeier, Mark David		25 Apr 1990			
Tegtmeier, Matthew	Alice				
Tegtmeier, Matthew		03 Feb 1981			

Tegtmeier, Matthew R.		27 Jun 1980			
Tegtmeier, Minna Wilhelmine Albertina		01 Oct 1856	Iden, Osterburg, Prussia	12 Sep 1867	Middleburg Twp. Cuyahoga Co. Oh
Tegtmeier, Miriam Ann	Camper, Paul	08 Apr 1946			
Tegtmeier, Molly Marie	Stull, Brad	24 May 1971			
Tegtmeier, Nina	Bartel, xxx	ABT 1915			
Tegtmeier, Norma	Pernoja, xxx	ABT 1915	Ohio		
Tegtmeier, Oscar		09 Jul 1914	Brookpark, Cuyahoga Co., Ohio		
Tegtmeier, Otto Friederich Heinrich (died in inf)		07 Jan 1879	Berea, Cuyahoga Co. OH	02 Jun 1879	Berea, Cuyahoga Co.,Ohio
Tegtmeier, Paul	Rice, Sandra	03 Aug 1948			
Tegtmeier, Randy James	Eubanks, Heather	24 Mar 1975			
Tegtmeier, Raymond Julius	Minichbauer, Laura Anna	07 Dec 1912	Brookpark, OH	Sep 1982	Wayne County, Ohio
Tegtmeier, Richard Elmer	Kestner, Sandy Louise	03 Jan 1924	Berea,Cuyahoga Co.OH	17 Oct 1995	Crossville, TN
Tegtmeier, Rose	Biller, xxx	ABT 1914			
Tegtmeier, Ruth	Davidson, Francis P.	ABT 1913	Ohio		
Tegtmeier, Ryan		11 Oct 1984	Columbus, Ohio		
Tegtmeier, Sara		ABT 1986			
Tegtmeier, Sarah Christine		16 May 1993			
Tegtmeier, Sharon Lee	Erro, Gary	04 Jan 1947			
Tegtmeier, Shawn	Michelle	ABT 1984			
Tegtmeier, Terry	Tegtmeier, Brenda G.	25 Sep 1949	Bolivar, Oh		
Tegtmeier, Timothy	Honaker, Pam	15 Sep 1955			
Tegtmeier, Todd Alan	Floyd, Wendy	19 Feb 1962			
Tegtmeier, William Carl	Papenhagen, Erna Henriette Sophie	15 May 1882	Middleburg Twnshp, OH	10 Apr 1955	Medina Twp., Medina, OH
Tegtmeier, William Edward	Westlund, Lois Genvieve	06 Mar 1920	Brookpark, Ohio	24 Jul 2000	Savanah, OH
Thompson, Andrew Scott	Geyser, Erin Christine	07 Aug 1977	Denver, CO		
Thompson, Ian Robert	Sharp, Kristi Lea	05 Oct 1979	Denver, CO		
Thompson, Keira Ashlea		27 Jul 2006	Denver, CO		
Thompson, Robert Eugene	Meier, Cynthia Ann	16 Apr 1950	Denver, CO		
Thompson, Trevor Daniel		19 Aug 2006	Colorado Springs, CO		
Truman, Abigail					
Truman, Alex					
Truman, Ashley	McMaster, Dan	20 Apr 1976			
Truman, David	Sara	12 Sep 1978			

Truman, Grace					
Truman, Jacob					
Truman, Jacob	Maggie	13 Sep 1974			
Truman, Jonathan					
Truman, Kaitlyn					
Truman, Paige					
Truman, Tom	Tegtmeier, Joan Charlotte	21 Jul 1946			
Truman, Tom		14 Sep 1972			
Untezuber, Nancy	Fasnacht, Glenn	03 May 1948			
Vickie	Papenhagen, Brian	ABT 1943			
Viers, Doris Laverne	Papenhagen, Norman Henry	15 Nov 1912			
Welnie, Rose M.	Tegtmeier, Gustav Adolph	1882		27 Nov 1937	Erie, PA
Wessendorf, Barbara	Wilcox, Rex	15 Nov 1952			
Wessendorf, Brandie Lynn	Matheson, Robert	26 Nov 1974			
Wessendorf, Bruce		21 Sep 1964			
Wessendorf, Jennie Lee		02 Apr 1978			
Wessendorf, Robert	DeFrancisco, Janice	02 Jul 1957			
Wessendorf, Roger	Papenhagen, Pauline				
West, David	Fairweather, Jean Marie				
Westendorf, Wilhelmina Marie Johanna	Papenhagen, Joachim Christian Johann	13 May 1849	Germany	05 Feb 1935	Ottowa Lake, Monroe Co, MI
Westlund, Lois Genvieve	Tegtmeier, William Edward	31 Dec 1922	Youngstown, Ohio		
Wilcox, Beth Marie	Garrelts, Nate	04 May 1978			
Wilcox, Eva Brittany		20 Feb 1988			
Wilcox, Rex	Wessendorf, Barbara				
Wilkes, Bruce James	Brenke, Sharon Sue	06 Oct 1947			
Wilkes, Gregg James		06 Sep 1971			
Wilkes, Teresa Sue		28 Apr 1976			
Williams, Janice Marie	Meier, Ronald Arthur	29 Mar 1946	Toledo, OH		
Woddups, xxx	Puls, LaVerne				
Wright, Rebekah	Miller, Jonathan Paul				

Index

978-0-595-44524-0
0-595-44524-1